More than a Pilot

A Pioneer in Mission Aviation

Claire Schoolland Mellis

Foreword by Dr. Arthur F. Glasser

Dedicated to our supporting
churches, family, and friends,
and to our colleagues
in Mission Aviation Fellowship—
all partners with us
in giving wings to the Gospel

Interior photographs are from the personal collection of Claire Schoolland Mellis unless otherwise noted.

Cover design and graphics by Eric Negron, Mission Aviation Fellowship.
Maps by Mary Epp and Eric Negron, Mission Aviation Fellowship.

Scripture quotations from the *The Holy Bible*, Revised Standard Version, Copyright © 1946, 1952, 1959, Thomas Nelson & Sons, New York. Used by permission.

ISBN 0-939925-19-2

Published by R. C. Law & Co., Inc., Chino, CA, in cooperation with Mission Aviation Fellowship, Nampa, ID. *www.MAF.org.*

Printed in the United States of America.

A word to my children . . .
John, Jim, Gordon, Gil, and Esther

As you know, my original purpose in preparing this documented account was to share, primarily with you, the events that were a part of our family's pilgrimage, because even you who are older would not remember details—nor would I, I suspect, apart from the letters that were saved. Still, without your loving support and encouragement, I'm not sure I'd have undertaken the project—or persevered to its conclusion. Thank you for so willingly spending time with me in discussing your perceptions of your father, our family, and of MAF. And I appreciate the participation of your wives, my dear daughters-in-law, who also took time to read the manuscript at various stages in its preparation. All the comments, suggestions, and proofreading have been most helpful. I admit I was touched when several of you allowed me to know of ways in which the account has been particularly meaningful to you. And what would I have done without your assistance in picture choices and layouts? I hope you feel as I do that this has really been a family venture. Finally, I'm grateful that you appreciate your father, his contribution to MAF and to the Lord's work generally. How thankful he would be to see each of you (together with your families) serving the Lord as His disciples and in leadership roles He has given you. What beautiful answers to our prayers (3 John 4). May God continue to direct your paths and may all of our lives bring glory to Him.

I love you,
"Mom"

Contents

****

Preface

Whatever Charlie Mellis attempted he did with all his heart. He was a true idealist, and ideals were not just theory for Charlie. Servant leadership, simple lifestyle, and religious communities in mission are just a few of the ideals he attempted to apply to his everyday life, sometimes at considerable expense to himself and his family. But Charlie was willing to listen and modify his ideals, most notably so when he began to look at the world through the eyes of his teenage children.

In *More Than a Pilot,* Claire Mellis quotes extensively from her late husband's letters as she describes the three years they spent in New Guinea, pioneering air services to missionaries in the then wild, mostly unexplored interior of that great island. Those were formative years for the Mellis family and for Mission Aviation Fellowship as well—years of attempting the near-impossible with extremely limited resources and equipment. The interminable, almost-daily changes from wheels to floats to wheels to floats on their single-engine Piper Pacer airplane, for example, required a level of patience and commitment almost beyond our present comprehension.

There were adventures aplenty: Stone Age people in a "Shangri-La" valley; flights over unmapped terrain; the search for a missing fellow mission pilot; the first landing on a tiny lake to establish a missionary bridgehead in the heart of Papua, then known as Dutch New Guinea. (My very first assignment as a new MAF recruit in 1955 was to develop the pictures of that landing.) But these adventures are merely the backdrop. This is a book about commitment and searching and personal growth.

More Than a Pilot has special meaning for me because Charlie Mellis played a major role in my own life. He was a mentor, friend, and my immediate predecessor as President of MAF. Back in 1969 he summarized his life values beautifully in a prayer which appears on the last page of this book. It is a fitting epitaph for this truly committed man.

> Chuck Bennett
> MAF President 1973-1987

Foreword

On the face of it, this book records the opening up of great stretches of Papua New Guinea and Dutch New Guinea [currently known as Papua] to missionary penetration through the development of an interconnecting air transport system. Its pages recount the anxieties, uncertainties, and dangers involved in surmounting the obstacles that stood in the way; the terrain was horrible, the weather unpredictable and navigational problems most complex. You will marvel at the raw courage and dogged persistence that characterized the leader and members of a small band of young people (actually, all were young!) in their efforts to make possible the evangelization of the vast interior of that enormous island. Young Davids stood before that massive Philistine giant and triumphed in the name of the Lord. This is a record of technical competence and flying skill, of vision and suffering, of prayer and faith, and of victory.

But this book also reveals the manner in which God deals with His people. It shows what happens when a young couple seek God's highest and persevere in their devotion. When the book begins, we find they have already been enrolled for some time in His School of Discipleship. They do not know that He has destined them for administrative service in the troubled decades that will follow, and on a worldwide basis. They will be called to lead just about the most complicated Protestant missionary organization in the whole world: Mission Aviation Fellowship. They only know that for the present (1952-1955) they must give the all-inclusive yes to His will. Hence, this book tells us how He dealt with them as individuals and brought them to the place where they could be trusted to function "not by might, nor by power, but by His Spirit" (Zech. 4:6). This is a book about leadership.

My first contacts with MAF were in Dawson Trotman's rented office in the Bible Institute of Los Angeles as World War II grounded to a halt. Just a desk and the trio of Grady Parrott, Jim Truxton, and Betty Greene: their dream was beginning to crystallize into precise vision. But the obstacles they faced and the uncertainties that dogged their steps were both many and formidable. As they began to move forward, however, breaking new ground every step of the way, God did a wonderful thing: He gave them Charlie and Claire Mellis. This meant that MAF soon began to take on the added imprint of their creativity, their single-mindedness and their venturesomeness.

We are all profoundly grateful to Claire for having produced this fascinating record of their service in the South Pacific during those formative years when God was preparing them for the sort of leadership in the world-wide missionary movement that would be both significant and lasting. Fortunately, she did not have to depend on her memory in putting down what appears in these pages. The extensive correspondence of those years has been constantly at her side. Without it, there might have been the unconscious temptation to indulge in what has been called "retrospective revisionism." After all, few of us are able to recall with accuracy and balance the impressions gained and judgments made years previously. So then, you will find here no elevation of the departed onto the heroic and saintly that largely characterizes mission hagiography. Just the straight-forward, unvarnished record. That's what makes it so valuable.

As stated earlier, this is a book on leadership. That is what makes it significant, particularly at this juncture in the Christian movement when good leaders are in very short supply. It is not that God is reluctant to raise up quality men and women. The tragedy is that not many potential leaders persist in their submission to the prolonged preparatory discipline under which He places them. They never fully enlist in His School. It is too rigorous. But when Charlie and Claire entered that School, they were determined to "please the Lord" (2 Cor. 5:9). Hence, as you read, keep asking yourself: What was involved in Charlie becoming "more than a pilot"? What did he personally learn?"

First, a leader must lead! This is his indispensable priority. For Charlie, this meant facing forward—carefully and persistently opening up new areas for MAF service. Although aircraft need constant maintenance, Charlie was not dominated by a maintenance mentality. With tenacity of purpose and consistency of endurance, he was always planning ahead. As a result, his younger colleagues never found him unprepared, taken by surprise, or given to rash, unreflective action in the face of the unexpected.

Second, a leader must train others. This is his greatest responsibility. The young people sent out from America to work under Charlie were highly committed enthusiasts. But he knew that zeal, dedication and a capacity for sacrifice were insufficient in themselves. These young MAFers had to be patiently and thoroughly introduced to the complexities of their assignments. Only then would they be able to cope positively with the crises that would invariably arise.

It is significant that Charlie never forced commitment or self-denial on them. Since they knew he believed in them, the sheer pressure of his example before them gave him more than he asked for. As a result of his unrelenting tutelage, they became almost hard-headed in their comprehensive knowledge of their assigned tasks. This was largely due to his capacity, in a non-routinized fashion, repeatedly to clothe the most profound ideas and basic rules in simple language, and then drive them home! Charlie produced many who, in turn, became prominent in the subsequent leadership of MAF.

Third, a leader must consistently model a winsome Christian spirituality. This is his most demanding task. Charlie believed that his personal walk with the Lord was crucial. But he related this dimension of his life intimately to his leadership role. He knew that he had to get on top of his work, and stay there. Only then would he know personal freedom for reflective thought on his work and holy converse with his God. He was pressed to secure full knowledge of each and every aspect of his many responsibilities. This is the Charlie we all knew. Somehow, we were never surprised when we gained the occasional glimpse into his devotional life. There was a simplicity about him; he reflected the sincerity, dignity, and industry of a contented person. He was frank and transparent—"an Israelite indeed, in whom is no guile" (John 1:47). And his frugal lifestyle was what you would expect of a man whose life was "hid with Christ in God" (Col. 3:3).

Fourth, a leader must be loyal to the organization he serves. Charlie cheerfully accepted the leadership God placed over him in MAF. His loyalty was coupled with the courage to admit his errors and the honesty to raise such a fundamental question as to whether MAF was doing the right work, rather than merely doing its work right. He never suppressed his capacity for self-criticism, hence remained free from the bull-headedness that all too often causes leaders to adhere obstinately to lines of action long after they have been proven wrong. And he sought to encourage this form of elasticity—or sensitivity to the Lord's leading—at headquarters. I guess the constant discipline of his mind was to be accustomed to danger (after all, he had been a bomber pilot in Europe during World War II). And withal, Charlie was a cheerful, pleasant person—engagingly so, for his charm was free from all artificiality.

I am sure you have appreciated my frequent reference to Charlie and Claire in this foreword, even though Claire intended that her manuscript was to portray him, and him alone. Actually, Charlie's contribution to the world-wide mission of the Church would have been far less had Claire not been his loving and supportive wife. Leaders, whether men or women, rarely attain their best if they do not know the tranquility of home life, the blessing of love given and received, and the companionship of problems shared and understood. Claire provided all these above measure. Their stability of character was a challenge to many. At Charlie's funeral, his eldest son John spoke most movingly when—in a break in his tribute—he abruptly added: "Dad was faithful to Mom." That "plus" said a great deal.

I only came to know Charlie and Claire long after their years in the South Pacific. By then Charlie was the president of MAF and had helped bring the organization through the tumultuous years of the '60s. I envied his competence, his relaxed style of leadership, his absolute clarity of thought, his abundant common sense, his ability to absorb knowledge, and his skill with the pen. There was an accuracy and simplicity to his prose. It reflected a distinct style, much genuine imagination, and the total absence of the redundant. He used to chide me whenever I sought his help with my editorials for *Missiology*, the journal we edited together. "Why do you take so long getting off the ground? Your third paragraph is where you really begin to say something!" And I would invariably agree. What a friend he was!

Charlie and Claire Mellis were those who thought positively and gratefully about their backgrounds. They loved their parents. They saw themselves as debtors to their generation, and believed in the possibility of their being used together for God's glory and the blessing of others. To meet them was to come into touch with a couple who knew themselves as truly caught up in the gracious arms of a loving God. They had no doubts about His having disclosed Himself in the utterly trustworthy record of Holy Scripture. They had no uncertainty as to the possibility of making a solid contribution to the evangelization of their generation. They were convinced it was downright sinful to approach life and its demands in a superficial and selfish fashion. The seriousness of life gave them a sense of social responsibility. Charlie's war experiences had deeply etched upon his consciousness the awful realities of evil and the demonic dimensions of human existence.

So they faced the fact that to pursue what they deemed to be the will of God meant risk, self-denial, and inevitable suffering (Col. 1:24). As you read the account, seek to get the full measure of its implications. Believe that the veil is being drawn aside for you to gain insight into the ways of God with those whose hearts are right toward Him. Covet their single-mindedness, their devotion to a duty rigidly defined, and their loyalty to authority, both human and divine, that is consonant with Christian discipleship. Believe that God desires to quicken in you the conviction that you too can serve this generation in the will of God.

But there will be a price. That is the message of this book.

Arthur F. Glasser
Dean Emeritus
School of World Mission
Fuller Theological Seminary
Pasadena, California

1
Letters Tell a Story

Why would we want to save all those old letters we had written over a 3-year period? Would we ever really look at them again? On the other hand, we were reluctant to throw them away, knowing that our parents had made such a point of saving them for us. They were convinced that someday our detailed accounts could be of special interest to the family—or perhaps have some historical value since they recorded the beginnings of Mission Aviation Fellowship's presence and air support for missions on the remote South Pacific island of New Guinea.

Our parents cared about us to the extent of becoming partners with us in the work of Mission Aviation Fellowship. They encouraged us through love and prayer and also generously contributed to our financial needs. This new assignment of ours no doubt increased their interest in MAF, but could this idea of saving these letter-records also have been prompted by God?

Well, those letters lay all but forgotten over the years . . . until shortly after Charlie's death in 1981 when I thought about them and decided that maybe rereading some of them would be a good form of grief therapy. As I began to sort them chronologically, I found myself pausing to read snatches here and there. Then paragraphs. Before long I was reading entire letters, and reliving experiences as memories surfaced. But perhaps more importantly, I realized our parents may have been right in thinking about their historical value—for our assignment in New Guinea, particularly in view of Charlie's leadership role there and throughout our lengthy service in MAF, did seem rather significant.

At the time we left for New Guinea, in 1952, Mission Aviation Fellowship was already well into its first decade of existence. The small unknown organization, founded by a few former military pilots, was now at work providing transportation for missions in Mexico, Ecuador, and Honduras. Within a couple more decades (by the end of the 70s), MAF-US and its counterparts in Britain [BMAF] and Australia [AMAF] were serving 150 agencies in 28 nations around the world with upwards of about 125 planes and even a few helicopters. The high cost of the helicopter operation, however, brought about a decision to turn that part of the work over to another organization.

Who could have imagined, at that time, that MAF would one day utilize sophisticated planes with global positioning devices that could provide almost instantaneous communication via satellites? Yet by the turn of the century technological advances had opened doors to new educational and ministry opportunities such as larger and more suitable aircraft, satellite and Internet communication networks, and distance learning capabilities. It's a different world!

From the very beginning, MAF candidates were required to meet specified technological standards for aircraft pilots and mechanics. And there was a recognized need almost immediately for some kind of orientation for the new recruits—to prepare them for living and serving in a variety of cultural settings. Initially, orientation was very limited in scope, and conducted informally. But as the organization matured, a more lengthy and comprehensive orientation program was instituted. It now includes an emphasis on language learning techniques and cross-cultural insights, in addition to specialized aviation skills. For career personnel, certain basic requirements remain unchanged: that of a personal commitment to Jesus Christ as Lord and Savior, a relationship to the Church (the Body of Christ), and some formal Bible training.

MAF's original purpose was to provide essential transportation for missionaries and evangelists (national and expatriot) which would make it possible for them to live and work in remote areas—whether beyond the reach of existing transportation or in areas where terrain or living conditions necessitated reliable air support.[1] Countless surveys were conducted to locate pockets of previously unreached people groups so that missions could strategically place their personnel. MAF's planes also carry school children, mail, building materials and other supplies; assist with agricultural projects; and respond during times of medical emergencies, disaster relief efforts, and evacuation.

Such aviation services were essential for mission outreach in New Guinea's rugged and mountainous terrain. In the 1940s and 50s, New Guinea's rugged and mountainous terrain presented tremendous and specific challenges—interior valleys could not be reached apart from air transportation. And this inaccessibility was underscored, at the time, by sketchy and incomplete aviation

[1]Barriers of various kinds continue to prevent the Gospel's penetration into some areas of the world. With the cooperation of many mission agencies, MAF conducted a five-year study called Operation *ACCESS!* designed to identify and locate those remaining barriers around the globe. This exhaustive research was completed in 2006. Survey results are available at www.operationaccessmaf.org

maps for the entire island; some portions were either blank or designated "unexplored territory."

MAF's initial efforts there were expected to expand. But I doubt that any of us, in 1952, could possibly have imagined the changes that occurred during the next 30 years. By the 1980s, MAF had more than 36 planes flying nearly 80,000 flights a year from some 20 bases—all on the island of New Guinea. Missionaries in Papua [formerly Dutch New Guinea, which became Indonesian Irian Jaya—then Papua], at one point found themselves literally overwhelmed by "people movements" that erupted in various locations, when huge numbers turned to the Lord all at once.

Before launching into the story of MAF's initial entry into New Guinea, I'd like to express deep appreciation for our many colleagues in MAF. Together we share a special bond as partners in our combined efforts to take the redemptive message of Jesus Christ to inaccessible areas in the world. I'd like also to acknowledge the thousands of others who have faithfully served with other mission agencies. Without these dedicated Christ-followers there would be no story to tell.

This account, however, will focus primarily on Charlie Mellis—his leadership role in the development of mission aviation on that island, and his administrative role at headquarters through the years. He was *more than a pilot*.

As I think about our 27-year involvement in MAF, especially our three years in New Guinea, I am very much aware of personal limitations and weaknesses, many of which will no doubt be apparent in the pages that follow. If we had the opportunity to try again with the benefit of hindsight, might we do a better job? Perhaps, but that is a futile question, for none of us can change the past. I do know that I am exceedingly grateful to a loving and forgiving Sovereign Lord for His unfailing patience, presence, and enabling. He faithfully worked with us (and, yes, I believe even *through* us) to enlarge His Kingdom and accomplish His purpose. I might add that it is with a very thankful heart that I will share our story, documented by those letters that were so carefully preserved for us and by memos and reports found in Charlie's files.

But first, I'd like to provide some background information. How did we come to be a part of MAF? And, what series of events led to our assignment on that distant South Pacific island of New Guinea?

2
Toward Airplanes for Missions

How did we get involved in mission aviation? A simple explanation might be to say that God brought to our minds ideas similar to those of other Christians who were beginning to think of using wings to take the Gospel to remote areas of the world. But there is more to it than that. Like other Christian airmen in World War II, Charlie (a B-17 bomber pilot) wished there were some way to use his government flight training to serve the Lord. But it wasn't until the summer of 1945 (after we were married) that we heard about a new organization called Christian Airmen's Missionary Fellowship.

As its name implies, CAMF was a fellowship of believers—pilots and others related to flying—who were committed to applying aviation to the Great Commission. Charlie was excited about the prospect. Eager to know more about CAMF, he wrote asking to become a member. Before long we began to receive the first few newsletters.

When the war ended in August of 1945 and it seemed clear that Charlie would soon be released from the Army Air Corps, we made plans to go to Chicago. Since Charlie had dropped out of Wheaton College to enter military service (already a private pilot, he chose to enlist in the Air Corps rather than wait to be drafted), it seemed only natural to think of returning to his studies once the war was over. But he could not put CAMF out of his mind. Should he perhaps offer to help out—at least temporarily—until others released from military service could take over?

As we understood it, CAMF's core group was very small, consisting of co-founders Jim Buyers and Jim Truxton (both Navy pilots), Betty Greene (a former Women's Army Service Pilot then managing the CAMF office), and Grady Parrott (a former Army flight instructor who worked full time in Los Angeles in a secular job).

Not long after we arrived in Chicago we learned that Grady expected to visit Wheaton College within the next couple of weeks, so Charlie arranged to meet him there. As the two of them talked, Charlie felt increasingly drawn to CAMF, its purpose and goals. Near the end of their time together, he decided to ask if

CAMF could use volunteer representation in the Chicago area. CAMF, of course, had no resources with which to pay wages or salary. Charlie knew this. But he was convinced that if this was the right thing to do, the Lord would supply our needs—even if it meant living initially on our savings. In making such an offer, Charlie was well aware of Chicago's strategic location: a considerable number of missions had their headquarters in the area, and interest in missions was high in many churches in that part of the country. Someone needed to provide information about CAMF.

Grady thoroughly concurred with Charlie's reasoning, but felt he should consult with the others in L.A. before accepting the offer. For Charlie, such a commitment meant abandoning, at least temporarily, any plans for further study. As it turned out, that decision had far-reaching consequences and permanently changed the direction of our lives.

Once the affirmative decision was communicated, Charlie immediately swung into action. He wrote letters, arranged to meet with pastors and mission personnel, and prepared to accept invitations to share about CAMF whenever and wherever an opportunity arose. Within a month or two, he found himself reaching out beyond the Chicago area to present CAMF's objectives and challenges to churches and groups farther away.

Meanwhile, living in Chicago those first few months was not easy for us. Our major problem was housing. Few options were available, due to the many being released from the military so soon after the war's end. Our abrupt change of plans meant that instead of moving into college housing, we had to arrange overnight accommodations one day at a time. Thankfully, the Lord enabled us to locate a place each night—usually after spending a considerable amount of time looking and inquiring. I admit this was harder for me than for Charlie—facing the unknowns of where we could overnight next. Of course moving every day and living out of our car meant we had no address or phone, nowhere to prepare meals, and no laundry facilities. And with no "base of operation," so to speak, there was little I could do or accomplish (except "wait") while Charlie made his contacts.

Finally, after nearly six weeks of those one-night stands, while visiting to share about CAMF with a pastor in Roseland, south Chicago, he and his wife—Dr. and Mrs. Harry Hager (also relatives)—invited us to stay with them until we could locate an apartment. To this day I vividly remember those feelings of homelessness that suddenly ended with the unexpected gracious invitation.

Being a part of their family for Thanksgiving certainly enriched for us the meaning of giving thanks.

During the Christmas holidays, which we spent in St. Louis with Charlie's parents, the Hagers phoned to tell us of an apartment that would be available to rent for a few months while parishioners of theirs were wintering in California. It was just a block from their house and near their church. Needless to say, we were overjoyed—and additionally thankful for this provision.

As the new year of 1946 began, we learned that CAMF was being given its first airplane—a Waco biplane—to serve the Wycliffe Bible Translators at their Jungle Camp in Mexico. Getting the plane there was made possible by additional gifts, some very sacrificially given by close friends of the work. Because Betty Greene was selected to fly the Waco to Mexico and stay to launch the program, there would be no one to staff the CAMF office in L.A. In anticipating her departure, Charlie was approached about taking over these office responsibilities. After thinking and praying about it, we both came to the conclusion that the Lord wanted him to accept. However, we could not make the move immediately because of the imminent birth of our first son (John) in March.

We arrived in Los Angeles in mid-May and learned that Jim Truxton's sister Margaret had invited us to stay with her temporarily. Her tiny apartment was within walking distance of the CAMF office in downtown L.A., across the street from Pershing Square. Margaret, along with Selma Bauman, both Biola students, took turns as CAMF's part-time secretaries. Betty Greene, with the Waco biplane, was already at work in Mexico. The two Jims were in other parts of the country—Jim Buyers, preparing to enter Princeton Seminary; and Jim Truxton, traveling on behalf of the work. Grady lived and worked in L.A. but was available for consultation. His proximity was especially valuable to Charlie as he settled immediately into office management.

Along with his office responsibilities, Charlie spent time looking into housing possibilities for our family. But post-war housing in L.A., we soon learned, was as scarce as in Chicago. The house search was complicated by two other factors: we had no car, and Charlie was reluctant to spend precious office hours at anything other than office work. In the end, the best of available options seemed to be a piece of property with two houses on one lot (not uncommon in L.A. at the time) about a mile south of the Coliseum, near well-known Figueroa Street. While not ideal, it had possibilities. Charlie reasoned that if we bought the property personally, it could provide housing not only for our family but for CAMF's office as well—temporarily, until the rear (guest) house was vacated, which he foresaw possibly accommodating a candidate couple as well. This location had additional advantages of being close to public transportation, and it was within walking distance of a bank and post office.

We (and the office) moved there in early July 1946. By September, CAMF needed a full-time secretary. Selma agreed to set aside her schooling at Biola in order to take the job, provided she could find affordable housing. We invited her to live with us—which she did. So within a few months our little house became not only our family's residence but provided space for CAMF's office, and for CAMF's first full-time office secretary.

After some months the house in the rear was vacated. Jim Truxton, with his sister Margaret and their mother, moved in there so that Jim could be closer to work. When the first candidate couple (Nate and Marj Saint) arrived, we were able to rent a room from the lady next door to house them. As for the front house, Charlie and I used as our bedroom by night the room the office occupied by day. (It had a double bed that slid underneath a built-in desk and an adjacent elevated closet.) Our two boys—John and his new baby brother Jim—slept in the bedroom; we had converted the "breakfast room" for Selma; and Charlie's mother, who was assisting us following Jim's birth, slept on a "roll-a-way" bed in the living room. We were totally out of space!

About this time Jim Lomheim was asked to serve in Mexico. And during the time the Saints were candidating, the office moved to the rear house, which then also became available for candidate housing. After the Saints left, the Hatcher family arrived for candidacy, and the Berry family was next in line. Throughout these first couple of years, all of us ate, slept and practically breathed "the work." A few friends (mainly volunteers for CAMF projects) joined us weekly for a time of prayer. They also helped with monthly "publication parties." Of course, our mailing list was not yet very extensive, but folding, sorting, and stamping even a relatively few thousand pieces of mail consumed a lot of time. Occasions like these served as both entertainment and social life, for none of us had much money. Somehow, meager personal finances didn't seem to matter—our motivation and enthusiasm for the Lord's work through CAMF knew no bounds.

Incidentally, in those early days, the allowance for a family of three was $100 per month (proportionately less for single persons). This stipend was paid in full—if sufficient gifts were received. If not, we shared what was available.

Shortages were carried over to the following month, except at the end of the year. January began with a clean slate; that is, no deficit was carried over at year's end. There were very few months when insufficient receipts prevented allowances from being paid in full, and only occasionally did a shortage last two or more consecutive months.

In 1950 a major decision was made to change the organization's name. Christian Airmen's Missionary Fellowship became Missionary Aviation Fellowship,[1] a name adopted by an organization with similar membership and purpose in Britain. This shared name has resulted in a lengthy and mutually appreciative and cooperative relationship between these first two MAF groups.

Not surprisingly, Charlie's plans for returning to college were put "on indefinite hold." MAF responsibilities consumed all his time and, in fact, the time and energies of every one of the relatively few involved. As funds for planes began to accumulate, a few friends of MAF—engineers and mechanics at local aerospace companies—volunteered to help with modifications done in a rented hangar at a small airport in nearby Hawthorne.

Between 1948 and 1950 there were several departures for "the field." Nate and Marj Saint left for Ecuador; the Hatchers joined Jim Lomheim in Mexico (although in separate programs); Betty Greene moved from Mexico to Peru to fly the Wycliffe Bible Translators' amphibian (a Grumman Duck); and the Berry family made preparations to open a new program in Honduras.

Early in 1950, shortly after Grady and Maurine Parrott joined the work full time, it was decided that our family should make an extended trip across the southern states so that Charlie could recruit pilot/mechanics at Christian colleges and present the work to interested churches along the way. To facilitate our family's moving around, we traded housing with the Berrys—that is, they moved into our house and we utilized their 33-foot house trailer.

At the end of the year, after traveling for nine months, our family returned to Los Angeles. Charlie and Grady shared office responsibilities and more or less took turns traveling to take speaking engagements in distant cities, and to meet with mission leaders in the East and Midwest. While in those areas they also represented MAF at churches and mission conferences. There were other requests to speak at local churches and fellowship groups in Southern California. Occasionally one of them traveled to the field. By 1951 Jim Truxton

---

[1]The name was changed again some years later to Mission Aviation Fellowship.

was working steadily in South America where he was joined by Hobey Lowrance, a former American Airlines pilot. Together they completed the survey in Ecuador that Jim had begun and then moved on to other surveys and feasibility studies in Colombia, Venezuela and Brazil.

At that point I'm sure Charlie began to wonder if he himself would ever fly on the field. He was content using his administrative gifts in the office, but how should he reconcile this with his earlier call to "go"? I've wondered whether he was perhaps a little concerned about whether I could handle an overseas assignment. We both knew I had come to missions by a very different route. As his wife I was lovingly committed to him and fully supportive of his work, but I had felt no specific call to missions. Nor had I had the same in-depth exposure to missions and missionaries as he had.

By contrast, Charlie's entire family had been a part of a church where the emphasis and priorities were missions. His parents continually invited visiting missionaries to stay in their home. And his father not only took time from his business to arrange meetings for them in the St. Louis area, but he provided projection equipment and necessary transportation as well. Beyond that, he had established a Trust Fund from which he made funds available for missionaries and mission projects he had become acquainted with during his frequent trips to visit those supported by his church.

As early as 1937, Charlie (at age 16) persuaded his parents to allow him to accompany his father on a trip through Africa. Traveling by carryall truck, they spent approximately eight months visiting as many missionaries as possible throughout that continent, many of whom had been guests in the Mellis home or were related to their church's mission program. They brought back dozens of reels of 16mm film to show to interested groups in the States. It is no small wonder that missions became a vital part of Charlie's life.

Charlie's interest in missions may have developed largely through his family, but he discovered when he spent two years working for his dad after graduating from high school that he did not enjoy working closely with his father in the family's building business. Were they perhaps too much alike? Or were his father's expectations too high? Whatever the reason, it was during those two years that he learned to fly—partly, he later admitted, to get into a field that his father knew nothing about. However, he loved flying and toyed with the idea of becoming an airline pilot. And yet, there was always a deep-seated awareness that God was calling him into missions.

One valuable insight came from working with his father: Charlie was drawn to, and had a knack for, some aspects of business. Later he marveled at how the Lord brought together for him in MAF three seemingly unrelated interests: missions, flying, and administration. In fact, he often remarked that he couldn't imagine being happier or more fulfilled than he was in MAF. I am convinced this is what motivated him to throw himself so wholeheartedly into everything connected with MAF. Talk about commitment! He had it: a commitment to the Lord and to the task.

In the six years that we had been a part of Mission Aviation Fellowship, MAF's services and programs expanded deeper into Central and South America. British MAF began working in Africa, and MAF of Australia's focus was the Pacific. We in MAF-US never dreamed that the Lord would use a tragedy halfway around the world to drastically change our organization's planning. Nor did we expect this tragedy would lead to a decision calling for a sudden and imminent move by the Mellis family. But that is exactly what happened!

3
The Challenge in New Guinea

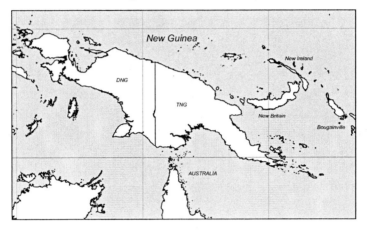

"Charlie, are you serious? ... You mean the decision is final? ... We're the family to go to New Guinea?"

I knew discussions were underway at the office about how to respond to an urgent request for help following a fatal accident in New Guinea. But I wasn't prepared for the Board's decision to send our family to New Guinea, particularly when I learned the target departure date–June 22 (1952)–was only eight weeks away! Yet I realized that the Board had few options, personnel-wise, from which to choose. Not only were MAF's few pilots already committed elsewhere, but the nature of the anticipated task in New Guinea required authoritative decision-making skills. Charlie was one of a few who would logically be considered. On the other hand, I thought about the recent arrival of our new baby (third son, Gordon), only a couple weeks old. Suddenly everything seemed so very complicated. I just couldn't imagine how we could possibly have our family of five ready to leave in just eight weeks for a two-to-four-year absence! Charlie, on the other hand, in accepting the assignment, was convinced that if we did everything we knew to do, the Lord would make it possible for us to leave on schedule.

Originally, the idea of becoming involved in work at such a distance from our shores was not a part of MAF-US's long-range planning. It was only when the urgent request for help came late in 1951 that our Board even considered moving beyond Central and South America. But what a request! MAF-US had struggled to get two programs operational by 1951–two planes and pilots in Mexico and one in Ecuador; and preparations for launching a fourth program in Honduras were nearing completion. Our Board was by no means certain a response to this request was even possible because available personnel and resources were already pretty well committed. Ultimately the question became, Was the Lord opening doors? If so, might He not expect a positive response?

Before final agreement, the Board decided to obtain more information. Grady Parrott (MAF President) was sent first to Australia to confer with AMAF's Council before going on to New Guinea to assess the situation there personally. It was important to look not only at current needs but also at possibilities for expanding services in the future.

By this time we at home had learned that New Guinea was the second largest island in the world (after Greenland). We knew it lay just to the north of the continent of Australia in the South Pacific. The island of New Guinea resembles the side view of a bird whose head lies at the north and west end and its tail extends south and east. At that time (1952) it was divided in half politically, into east and west segments. The eastern half–known as Papua New Guinea–was currently under Australian control by mandate of the United Nations following World War II. It was designated the Territory of New Guinea (or, simply, TNG). The western half–today a part of Indonesia–was in 1952 a colony of the Netherlands, and known as Dutch New Guinea (DNG).

The Australian-mandated portion of the island (eastern half) had been the scene of mission activity already in the 1800s when Lutherans arrived there from Germany. This mission activity increased later when Lutherans from Australia and the United States came to join them.

During WWII the entire island was affected; mission personnel were either interned or evacuated. When the war ended, the Lutheran Mission returned to its mission activities and eagerly sought to move into previously unreached areas. But this was recognized as hardly feasible apart from adequate air support.

To secure this vital air support, the Lutheran leadership contacted Mission Aviation Fellowship of Australia (AMAF), and in 1951 AMAF sent its first plane and pilot to serve them. However, to begin this, their first field operation, AMAF had to stretch both its personnel and financial resources to the limit. At that point, the organization had only one trained pilot available (Harry Hartwig) and funds for just one airplane (an Auster). Realizing they needed help with maintenance, since Harry was not a trained mechanic, they had asked for the loan of a MAF-US pilot/mechanic to assist him.

It so happened that Bob Hutchins, a former U.S. Navy pilot, had just completed his mechanics training and was ready for MAF candidacy and an assignment. When the New Guinea challenge was presented to Bob and his wife Betty, they accepted.

The Hutchins flew first to Sydney, Australia, where they helped at MAF headquarters during the final months of planning and preparation. Then, in April of 1951, Harry and Bob together ferried the Auster to New Guinea, stopping briefly at the Lutheran Mission headquarters in Lae before flying on to Madang, where the plane was to be based. Their wives (Margaret and Betty) spent three weeks traveling from Australia by ship to Madang.

AMAF's Madang-based program was underway only a few months when in August of 1951 we in Los Angeles got word that the Auster had crashed on a flight into the Highlands. Harry, flying alone, had been killed and the plane destroyed. We in MAF-US were stunned, but for AMAF the loss of both pilot and plane was devastating. No other pilot was trained or ready to take over, and replacement funds were all but nonexistent. AMAF's situation seemed desperate. By year's end, AMAF leadership contacted our L.A. office to inquire if we could help. Would it be possible for MAF-US to somehow reestablish the air service and assist AMAF back into the aviation picture there in New Guinea?

After the accident, Bob and Betty Hutchins remained in New Guinea while awaiting the outcome of the various discussions. Their presence enabled Grady to enlist Bob's help in studying the terrain and population concentrations, to ascertain equipment and personnel necessary for accomplishing the mission's objectives.

As it turned out, Grady had hardly set foot in New Guinea before he was conscious of a series of doors opening, one after another. His immediate impression was that the whole island was ripe for mission aviation. If this were proven true, MAF-US could conceivably have its hands full very soon, for much developmental work would no doubt follow in the wake of the initial program activity.

Grady and Bob began their study by arranging a few flights with local commercial operators to look over the Central Highlands. Then, as they met with Lutheran Mission leaders to discuss the situation, they learned that the

Lutherans were prepared to purchase whatever plane MAF recommended (a Cessna 170), if MAF would supply the personnel. The Lutherans also graciously agreed to make their plane available on a limited basis until such time as additional planes and pilots would be forthcoming. Bob and Betty agreed to stay on, even though Bob's experience as a pilot was considered minimal. For this reason, it seemed wise to send someone who could take primary responsibility as lead pilot. But, in anticipation of additional requests for service from other missions, it would be good to have someone on site who could make administrative decisions on behalf of the organization as well.

Thus far, Grady's investigations related only to strategy for serving the eastern half of the island—the Territory of New Guinea (TNG). But just across the border to the west lay Dutch New Guinea. While he was in the vicinity he decided to try to determine potential need there as well. So, after finishing his preliminary study of the Territory, Grady managed to find a ride to the western half of the island (DNG). Although there was some mission activity (primarily in coastal areas) on the part of the Dutch Reformed Church, that half of the island had remained all but closed to the evangelical message—with one exception. Now, in 1952, some closed doors seemed poised to open, perhaps a crack. In anticipation, several missions began assigning personnel to Dutch New Guinea even though they knew full well that once missionaries arrived they would be unable to move into the interior without aerial support. But available maps and charts for DNG at that time all indicated that much of the interior was *unexplored*. Moreover, its inland mountainous regions were surrounded by flat swampy jungle areas, reminiscent of medieval moats. What a challenge!

The one exception to the complete closure to missions was a place near the Wissel Lakes, toward the western end of the mountainous mid-section. There, one mission (Christian and Missionary Alliance) had begun a work. Any penetration inland from there, however, was deemed impossible apart from air support.

When Grady arrived in Hollandia (DNG) he met with representatives from several missions—i.e., Christian and Missionary Alliance (C&MA), the Evangelical Alliance (TEAM), and the Unevangelized Fields (UFM) missions. They greeted him with optimistic news. Governmental attitudes toward mission entry seemed to be softening; several missions previously denied entrance now had permission to send personnel. What was perhaps more gratifying was that it seemed obvious that these mission representatives were beginning to see

MAF as the key to unlocking the whole of DNG's interior.

The implications were staggering. Could MAF even begin to meet such a challenge? Before allowing himself to get completely carried away, Grady decided to confirm these seemingly more relaxed attitudes; he needed to talk directly with the Dutch government officials. In doing so, he was pleased to find genuine interest in MAF's technical participation in developing air services into the interior.

As a climax to his investigations, Grady arranged a flight over the Baliem Valley just before he left the island. What he saw was an isolated but well-populated valley with an advanced Stone Age civilization. The vast valley, discovered by the Archbold Expedition shortly before World War II, had received a lot of attention near the end of the war when the U.S. Air Force made a glider snatch to rescue several airmen who had gone down in that valley while on a sightseeing flight. It was then that the valley acquired the name *Shangri-La*, and the time when evangelical missions began to pray about entrance into that valley. But the doors had remained closed. Now, at last, it seemed their prayers were being answered. In fact, all indications seemed to be pointing to its being God's time for MAF to enter the picture.

It was an excited Grady who returned to L.A. to share this tremendous challenge with MAF's leadership and constituency. All his investigations had more than confirmed a need for mission aviation, but the task suddenly seemed much bigger than first anticipated. That it would prove a big responsibility, none of us doubted. But I don't think any of us really understood at that moment all that would be involved—even though the list included: establishing relationships with AMAF and with many other missions in addition to the Lutherans, securing government permissions to operate, determining personnel needs, recommending equipment, conducting surveys to determine locations for mission stations and airstrips, overseeing the programs as they developed, studying expansion options, coordinating the various programs, and more.

It couldn't have been an easy decision for MAF's Board to make. Mission aviation was so relatively new and the organization lacked precedent-setting experience. Nevertheless, a decision was reached and then announced in MAF's May newsletter, *Wings of Praise and Prayer:*

> After PRAYerful consideration, we've decided to send MAF Secretary, Charlie Mellis, and his family to develop missionary aviation needs in this area. Charlie's first job will be to work with Bob Hutchins flying the Cessna in Australian New

Guinea. Because the Cessna will be arriving in New Guinea soon, Charlie and Claire face a tight schedule to leave Los Angeles by June 22 ...

As I have indicated, the Board's decision came in mid-April and we faced a June departure. To me, the eight-week preparation time seemed on the one hand totally unrealistic; and yet on the other hand, I realized the plane service was needed *yesterday*!

At any rate, once the decision was made, and since time was at such a premium, Charlie began to formulate a plan to meet this demanding schedule. If he was at all apprehensive about going, I was not aware of it. I just know the idea of going was more of a struggle for me. It was probably a good thing we were very busy, for it gave me little time to dwell on any negatives.

Charlie, of course, was in his element—planning and organizing all the details. He loved putting his energies into work for the Lord, and he loved MAF—which he considered a welcome change after military service. He happily worked long hours—as did many of the other early MAFers. They all drove themselves hard; there were so many things to do and so few to do them.

However, his intense and single-minded devotion to the work became at times a sore point for me. Even though I knew his family was important to him, I occasionally felt we were excess baggage. I'm sure Charlie only intended to put the Lord first, but I had a hard time trying to figure out just where our family fit in. Should I question his priorities when he seemed so happy in MAF and was obviously fulfilled in his work? Yet, to be honest, I felt left out. Why was that? Did I really have so little to offer? (I knew nothing about airplanes and not a whole lot about missions.) Or was I just being selfish, unwilling to let him put the Lord's work first?

Some years later I realized that woven into this situation was my own understanding of the husband/wife relationship. Both of us had grown up with rather traditional views of a wife's role (primarily household duties and child care). "Housewives" were not expected to make particularly significant contributions when it came to discussions of important issues or business matters— even though many of us were college graduates. I usually managed to accept the situation, but unresolved questions continued to surface periodically through the years. In fairness to Charlie, however, let me say here that some years later he came to recognize an imbalance existed in his priorities regarding the family, and—conscientiously, as always—he endeavored to make appropriate changes. More about this in the final chapter.

But, back to our preparations to leave in 1952. Charlie planned and organized our activities, I helped execute them, and our MAF colleagues pitched in when they could. It was a demanding schedule. Passport applications, medical checks, immunizations, shopping, and decisions about what to take or leave, the boys' schooling, etc., etc. and packing!

We even managed a whirlwind cross-country trip in those eight weeks. Since Charlie enjoyed combining as many objectives as possible into one activity, he now reasoned that if we rented a Cessna 170 (like the one ordered for New Guinea) we could not only make a quick trip to see our parents and interested churches in the Midwest, but he could at the same time update his flying skills (including navigation) and even practice loading and tie-downs. Naturally, the rest of us were enthused about flying as a family, and we had a wonderful and memorable—though hurried—trip.

Suddenly, it was June 22 and time to board the Pan American Stratocruiser waiting at the gate at Los Angeles' International Airport. We were breathless, but ready to go—with the Lord's enabling!

Charlie's planning, however, hadn't ended with reservations and plane tickets. He had researched travel arrangements and found he could reserve the forward compartment of the plane (at that time equipped with upper and lower berths for sleeping) for our family. Though determined to keep expenses to a minimum, he was always alert to available opportunities. It really pleased him to discover this possibility for the family's enjoyment. He wanted the trip to be special. In fact, it was travel times like these that we all loved because, for once, he was *all ours*. We didn't have to share him with anyone else! What made it even better was his obvious enjoyment of his family while we were traveling. And we were off to a family adventure and challenge!

4
Half Way Around the World

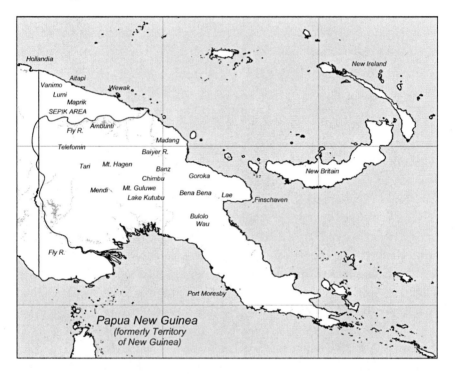

Now and then in the midst of our preparations I had tried to imagine what it would be like to work half way around the world in totally unfamiliar surroundings only one week after leaving the States. I wondered how we would cope with such things as the tropical heat, learning a new language, managing household help. Just thinking of all those things was rather frightening. I told myself it was futile to borrow trouble by worrying ahead of time. Besides, weren't we confident that the Lord had directed our going and would see us through? We determined to throw ourselves wholeheartedly into the challenge, and take one day at a time, if necessary. That strategy sounded great—maybe even noble! However, we were to discover that day-by-day trust isn't always as easy as it sounds, particularly when events take turns that are hard to understand.

After an overnight stop in Honolulu, and a multi-hour stop for plane maintenance in Fiji, we flew on to Sydney, Australia, where we were met by a few representatives of Australian Mission Aviation Fellowship (AMAF). They saw us to our downtown hotel, located near offices where Charlie needed to finalize the paperwork for our New Guinea visas. The next day, after completing the paperwork, Charlie flew on alone to Melbourne to spend a couple of days conferring with the AMAF Council.

When he returned to Sydney, he gathered up the family and we were soon airborne—this time headed for Port Moresby, the capitol city of the Territory of New Guinea near the southeastern tip of the island. Here we went through customs and changed planes for the two-hour flight north to Lae. In Lae we met the leaders of the Lutheran Mission and spent the day (Sunday) with personnel at their headquarters. The following day—exactly seven days after our departure from Los Angeles—we flew the remaining two-hour leg to Madang, our destination.

The day was overcast and the flight seemed short. We gained altitude to cross a ridge of mountains and then almost immediately began the descent to land. With so much that was new, I'm sure we didn't fully appreciate the beauty of Madang's coastal setting. I hardly noticed the coral reefs in the waters below, but I did note the presence of graceful palms, vivid green hills and lush tropical foliage along the coast. The scenery was indeed beautiful, but I was also very much aware of being a long, long way from home.

As we taxied to the terminal we spotted a familiar face. Bob Hutchins, a fellow MAFer, was there to meet us. He helped us collect our luggage and ushered us aboard an old gray truck, a war-weary weapons carrier that had somehow survived the fighting. It was one of many vehicles declared surplus by our government after the WWII hostilities ceased. Acquired by the Lutheran Mission, it was assigned to their aviation department since it could nicely accommodate and transport passengers and cargo back and forth between the airport and the mission's supply store in town.

The road from the airport into Madang wound around a good-sized bay. The relatively few local roads look much like our gravel roads but are graded with crushed coral. These coral roads apparently drain well and don't tend to become slippery or muddy, but they do have the disadvantage of being extremely dusty when dry.

In 1952 about 200 Europeans lived in and around Madang. Most were Australian government officials or civil aviation personnel. Other European residents were related to the Lutheran Mission, and lived on a number of stations clustered within 10 miles of Madang—for example, a technical/industrial school for young men at Baitabag, a plantation and print shop at Nagada, a hospital at Jagaum, and a girls' school at Amele. These stations were accessible by road, although none of them were in as good a condition as the well-traveled one between Madang and the airport.

As we were leaving the airport, one of our boys excitedly pointed to a wrecked plane on the far side of the field. There, partially hidden by the growing grass, lay a moth-eaten Japanese Zero—no doubt lying just where it fell when shot down.

We were to discover other war relics around town—grim reminders of the heavy fighting on the island that had ended less than seven years before we arrived. We saw bullet holes in some of the buildings, an old rusted-out tank almost covered over by tropical vegetation, shell damage at the lighthouse on the "point," and a rusted skeleton of a ship half submerged and half above the water line in the harbor. Live grenades still turned up here and there, which were given to the authorities to detonate. Some months later, when we moved into our new house, our sons John and Jim discovered portions of tank tracks in our backyard that were all but concealed by the encroaching tropical growth. John also recalls finding an unexploded shell. We learned that missionaries who remained in New Guinea throughout the war were interned by the Japanese on one of the islands in Madang's harbor.

When we arrived at the Hutchins' house—one of the Lutheran mission's houses—Betty greeted us warmly, with breakfast on the table. Bob and Betty told us we were to live with them temporarily, until the first of the two new houses being built across town for the mission's aviation personnel were completed. (They themselves would move into the second new house when it was ready.) Unfortunately, as so often happens, construction was behind schedule, slowed by shipping delays of building materials and other hard-to-obtain items from Australia. It could be several weeks yet before the houses were finished.

The house Bob and Betty currently occupied was good-sized, however, and could accommodate our two families. It was rectangular, with the kitchen, three bedrooms and a shower room across the rear, and the living room/dining area and an office across the front. A laundry shed and outhouse were adjacent to the house. The house had screens throughout, but no glass in windows or doors.

We had running water in the house, as long as it rained often enough. Most houses had at least one huge corrugated aluminum tank positioned on a platform next to the house to catch the runoff rainwater from the roof. Pipes near the bottom of the tank brought the rainwater into the house–water which we could use without first boiling it. Although we managed to adjust to the out-house, it didn't take us long to start looking forward to one luxury feature of the new house: an inside flush toilet! We did have electricity–from 6 a.m. until midnight–supplied by the city. But everyone also owned kerosene lamps and flashlights for times when the power was shut off or there was a power failure. And no one went anywhere at night without a light of some kind because of the possibility of snakes.

Madang's "downtown" was only a few blocks away. The shopping/business district consisted of a couple of Quonset huts on one street that housed a bank and a store, and there was a second general store on a nearby street. These catered primarily to Europeans. Located separately was Chinatown, where a number of tiny shops were stocked with goods that attracted the native popu-lation and the tourists that arrived by ship. There was also a large wharf in the vicinity where the two ocean-going ships from Australia docked. One of these, the Bulolo, was a passenger ship that usually carried a considerable number of tourists, in addition to residents who were coming or going from the Territory. The other ship, the Malekula, was a freighter which could accommodate a few passengers as well as its cargo. Beyond the stores was Madang's new hotel. And beyond the hotel, near a lighthouse on the point, was the newest (resi-dential) section of town. It was here that the mission was building its two new houses for the aviation families.

Papuans (those from various areas in the Territory of New Guinea) spoke such a variety of languages that it was necessary to establish a common trade language: Pidgin English. Pidgin is very interesting. Its written form looks like a foreign language, but when one tries to read it using phonetic sounds, he dis-covers that many of the words sound very similar to English. For this reason, understanding it is not really too difficult. Using it correctly is more of a chal-lenge, because there is a proper grammar and word order. The more we got into it, the more we found it delightfully descriptive.

The weather? We were prepared for the fact that it would be very hot. In fact, our four-year-old Jim had told people in the States before we left that it would be "boiling hot" in New Guinea. I'm not sure where he picked up that information, but maybe because we were prepared for the worst we didn't find the heat too bad. Evenings were quite pleasant, and at night we usually needed at least a sheet over us. But weather patterns for flying were something else, as will be apparent in due course.

Living in the tropics required taking weekly anti-malarial drugs. We didn't anticipate some other problems—like the boils that suddenly appeared on our three-month-old Gordon's head within a week or two of our arrival. A penicillin shot came to the rescue, thankfully; but we had to go through the whole procedure over again every couple of months for a while. For Jim, it was the ulcerous sores that developed on his arms and legs, presumably from his scratching insect bites—which then became infected. Flies were a particular nuisance because it was so hard to keep his sores clean and covered. His activity, plus the high humidity, kept band-aids and other bandages from staying in place.

We loved the available tropical foods, especially the papaya, pineapple, mangoes, soursop, taro, bananas, to mention a few. There was also a refreshing lemonade made from *mulis*, a cross between a lemon and a lime.

One other food item we came to appreciate in a new way was fresh meat. There was a limited variety of *tinned* meat, all of which got to tasting the same. And there was some "freezer meat" shipped from Australia—which was too expensive to have very often. The mission, however, had some animals on its plantation and occasionally butchered one. Soon after we arrived we were included among the mission families to receive a portion of a butchered 15-year-old bull. It was left to individual families to further cut their portions and package them into meal-sized amounts. Bob and Charlie tackled the cutting while Betty and I did the packaging. How we enjoyed the fresh meat, even from that old a bull!

On another occasion we were given a different kind of fresh meat when a couple of Papuans, together with the Lutheran store manager, caught a tortoise and shared part of it with us. To catch it, one of the men dived into the water, managed to put a rope around its neck and then all three worked to haul it in. We thought the tortoise was huge, but our kitchen helper said it was really only a small one compared to others he had seen. None of us was particularly enthusiastic about the taste, but we tried to appreciate the fact that it was fresh meat.

Everyone in New Guinea seemed to share one common concern: the mail. We could expect mail to arrive (or be sent out) twice a week—if the DC-3 planes were on schedule. They could be delayed hours, and sometimes even days, by weather or maintenance problems. These delays caused all kinds of frustrations and affected all of us at one time or another. Surface mail arrived by ship—every two to three weeks.

Our sons John and Jim soon began to look for interesting diversions of their own. They watched local activities and were included in a ball game now and then. But with all of us so caught up in the excitement of getting the Cessna ready to fly, the boys decided they'd like to assemble a Cessna of their own out of some available scrap lumber. Charlie saw to it that they had a hammer and nails, and they set to work. First they built a fuselage big enough to sit in and then somehow attached wings and a tail. John constructed a landing gear. But to be complete, it also needed lights on the wing tips. So they got out their crayons to draw a red light on one wing and a green light on the other. Jim drew lines to mark the ailerons, flaps and rudder. Still, they weren't satisfied; it lacked a couple of finishing touches—custom stripes along the sides and an identifying name, *Cessna Jet,* printed on it. Bob gave a hand with the prop, nailing it on so it would spin. At last, after a final inspection, they agreed it was ready to fly.

John stood out in front calling out "Switches off," "Clear," "Switches on," "Contact," to John, the pilot. John had had the foresight to plan the cockpit with the starter inside the cabin, which meant he could both start the plane and be its pilot. Although their project had taken quite a bit of time, at least their Cessna Jet was operational. Disappointingly, the Cessna 170 we had come to operate for the Lutheran Mission remained grounded, waiting for red tape to be unsnarled. How much longer would that take? When would it be permitted to fly?

5
Unraveling Red Tape

Our first several weeks in Madang were frustrating. The plane had arrived; and Bob had it assembled. It was ready to fly except for a few minor details. Neither Bob nor Charlie had reason to anticipate additional paperwork would be required. They fully expected the certification of Charlie's pilot license by the authorities at the Department of Civil Aviation (DCA) in Port Moresby to be routine. But now, in making inquiries about how soon he could expect this certification, rumors indicated that the licensing process could take months. Meanwhile, the plane had to remain idle in the hangar. We found it hard to wait.

This waiting period did prove valuable in one way. Charlie had been eager to get better acquainted with the local DCA officials and with the operators of commercial air charter operations there in Madang. He hoped to establish good rapport with them, knowing they were fellow aviation enthusiasts. There would undoubtedly be occasions in the future when they would need to call on each other for some kind of assistance.

The operators were all very helpful in answering questions, particularly regarding paperwork. But they questioned him too; they asked about MAF—the pilots, their training, equipment MAF used, and its operating procedures. The DCA officials asked about the Cessna's specifications, including its performance levels, since this was the first plane of its kind to operate in New Guinea. Charlie began to wonder if there was something behind all these questions. He had the feeling that DCA was going to be especially cautious in granting permissions related to mission flying following the AMAF accident. That was understandable, for they were charged with the responsibility for air safety throughout the Territory, and they had no first-hand knowledge of MAF-US's reputation. They obviously believed they had no choice but to follow the rules.

Everything we had experienced thus far underscored the fact that we would need to prove ourselves to the Australian authorities. Evidently those in the L.A. office realized this too, and wrote to remind Charlie of that fact. He responded a week after our arrival by saying, on July 7, 1952:

Your thoughts about diplomacy and careful approach to aerial survey are well-taken. We're having a real test of patience right off the bat. All last week we had to wait for the aircraft surveyor for Madang to get out of a sick bed. He was back in his office today—we waited two hours there.... What a lot of paperwork! He sent another radiogram to Moresby today to ask if I can go ahead with slow time and test flight while waiting for my license to be returned. We may get in the air tomorrow. But there will be no flights away from Madang until I have license in hand and the plane has Australian registration. Even that will only be private registration. We can't do any work for other missions until we get our charter license, and that isn't even applied for yet—we need the test flight information first. But we'll have plenty to do for the Lutherans since we're only planning on one trip a day for the first few weeks—until we get our bearings real well.

The Cessna 170 had no radio. Although the fellows realized that a radio would be a comforting accessory, they also knew that arrangements to install one would not be a simple matter. If they chose an American-made Lear radio, for example, they would be faced with mountains of paperwork to get it approved by DCA. If they chose either a British- or Australian-made radio, they would be saddled with heavier pieces of equipment that would cut down payload.

Beyond the matter of equipment choice, there was the additional factor of radio maintenance. If the mission's radio man was to take on the responsibility for maintaining the plane's radio, he would not only need further licensing by DCA, but would also have to sign a certificate of safety on it every seven days! That latter requirement in itself would obviously take valuable time away from his other duties, and could become a real nuisance factor for him as well.

In addition to the problems created for the radioman specifically, there were certain other DCA rules that applied when a plane had a radio. In the first place, it had to be in working order whenever the plane took off. So, if it was not working on a particular day, that day's flying might be lost by the time the radio man could get to the airport from his station and then spend the time necessary to fix it. All things considered, Charlie decided the radio matter had to be tabled for the time being. He was not abandoning the idea, but for now, other problems had to be resolved first.

The Lutherans, meanwhile, published the characteristics of the new Cessna, perhaps to explain to their constituency the reasons for its being chosen to replace the Auster. In one of their little magazines they passed along information given them by MAF which stated that the Cessna 170 was probably one of the finest American planes available for use in mission work, with its 45 horsepower engine, 15,500 ft. ceiling, and cruising speed of 120 mph. Empty, it weighed 1200 lbs, but it could be loaded to a gross weight of 2200 lbs. As a four-place plane, it was thought roomy enough to meet most emergencies.

Even though the plane was still hangar-bound, the Lutherans saw no reason to postpone its dedication. The dedication service was scheduled for a Sunday afternoon in July. Bob, Charlie and their Papuan helpers got busy and spent the whole preceding week cleaning and polishing it (while waiting for Charlie's license to show up). Charlie reported their cleaning procedure to the office:

> We were all interested in learning how easy it was to get the preservative off the airplane at this end. It does wash right off with kerosene all right. If the airplane were stamped out of one big piece of aluminum, it would be a snap to clean it up. However, it's really a job to get it off the seams and from around every single rivet. We've put a lot of man hours into this already and we still aren't through with the job. After we finish cleaning around the rivets and seams with gasoline, we are polishing the surface with an alcohol, Bon Ami and water mixture—and getting excellent results. After washing the Bon Ami off with detergent and then with clear water, we are putting the carplate on it. It's really going to look beautiful at the dedication Sunday.

And it did. The plane really glistened. But I think everyone was disappointed it was not yet flying. Nonetheless, a good crowd assembled; quite a number of missionaries, about 300 Papuans, some Australian officials and Chinese residents. Most of the dedication service was conducted in Pidgin English. There were hymns, a prayer, speeches by Papuan pastors and by Lutheran Mission representatives. When it was Charlie's turn, he spoke briefly in English and someone translated for him into Pidgin.

A few days after the dedication we heard Charlie's license was on its way from Melbourne. That was the good news—which, unfortunately, was followed by some bad news. A wire from the DCA office in Port Moresby informed Charlie he needed another physical exam—to be taken in Moresby. This meant further delay, since airline service between Madang and Port Moresby was limited to twice a week. The news was especially disappointing because we thought we had anticipated the need for a physical in New Guinea by having one in the States just prior to our departure—which we understood would be acceptable there. The whole situation was terribly frustrating! Had we known this was going to be required, we could so easily have stopped in Port Moresby long enough to take care of this when we arrived. Now there was no alternative but to make a reservation for the earliest possible flight—and wait for results.

During those few days of waiting we took the opportunity to visit a couple of mission stations near Madang, the technical school at Baitabag and the hospital at Jagaum. In addition, Betty and I accomplished one project for the program. We made two sets of seat covers for the plane so that one set was available to use while the other set was being laundered. The project sounded relatively simple, but the sewing ended up taking longer than we anticipated since neither Betty nor I were very adept at using her hand-powered Singer.

Charlie's trip to Moresby and his physical exam went without a hitch. While it had been hard for us to view that trip as anything other than a nuisance, we felt a bit chastened later when we realized how much that timing contributed to our getting started. At that moment, however, the fellows were just happy to finally begin flying, even if only locally. They understood that permission for the plane to leave the Madang area was to be withheld pending completion of its Australian registration—the new letters (VH-AMF) had been assigned, but the official papers had not yet arrived in Madang.

As the local flying got underway, a daily schedule began to evolve. Mornings were devoted to flying since the weather was at its best during those hours. By afternoon, clouds had formed and the accumulated build-ups were often accompanied by stormy conditions which made flying more uncertain and, on occasion, hazardous. Afternoons were spent servicing the plane and loading it for the next morning's trip. Correspondence and paperwork were relegated to the evening hours, as was time for family and visitors. But by that time the pilots were usually very tired and ready for sleep.

The preliminary flying accomplished more than one purpose. It provided the engine with an adequate amount of slow time; allowed opportunity for Bob's checkout in the plane (since he had not flown a Cessna before); and because this was the first Cessna 170 to fly in either Australia or its Territory, it provided the plane's performance figures that DCA required for its files. But the fellows felt as though they had passed a real milestone when the registration papers came through and the U.S. numbers could be replaced with the Australian letter-registration.

Once the local flying was finished, application could be made for the charter license which was needed in order to serve other missions. All they lacked now was clearance to make trips into the interior. At first, permission was given verbally, as Charlie reported in a letter to our parents:

By this time the local aircraft surveyor had said, "Go ahead with your familiarization in the highlands—and if anybody objects, tell him I said so." ... We went ahead
on Monday. But there was a question whether we should carry loads.
(Familiarization with route is a required thing in this place, and a mighty wise procedure. Maps are practically useless—there's no way to navigate but to know personally the various peaks, gaps, gorges, valleys, etc. Since Bob had had over a hundred hours in the highlands, they are letting him ride with me—ordinarily it's one
of the older hands [who rides along].)

One day, when Charlie and Bob were talking with the aircraft surveyor in
Madang, he suggested they might want to take "a little ballast" on their familiarization trips. That hint was all they needed to realize it was apparently all
right to begin carrying loads. However, because this was not "official permission," the two pilots were hesitant to leave the Madang control area—such as
going to Lae, for example, which they would have found helpful at this point.
If the DCA men there, with more authority, should question the operation, the
good relationships that were being built could easily be spoiled. Aside from
getting to Lae, they didn't feel at all constricted because flying within the
Madang control area gave them access to all of the central highlands, which
was their main area of operation anyway.

All the operators at New Guinea airports seemed to know who was moving
where by plane—if not in fact, at least by rumor. So when Charlie heard that an official from Lae would be arriving in Madang on a particular DC-3 flight, he and Bob
decided to delay their early morning takeoff to Kerowagi long enough to meet the
plane. It was a real surprise to discover that the VIP stepping off the plane turned
out to be the Regional Director of DCA—the top man in New Guinea flying.
Charlie had met him when he went to Port Moresby for his physical and they had
had a good chat at that time. It was soon apparent that the Director assumed the
Cessna was already flying into the highlands—and he raised no objections.

Later in the afternoon, the aircraft safety man (also from the regional office
in Moresby) wandered over to the Cessna's hangar. Charlie had not met this
man before but had talked with him by phone when he was in Moresby for his
physical. Charlie was sure he wouldn't miss noting that the plane was loaded for
a flight into the interior. He and Bob had attempted their planned flight to
Kerowagi after meeting the DC-3 that morning, but had turned back because of
weather. So the plane remained loaded for another try the next morning. Again,
Charlie fielded a good many questions about the plane, but no question was

raised about carrying loads into the highlands. As they talked, Charlie decided to offer him a little ride the next morning before leaving Madang. If this official was satisfied, they could feel cleared to go ahead full bore with flight operations.

By this time Charlie and Bob began to realize what had been happening—the Lord was opening the way, one step at a time. The various delays had served to provide time to become acquainted in a more relaxed fashion with both commercial operators and DCA officials in Madang. His being forced to comply with DCA's regulations in terms of that physical exam turned into a positive experience. Mere acquaintances became friendships, which then were strengthened through the contacts renewed in Madang. Even his return flight from Moresby back to Madang had surprise elements. Normally, cargo flights between Moresby and Lae disallowed passengers. Not only was an exception made in this instance, but he was invited to ride in the "wheel house" with the pilots. This gave him a good chance to check out that particular route—until an undercast hid the ground during the last part of the trip.

Because the connecting flight on to Madang from Lae would not be leaving until the next day, Charlie had the whole afternoon to spend with the Lutheran leaders in Lae to discuss aviation program financing. He found it especially helpful to talk about these program details in person, and came away feeling a good working relationship had been established.

Cargo flights north from Lae to Madang, and on to Wewak, occasionally carried some passengers utilizing bucket seats—seats along the sides of the cabin which left the space in the middle for cargo. Charlie's flight was scheduled to make two stops between Lae and Madang, one of which was in the highlands. Again he was delighted to be able to check out another route by riding up front with the pilots.

We probably shouldn't have been surprised by all this; we should have suspected that the Lord was directing the timing. Evidently we had become so consumed with our frustrations when our own careful planning fell apart that we failed to realize that God might have had a different agenda. It was humbling to discover that those delays actually contributed to a better start for the program. In this instance we were clearly shown reasons for our "whys" but we were going to face other occasions during our New Guinea sojourn when we did not understand—and would receive no answers to our questions of "Why?" or "When?" For the moment, however, we were exceedingly thankful to be on the threshold of actual flight operations. It was an exciting moment indeed!

6
Highland Flights Begin

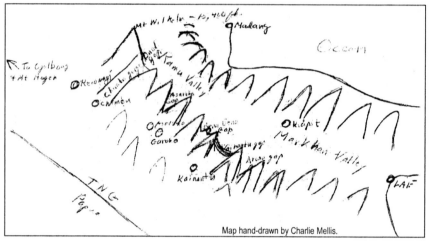

Map hand-drawn by Charlie Mellis.

The Cessna's first full week of operations into the interior began on Monday, August 4, 1952. It was a day we had looked forward to. Although we had been in Madang a little more than a month, it seemed much longer. The preliminary familiarization flights had served to acquaint Charlie not only with the terrain, landmarks, and locations of airstrips in the highlands but with the characteristics of the various airstrips as well: such as length, slope, type of surface, obstructions, and wind patterns for landings and takeoffs. He learned routes and thought through alternate strategies for emergency situations or weather-related problems.

At the end of that first week of operations he drew a map to send along with his letter to our parents. In the letter he described those first few trips:

> Monday we made an easy run down the Markham Valley to Kiapit. We flew south out of Madang, along the coastal ridge that is only about 5,000 ft. high. But where the coast bends east, the range rises to about 11,000 ft. We skirted the edge of that higher ground and broke out into a long valley which was only a little over 1,000 ft. at its highest point (where the water flows in two directions). After we crossed the coastal range at 6,000 ft., it was a long downhill coast to Kiapit.

30

From there we went on up to one of the easiest highland points—Kainantu—through a low spot even farther southeast than the Arona Gap. After we shot a few landings at Kainantu (the strip has its peculiarities, but it's a good strip), we looked over some of the other fields in the area and then headed home through the Arona Gap because the Kainantu Gap (hardly a gap—it's really only a slight dip in the ridge) was partly cloudy.

Tuesday we headed for Asaroka through the Asaroka Gap. (It was in coming out of that Gap too low that Harry was killed.) The Asaroka Gap is quite a sharp narrow gap with mountains over 10,000 ft. on each side. Since we flew at about 10,000 ft. that day we hardly noticed we were in the gap. This is one of the best routes into this part of the Highlands, although the Bena Bena Gap is a wider, more distinct landmark, and is more often open as far as weather is concerned. But it also takes longer to get in that way. What we usually do is to go over and take a look at Asaroka Gap first. If that's not safe, we fly down to Bena. If that is closed and the trip is urgent enough, we use the Arona Gap. There are no set routes! Everything depends on weather—and New Guinea is a regular weather factory, with all its high ridges and ranges.

My sketch doesn't show it, but the mountains don't end when you've crossed the main range (the one with all the gaps marked). Garoka and Asaroka sit in a fairly good-sized valley where the valley floor is from 4,000-5,000 ft. For the most part the highlands consist of just one ridge after another, so we really need to know our way around. When the weather isn't good, the ridges can get to looking very much alike, since you don't see them in perspective. That's why this enforced familiarization is a good idea. In fact, we are doing more than is required.

Wednesday's trip was my first solo (incidentally, just one year from the day of Harry's accident). I went back down to Kiapit with a load—then shuttled the two loads that had been left at Kiapit but were meant for Kainantu. Since I got a late start that morning, and because shuttling takes time, I didn't get back until 4:30 p.m. A long day! I ran into a lot of haze and smoke that I had to work my way around—the people burn off their fields this time of year and it really fouls up the visibility.

Yesterday's trip was probably the prettiest of all—over the Bundi Gap, just south of Mt. Wilhelm (the highest point in TNG, I guess) and down the steep Chimbu Gorge to Chimbu. It's an almost breathtaking sight. To top it off, Chimbu itself is a regular little garden spot, nestled down in a tiny valley. We in Madang get most of our fresh vegetables from Chimbu [as backloads]....

The highlands are really beautiful. The climate is wonderful and the air cool and crisp. Although the ranges are covered heavily with trees (they are not quite what you'd consider jungle—the real jungles are along the coast and northwest of Mt. Wilhelm), the valleys of the highlands are mostly grassland.

Routine flight operations were underway only a couple of weeks when on August 20th (scarcely two months after our arrival) we received a letter—an official invitation—from the Unevangelized Fields Mission headquarters in Australia asking us to serve their missionaries in Dutch New Guinea, across the western border from the Territory. They had only one or two families on the coast of DNG then, but hoped to move them inland before too long. That letter made Charlie eager to get over to DNG to begin preliminary discussions with both missionaries and government officials. Getting to DNG, however, was not a simple matter. The Cessna of course was too busy to borrow for the trip. But to go by airline, one had to fly south to Australia first, and then take a flight north from Sydney to Hollandia. Alternately, one could charter a flight from the Territory by contacting a local commercial operator. Either way (whether by charter or airline), making such a round trip was expensive as well as complicated and time-consuming.

When Charlie heard that charter flights occasionally had room for an additional passenger, he decided to inquire about riding along on someone else's charter. It would certainly be less expensive, but it could mean a very abrupt departure. Still, it was worth a try. So he packed (partially) to be ready to leave on short notice.

The timing of such a trip seemed to be confirmed a few days later when we received a letter from one of UFM's missionaries living in Dutch New Guinea. He asked Charlie to come "sometime in August" to fly the Governor over the Baliem Valley. He suggested August because the Governor planned to visit Holland in September and very much wanted to see the Baliem before he went.

How Charlie wanted to make that flight! If he could get there, he could see the Valley for himself at the same time. He lost no time in wiring back that he would come—by charter if necessary!—if his entrance into DNG could be arranged without a visa. Needless to say, he was terribly disappointed to learn that the Governor had been able to make other arrangements, by going with a pilot who happened to be in DNG at that time—which saved his having to charter a plane from a distance.

The incident, however, seemed to indicate an increased interest and willingness on the part of government officials to ease restrictions for entering uncontrolled areas. Taking note, the missions began to accelerate plans for advancing into DNG's interior. Only one stipulation remained—that of adequate air support. To Charlie, this sounded like a clarion call for MAF's participation. Also, it was the kind of assignment that MAF liked best—an assignment that depend-ed upon MAF's services.

Because events suddenly seemed to be snowballing, Charlie wrote to the L.A. office to ask about starting a fund immediately to provide a survey plane for DNG. MAF had many pressing needs in Latin America; but then again, it would take time to gather funds, and additional time to order, deliver, modify and ship the plane across the ocean. It seemed wise to think and plan ahead.

Meanwhile, August gave way to September. The Lutheran program expand-ed with additional airstrips and an increase in flights. Charlie commented on the busier schedule in a letter to our parents dated September 2, 1952:

> Last week the weather really messed us up. During the first three weeks of August we only had to turn back once for weather. Last week [we turned back] three times. Even when we got through, it was a fight all the way. We earned all our flying time last week.
>
> Yesterday I had my longest day—3:40 hours flying time. As often happens on Monday, the plane wasn't gassed or loaded. So we got up at 5:30 a.m. and still I did-n't get off the ground until 8:30 (last-minute maintenance consumed half an hour). I didn't drag back here until 2:15 p.m., even though we are seldom out much after noon. Then, last night, we heard a U.S. news commentator on the radio remind us that it was Labor Day. Now he tells me! I should have been playing tennis!
>
> We have been getting earlier starts the past 10 days. We are now shooting for two trips on Tuesdays and Wednesdays. But in order to get the two trips in, we have to be off the ground for the first one pretty close to 6:30. That gets the second one out of here about 9:30. If the second one isn't started by that time, it prob-ably won't get through.
>
> Bob and I alternate on these. At first we both went out early. I worked on paper-work while he was gone, and he worked on mechanics projects while I was gone. But, getting up at 5 a.m. every morning was getting quite old for both of us. (Even when we didn't make the two trips a day, we found it was best to get off early—there wasn't so much of a fight with weather.)
>
> So last Friday, the store manager (the man who schedules the loading) bought a bike for the aviation program. Now the early-trip pilot takes the weapons carri-er out to the airport. About 8:30 the other one takes the bike across the bay by boat and peddles the half-mile distance from there to the hangar. (The trip by road around the bay is five miles.) If the one making the first trip is unusually tired, he can come back by bike and boat and leave the truck for the one making the second trip.

I was interested to note our first month's flying time. Beginning with July 28, we flew 7 hours to month's end; 60 hours in August. All but 10 of the 67 hours were out over yon hills and jungles. I would guess I logged 50 of them myself.

Occasionally whole days were spent completing delivery of loads that for one reason or another were dropped at undesignated locations. If weather or some other problem prevented delivery, the pilots preferred to leave the load somewhere near its destination rather than bring it all the way back to Madang.

Ordinarily no flights were scheduled for Saturday afternoons, although the pilots were always on standby for emergency requests. Instead, they tried to build a little relaxation into their lives by playing baseball in the park in town. Several groups formed teams and played against each other. Mission personnel made up one team. Other teams were comprised of government employees, personnel from commercial businesses in town, and men from Madang's Chinese community. These games provided welcome diversion after a heavy week of flying, and also gave the families a chance to socialize.

In mid-September Bob made a trip to Asaroka to retrieve usable parts from the Auster wreckage that had been previously salvaged from the crash site. He stayed overnight, and when he arrived back in Madang early the next morning, Charlie had a load waiting for the next trip—to Kerowagi, with a stop at Chimbu on the way back.

The Bergmans, a very friendly German missionary family, lived in Chimbu. Not only were they hospitable, but they seemed to enjoy the opportunity for fellowship whenever the plane was due. They inevitably insisted the pilots come up the hill to the house for at least a cup of coffee. Although the pilots also enjoyed the fellowship, they were usually a little wary about the normal pattern of deteriorating weather conditions between Chimbu and their next stop. On this particular morning, Charlie accepted the inevitable gracious invitation. By the time he had the engine running and was ready for takeoff, he realized it was almost 10:30. The account of his trip home shows the reason for a reluctance to stay anywhere very long for a coffee break.

> I climbed up the Chimbu valley; there were gaps under the clouds at the top of the pass, but they are often misleading. When I got there, the gap looked pretty small. I flew over to look at another one close by that was just a little higher. It looked better, but when I was just about across, I didn't like the looks of it and turned back. Since I was already up at 10,000 feet, I hated to lose all that altitude by going back down to Chimbu to follow the valley over to Asaroka because I

didn't know whether I'd be able to go across the main range there. So I decided to climb, and cut straight across to the Asaroka valley. I didn't have to worry about the terrain, but I had to top the clouds. By the time I crossed the main ridge, I had 14,500 ft.—the highest we've ever flown over here. I began to feel the altitude a little, but not much. It's wonderful to know you have that kind of performance when you need it. It took me 1:10 hours to get home—a 45-minute trip in clear weather.

In late September there was a request to fly to Mendi—the deepest penetration inland yet. Mendi was a comparatively new station, opened by the Australian Methodists. Since neither Bob nor Charlie had yet been there, one of the Territory's more experienced pilots was to go along to show them the route. They planned to ask him to check them out as well on a few other strips where they had not previously landed.

Mendi is quite a distance southwest of Madang, well beyond Chimbu. At that time its surrounding area was still considered restricted, having only recently been "policed," which meant that government permission was needed by anyone intending to spend a night there. Their initial trip to Mendi went well, but the day brought other complications. Charlie wrote:

> What a day! We flew 4:45 hours today—the most yet. Bob went along, so actually there were three of us, all pilots, making the trip. But I did all the flying. The familiarization pilot wasn't checked out in the Cessna and Bob's arm was sore, though his fever was gone. In fact, his arm began to swell.

> By the time we got home, about 3:45 p.m., we were all dead tired, but we picked up our families and headed for the hospital—which took the best part of an hour over that terrible road. I had to drive the old weapons carrier of course, because of Bob's sore arm. The doc diagnosed Bob's problem as blood poisoning and sent him home to bed to stay a while …

> As we started home it was beginning to get dark. It was then that we discovered the generator wasn't charging enough to keep the lights going for very long. So we drove along in second gear with one of us holding a flashlight—until we got to the main road, where we turned on the car lights and raced for home. Was I bushed!

> There are two trips scheduled for tomorrow. I'm to pick up an expectant mother (possibly of twins) on the first trip, to bring her to Madang. Then I go to Lae. But I'll stay there overnight if I'm too tired, and come back here the next day. That day I'll cut back to one trip—for sure.

Another trip late in September—to Lae—involved a medical emergency and an aircraft reported missing.

After my return from Chimbu last week (we flew 17.5 hours in 6 days that week), I got a sore throat and felt positively rotten. I probably should have stayed home that next day, but we were already down to one trip a day with Bob in bed, so I went anyway. I told myself that after all, it was only a short trip. The next day was another one-trip day, and then Saturday I added a second trip—to Lae—in the afternoon. By then I was feeling a lot better, and besides, the trips to Lae were getting to be "milkruns"—with passengers both ways and no freight to manhandle.

However, when I got to Lae with not too much daylight left in which to get back to Madang, I found that my expected return passengers had not yet arrived from Finschaven; the plane they were to come on was too full.

The mission, assuming I would be returning to Madang yet that day, substituted a load of freight for me to drop at Kiapit. I called it off, for several reasons. I would be pushing the daylight limit too close if I dropped a load of freight too. The weather in that direction wasn't very good, and I was too tired. I decided to stay overnight to wait for the passengers. We could make the trip to Madang on Sunday afternoon.

As we taxied out for takeoff about 3:45 p.m. (Sunday), a fellow came running out of the tower waving wildly. He had just gotten a message from Kiapit (right on our route, 30 minutes out of Lae) that a Papuan woman in childbirth was dying.

We took a few minutes to decide how to respond. Then we realized that of my three passengers, one was a lady doctor, one a nurse, and the other a Papuan carpenter.

We decided to take the carpenter as far as Kiapit, and leave him there for now (we could pick him up the next Friday) so there would be room for the Papuan woman—providing she would travel without her husband, and providing she wasn't a stretcher case. That we would have to check on.

At Kiapit the doctor examined her and said that while she was not in critical condition, the baby did need to be taken.

About that time a DC-3 arrived and landed. Its pilot had reported the case to the authorities in the first place. In fact, he had landed there when he saw a signal out on the strip. But he was already assigned to search for a missing aircraft so couldn't return to Lae with the woman.

Now he was returning from the search (the plane was found unscathed) so he was able to load the woman aboard on a stretcher and take her to Lae. That meant we could shove off for Madang.

We soon found ourselves running into heavy rainstorms. I got around the first one, but couldn't make the second one—it was just too thick to fly through. So back we went to Lae. We tried again the next morning (Monday). The weather was still a mess, and once I almost turned back. But we made it. By this time Bob was feeling much better and could take over the rest of the flying that day.

We found out later that the plane reported missing had only landed on a radio-less airstrip to wait out the weather. But he had been gone long enough that a search got underway.

The fellows found they frequently had to change plans abruptly. Unexpected events had a way of coming one right after another, so their schedules had to be at least somewhat flexible. Charlie's letter continued,

The next day there was an accident at Chimbu. We first heard about it when the local aircraft surveyor called us to see if we could take him in to investigate the accident. We were already scheduled and loaded for a trip to Chimbu for that next day anyway, so Bob just removed some cargo and took him along.

The plane involved was a Dragon. It had landed at Chimbu at least once (earlier) the morning of the crash. In fact, he was there when I was, and we had passed the time of day between my landing and his takeoff.

When he came back that afternoon, the wind was whipping up pretty strong (we avoid Chimbu in the afternoons generally), and he couldn't get on the strip—he kept floating because of the tailwind. He finally forced his wheels on the ground, but when he bounced badly, he added power to go around.

However, the Dragon doesn't have too much excess power to both climb the slight hill and fight the downdraft on that end of the strip. (Takeoffs are generally in the opposite direction.) He did manage to clear the end of the strip, but couldn't clear the ridge a quarter of a mile farther on. I hear the plane is a wreck and that the pilot broke his leg in two places—which isn't really surprising. The pilot of a Dragon sits right up in the nose with nothing to absorb shock—quite a contrast with the Cessna whose long nose could soak up the blow.

When Bob and the aircraft surveyor reached Chimbu, he heard that a missionary family from an outstation was on its way there with a sick child. So he decided to wait for their arrival. They didn't arrive until about 4 p.m. so Bob thought it best to wait there overnight. Next morning they were greeted by a rare morning when Chimbu is fogged in. It's almost always open early. But Bob and his passengers did make it back before noon and we got in another trip yet that day. Since then things have been more routine once again.

About that time a number of missionaries began to schedule trips which called for moving them around within their own areas. They regularly visited a number of villages to encourage the congregations in each place. Before MAF's arrival, all this had been done on foot. But some of the ground they covered was extremely mountainous and therefore difficult to trek. We began to help by transporting them one way. Either the missionary trekked to his most distant village and then was picked up at the airstrip nearest that village and taken home, or the plane delivered him to an airstrip at the far end of his trek and he visited villages as he worked his way home on foot.

Occasionally the fellows had something other than weather to think about. For example, Bob took off for Chimbu one day in early October but couldn't get through on account of the weather. When he tried again later that morning he ran into another problem. After about five minutes into the flight he became aware of an irregularity in the engine noise. There was nothing to do but turn back. (You can't pull over to the side of a cloud to check the engine!) He changed the plugs and checked everything over. It checked out OK, but by that time it was too late to make the trip yet that day.

The next morning Charlie checked it, and again it seemed OK. But about 10 minutes out, when he checked it again in the air, he found one mag was still slightly rough. At first he debated about going on anyway, but decided that to be fully safe he should return to Madang.

Bob worked on it the rest of the day and finished the next morning. By 9:30 he was ready to try once more for Chimbu. Then, just at the end of the runway, before takeoff, a brake started to act up. So, back he went to the hanger where he spent the rest of the day correcting that brake problem and finishing up some other work. By evening when he test flew it, everything was perfect.

Suddenly it was Friday. Most of the week had been eaten up with maintenance, and they were far behind schedule. How could they catch up? They decided to try three trips a day! Charlie managed an unusually early start by taking off at 6:13 a.m. He arrived at Chimbu just before 7:00 (in time for a second breakfast!) and brought the waiting family back to Madang.

Back at the hangar he loaded again for another trip to Chimbu. This time he brought back vegetables. After the second trip, he and Bob loaded a third time, and Bob (who had eaten an early lunch) took off for Lae with a couple of intermediate stops. By the time he returned that evening, it was 13 minutes before six—a long day, especially for the plane which spent six and one half hours in the air.

Needless to say, there was no time off that Saturday; instead, it was a full catch-up day of flying: a load to Chimbu, a missionary to move from Chimbu to Asaroka, a load from Asaroka to take back to Chimbu (the load dropped there the previous week when they couldn't get to Chimbu), and a German missionary to take from Chimbu to Bundi to begin his trek. A very full day. But it brought a good feeling, to end the week accomplishing at least the minimum amount of work scheduled for that week. And it was particularly satisfying to be able to do it in just two days.

Sometimes when life seems busiest, there is always one more thing to do. That same busy week was the week that the furniture for the new mission houses arrived in Madang. It needed to be assembled. Charlie had agreed to oversee the assembly at the technical school (at Baitabag) when he wasn't flying. So while Bob worked on the plane, Charlie spent most of his time at Baitabag working on assembling the furniture. The houses were now nearly finished, and we would soon be moving into one of them.

With all there was to think about, Charlie had not given up hope of going to Dutch New Guinea. He still had his suitcase half packed, just in case a Beechcraft headed for Hollandia might pass through Madang. He was so eager to confer for a few days with Fred Dawson of Unevangelized Fields Mission.

Although no hoped-for DNG-bound plane had shown up, Charlie decided he would be better prepared to go another time if he secured a Dutch visa. Having one in hand would avoid having to seek special permission if a future opportunity to go did arise. But when would that be?

7

Aided by a Dragon and a Dove

Charlie was beginning to feel it was urgent that he get to Dutch New Guinea to make contacts in person. He continually reviewed every scenario he could think of that might be a transportation option. He couldn't change the airline schedule. Flights north from Port Moresby stopped in Lae and Madang, before continuing on to Wewak. But there in Wewak, all flights turned around and headed south again. It seemed his only hope lay in somehow getting aboard someone's charter flight.

Suddenly a new idea surfaced. Suppose he flew to Wewak. Might he find a ride more easily from there to Hollandia? Was it even worth a try? Convinced it was, he made a reservation for the Friday morning flight (October 17, 1952), fully aware that he would probably be spending at least the weekend in Wewak—and perhaps longer—before a ride from there to Hollandia might materialize.

The idea had merit, but I found it hard to see him go when everything seemed so indefinite. On the one hand it was a necessary part of his job to explore alternatives, but there were so many unknowns connected with it. My emotions rose and fell. I told myself if he didn't get a ride he would return before very long. But if he did find a ride, when would he be able to find a ride back again? (I recalled that just a year earlier Grady had had to wait in DNG three weeks before he managed to find a ride back to the Territory.) Then, in addition to the indefiniteness of his return, I had to face the fact that any contact between us over that indefinite period of time would be all but impossible apart from an emergency.

However, his decision was complicated further by a couple other factors. For one thing, the new house we were to occupy was now finished and we needed to move. Housing in Madang was always tight, and the rooms we occupied at the Hutchins' house were needed for others. A second complication was that in two weeks an Australian MAF family (Charles and Dorothy Rasmussen with Jeanette and Glennis) were expected to arrive, to work with us in the Lutheran program. Charles was a qualified pilot/mechanic, and their coming was to be the first step in AMAF's reinvolvement in the New Guinea aviation picture. In order to allow adequate time to arrange transportation to and from DNG, make the necessary contacts while there, and get back in time for Rasmussens' arrival, Charlie figured he needed to be on his way almost immediately.

Because Charlie didn't want to leave Bob with the entire flight load any longer than necessary, our move was sandwiched in between flights over those few days, beginning on the Monday before Charlie's Friday reservation for Wewak. Of course we were by no means settled when he left, but we had moved.

Knowing Charlie, I was sure his thoughts during the entire moving process, and even while flying that week, were already focused on anticipated discussions with missionaries and government officials in DNG—and on everything involved in formulating a response to requests for MAF's service. Interestingly, though we weren't aware of it at the time, Grady Parrott wrote a letter that very same week to MAF's constituency in the States (dated October 15, 1952) in which he outlined the usual procedure for establishing an MAF program:

> Following a request for service in a given area, MAF first goes in for an on-the-spot survey. This survey must establish the need and practicability of an air-aid program. A closely calculated rate per mile is determined to cover plane operating costs. Assuming a decision is reached for air assistance, MAF then moves ahead to establish a service tailored to meet the field problems.
>
> We look for the Lord's provision of necessary funds. There's the matter of capital outlay—the plane, radio, shop, house and hangar. Support for the MAF pilot and his family will be needed. Problems sometimes arise causing delay and extra expense (government negotiations, etc.); but in the providence of God a new air operation is soon in action, and the Gospel moves ahead.
>
> As flights are made for the missionaries, they pay into the plane fund according to the established mileage rate. This plane fund remains a permanent part of that particular field program. From it the plane's operating expenses are paid. Since the calculated mileage rate covers not only running costs (fuel, maintenance, insurance, etc.), but also includes depreciation on the plane itself, it follows that the more the plane is pressed into service, the more reserve is proportionately built up toward its ultimate replacement. That means that once the Christian people have put a plane on the field through MAF, it becomes a self-sustaining unit from there on out. This self-replacement feature means good equipment for dependable, continuous service. In hazardous areas that's an important consideration.
>
> You see, the same funds which the missionaries would otherwise spend for mule hire and feed, and for native carriers and canoes, are now diverted to the faster, more efficient air transportation. Incidentally, the mileage rate does not include the MAF pilot's allowance, nor anything for MAF's headquarters which institutes

and directs the various programs. Those costs are taken care of through gifts of individuals and Christian groups who wish a part with us in this pioneer advance.

Charlie did spend the weekend in Wewak. On Monday he heard about a plane—a Dragon, belonging to Mandated Air Lines (MAL)—that was going to Hollandia. Better yet, it had room to take him!

His days in DNG were very full. He resorted to making copious notes, for there was no time to organize his thinking—he'd have to prepare a written report to the L.A. office later. He did, however, manage to share random thoughts and observations in a letter to our parents written from Sentani (the small community near Hollandia's international airport).

SENTANI, HOLLANDIA, October 28, 1952—This dateline will be our address one of these days—as the Lord continues to work. And He surely has worked this week! I don't know when I've seen such evidence of the Lord's help in such a short space of time ....

Last Tuesday and Wednesday I spent a total of about three hours with the Director of Civil Aviation. I've also had several other chats with him since then. As a result of these, he has granted us a beautiful site on the airport for building a house and hangar—subject to the approval of the Resident—the site of our own choosing. In addition he offered to recondition a road that runs one and a half miles from the end of the strip to the large, fresh-water Sentani Lake where we can launch our plane when we operate on floats. He also wants to recondition a decayed army jetty at the end of this road for loading government flying boats. We will be able to use it too for our seaplane. He gave us the liberty of bringing in the plane under any registration we choose.

Friday we (Fred Dawson and I) went to see the "Resident" (DNG is divided into about four or five areas, with a Resident at the head of each) who is about next in rank to the Governor. He confirmed that we could have any land on the strip that the Director of CA [Civil Aviation] approved. He also approved visas for us and for the other couple that will join us—indefinite visas if we want them. He further gave us permission to house ourselves in a government building near the strip while we build our own housing. (I'm staying there now; it's quite a bit more primitive than our house in Madang, but it's a wonderful provision for which we can praise the Lord.)

Later that morning when we were down at Hollandia Harbor, Fred Dawson (the missionary we'll be working most closely with here) recognized the Governor's Adjutant entering the bakery. We invited him to have a cold drink with us and chatted for about half an hour.

Next we called on the man in charge of customs. He has to charge us 1% on the plane (expensive, isn't it!) but hinted broadly that we would probably be exempt from everything else.

Sunday evening we had tea with Dr. & Mrs. Schregardus. He's the head of all government technical departments, including aviation. We probably won't have much to do with him directly since he leaves all aviation matters in the hands of the DCA. But he's still the chief, so a very good man to keep friendly with.

Then, yesterday morning, for the grand finale, we called on His Excellency, the Governor [of Dutch New Guinea]. This was the first time I had occasion to wear the coat to my cord suit (though I've often carried it with me, not knowing when I might need it). You must wear a coat to visit the Governor. But you need not melt, for his office is air conditioned (the first air conditioning I've seen since leaving the States). Incidentally, the Governor's Palace is the building that previously served as General MacArthur's headquarters when he directed the Pacific campaign from here during World War II.

The purpose of our visit was to explain to the Governor our need for the road between the strip and the lake since the DCA [Department of Civil Aviation] will have to get funds for this project subject to the Governor's approval. The Governor approved readily.

Taking them in reverse order, I discovered that I arrived here—humanly speaking—at about the worst week possible. While these officials were available, they had plenty of other things on their minds. A few problems had just arisen (which I can't go into now) which not only absorbed their attention but could easily have turned them against letting missionaries go deeper into the interior—the obvious purpose of our work. But in spite of this, I felt we got a tremendous reception.

The other evident factor was that these different department heads must have conferred on the subject and the word had gone around to encourage us (although no doubt this occurred before the problems arose)....

With no light planes in the country, they're obviously eager to see what the light plane can do to help open up the interior; and we are the guinea pigs. I couldn't possibly have an assignment more to my liking. With the Lord's help, we can easily prove its value. Of course, they won't just sit by on the sidelines and watch; they will want to charter our plane. We'll be praying that they won't overdo this, but it won't bother us at first since the mission work usually starts off a bit slowly.

While these evidences of the Lord's preparation are thrilling, they still miss the heart of the work here. However I soon got to feel the pulse of the heart. A few days before I arrived, a UFM [Unevangelized Fields Mission] family with four small children had set out for their interior station at Sengge. They haven't reached it yet. In fact, they won't until Saturday. That's two whole weeks!

Their trek was made somewhat safer by their carrying a 2-way radio which they use to contact the government radio station here every other day. I was at the station when they made the contact the evening I arrived. Hans Veldhuis said they were making good progress, although that particular day they had been wading through mud all day, frequently sinking in to the tops of their jungle boots. (Fred Dawson told me that they each completely wear out a pair of jungle boots every time they make the trip one way—walking isn't cheap either!)

The night before, their little girl of about four had fallen out of her cot without waking up—just kept on sleeping on the floor apparently. Later she woke everyone up with a scream. A snake had bitten her on the thumb. Hans quickly put a tourniquet on her wrist and slashed the thumb with a razor. She was pretty sick for a few hours, but had completely recovered by morning.

Frankly, I felt rather ashamed for thinking of this place where I'm staying as primitive. So when they asked me to say a few words, I could only tell him to get that airstrip out there finished quickly and I'd do all I could to stir up an airplane in a big, quick hurry.

In the radio contact two days later, we learned they were still in about the same place—pinned down my mud and swollen streams from heavy rains.

That's the pulse—but it's still not the heartbeat itself. For Sengge is really comparatively near the coast. Actually it is only one-third the distance to the well-populated Baliem Valley (Shangri-La)—and the Baliem, in turn, is only one of the populated areas that is totally unreached. I knew this was wild country, but I hardly realized how much of it was so completely untouched. This is one place where the missionaries certainly aren't exaggerating when they say they can't do the job without MAF's help. …

From what I've told you so far, you'll think all I've done the last week is to get challenged and sit around sipping coffee with the Dutch. I really have done more than that: I've had to lay out tentative house and hangar plans, plan how they'll fit on the tarmaks, etc. I've been checking on what building materials are available here, and what we'll have to ship from the States.

Lumber is the big problem. Apparently there is only one fellow here who has a saw mill, and I hear he is a bit independent. But I also heard he needs new saw blades so I made a deal with him to bring him saw blades (which he can't get for lack of dollar allotments) as partial payment, if he in return will get our lumber promptly.

I talked to Shell's head man here; he's ordering a six-month supply of the kind of gas and oil we require—ordering it now so it will be on hand by the time we need it.

In short, I've spent the week trying to turn plans into action. I came up here to survey the situation, but have ended up getting the ball rolling. Fred said the officials had already been asking him, "When is the plane getting here?" They somehow seemed to expect, when they met me, that the plane was already here. I told all of them that we would try hard to be here by February [1953]. Then I suddenly realized that February is tomorrow—so I'd better get cooking if we are going to get here anywhere near that date.

The thing that leaves me a little breathless is realizing what this setup is going to cost. The plane will come pretty close to $6000, boxed and shipped. Lumber is so costly that the hangar will cost over $1000. The simplest possible house (with no luxuries except a flush toilet—and that won't cost us much) will cost a good $1800. We'll probably need two families here for at least a year, and after that there will be a constant flow of guests, so it almost seems we'll need two houses— but I'm sure the second one will have to wait a while. Then, we need a few tools, possibly our own power plant (small), more spare parts than we stock in close-by South America (including a spare engine), and last—but far from least—we'll just have to have a small pickup truck. Hollandia Stad [city] is a good 15 miles from the strip, and Hollandia Harbor is at least 10 miles beyond that. We'd be working with our ankles tied together without a truck. It all makes my head swim!

… I'm finishing this letter by kerosene lamp and it's hard on the eyes. Also, I need some sleep. I hope to get a flight to Madang tomorrow, but may first help out on an air-drop at Sengge.

Charlie's estimate of bringing a plane into DNG in February (of 1953) turned out to be very premature. The Lord was going to provide air service for Dutch New Guinea, but our move was not going to be by one dramatic leap across the border from Madang, as we envisioned it that November. Had we known all that had to transpire before actually arriving there, we might not have had the patience to see it through—nor the opportunity to work more closely with AMAF.

But, I'm getting ahead of my story.

Charlie managed to find a ride back to Madang aboard a Mandated Air Lines Dove, after only nine days in DNG. He returned to find Bob in the midst of a very busy flight schedule. The Rasmussen family was due shortly. And we were about to experience our first Christmas in New Guinea.

8
A Different Christmas

In mid-November, flights increased to two trips a day, and Charlie was surprised to note that according to his log book he had now flown nearly 150 hours in New Guinea. He and Bob continued alternating the early flights, but both flew every day. They tried to keep Saturday afternoons free to relax and unwind by playing baseball. The town's four-team league had shown improvement along with consistent enthusiasm.

Charlie had returned from DNG, but he was busier than ever—and was away from home a lot. His spare moments were spent writing or dictating letters and reports which I transcribed/typed, and we managed to have a fistful of letters ready to go each time mail was dispatched on the infrequently scheduled airlines.

My days were full as well. In addition to doing all Charlie's typing and keeping the household going, I home-schooled John and Jim, and also tried to keep Gordon, our pre-schooler, occupied and out of mischief. Life in the Mellis household had its share of frustrations. One letter I wrote to our parents during a week of heavy flying soon after Charlie returned from DNG went like this:

> Everything is under control in the kitchen—temporarily—although this has been one of those days when everything goes kinda wrong. It started when Jimmy got a bit smart this morning at breakfast. Hot coffee spilled on his arm when he bumped into it and the cup fell to the floor (and broke, of course).... We didn't get the borrowed washing machine in time—a misunderstanding. So we did the most essential pieces by hand. ... Charlie had to stay in the highlands overnight—it got too late to come all the way back to Madang before dark. So when he did arrive this morning, he had to go right out on another trip—to Mendi, the place farthest away! Now he won't be home until at least mid-afternoon. ... We were scheduled to have company for dinner, but plans were changed; we'll still have company, but not the ones that were originally scheduled. ... Johnny's athlete's foot is a lot worse. We've been treating it with sulfa powder which seems to help slightly. But we've about run out of ideas. ... Rasmussens arrived and his check-out in the plane begins tomorrow!

Interruptions added other frustrations to our busy schedule. In addition, the second house was completed, which meant that a number of families had to play musical chairs with houses. Bob and Betty Hutchins moved next door to us (to the new house), another family moved from an apartment into the house Bob and Betty vacated, which in turn left that apartment available for the Rasmussen family.

During the final weeks of 1952, several events provided memorable experiences—but for a variety of reasons. The first was a trip to the hospital at Jagaum. The road had hills and curves, but we hadn't remembered it like this. Somehow the trip seemed much worse than usual. At least something was different. As we bumped along, we got to wondering if something might be wrong with the vehicle, so we stopped to make a visual check. Oh no! The right rear wheel of the weapon's carrier, which normally had five or six bolts to hold it on, had only three bolts, and two of those were sheared off so that the wheel was secured by only one bolt! What should we do? Estimating that we were probably at least half way, we decided to go on—very slowly—using four-wheel drive to take as much strain off that wheel as possible.

Those last few miles seemed to take forever, and we all worried about the final half mile—a downgrade with a tiny bridge at the bottom before the last steep hill climb to the hospital.

Certainly not much could happen at this slow speed we thought—apart from maybe a sudden bump if the last bolt gave way and the wheel dropped to rest on its brake drum. But, we were after all getting closer, and could even walk the final distance if necessary. Thankfully the bolt held, and it was a relieved group of us who got out as we pulled to a stop at the closest house.

While we took care of our hospital objectives, a mission maintenance person repaired it using other bolts that would hold the wheel on, at least until we could get home. We were easily persuaded to stay for supper since it had started to rain. (The weapon's carrier had a roof, but was not closed in.)

The rain had stopped when we left for home, and we had driven most of the way to the main road when we met Bob and Charles R. coming toward us in a jeep. They became concerned when we hadn't returned, and had tried to call Jagaum. But the hospital's phone wasn't working, so they had come to look for us, bringing along a spare tire, petrol, tools, etc.—not knowing what our problem might be. We were especially grateful for their concern. After our earlier experience, we didn't at all mind being escorted home. Interestingly, just as we reached home, the rain began again, and became a pouring rain that continued all night. Needless to say, we thanked the Lord for a lot that day, including a nice full tank of rainwater.

A second memorable event was the opening of a bakery in Madang shortly before Christmas—with daily delivery of fresh bread right to our doors. At first, only bread was available, but rumor had it that when additional equipment and supplies arrived from Australia by ship, we could expect other baked things for sale as well. Meanwhile, the fresh bread, together with another round of fresh meat from the mission's plantation (beef from a two-year-old animal this time) convinced us that life on the mission field was suddenly looking up!

For the first couple of weeks after the Rasmussens arrived, Charlie took Charles R. along on his flights to familiarize him with the plane, routes and procedures. After Charles R. was checked out, Charlie planned to devote a week to neglected correspondence. But that idea had to be abandoned when the fellows suddenly realized they had forgotten to inform the insurance agency in Lae of the new pilot on the program. It was an oversight that meant Charles R. had to be grounded temporarily until everything was straightened out. So, to keep Bob from being overloaded, Charlie returned to flying—which then led to a third memorable event.

The Sunday before Christmas a call came through early in the morning requesting an emergency flight. Charlie took the flight because Charles R. was still grounded and Bob had a Sunday school class to teach. Charlie's account of his trip made it sound like quite an experience.

> The strip I went into is in the Ramu Valley—just a little north of our northern route. Up that way it's all restricted territory still, though there have been patrols in that area for a while. In fact, they have just recently opened this airstrip to keep the patrol officers supplied. It was my first trip to this strip—Bob had been there once. The patrol officer who was there when I got there had apparently just gotten in that morning and found this girl there. (She was about 15 or 16.) She had been sent there by another patrol that was patrolling south of there.

> I gathered there hadn't been any real skirmish—some policeman just got trigger happy when he interpreted some actions of the local people as unfriendly. I don't know how many shots were fired, but this girl got one in the thigh that apparently shattered the bone and left part of it sticking out. I didn't see the wound, but from the way it was bandaged, it sure looked ugly.....

As Charlie flew the wounded girl and her companion back to Madang for medical treatment at the hospital, he began to wonder if the time wasn't approaching when the mission would try to place someone in that area—especially now that an airstrip was there. However, climate would no doubt be a factor; it was too far from the coast to receive ocean breezes and at too low an altitude to benefit from the cooler mountain air, which would probably make it the most undesirable climate in New Guinea. Still, with people there who needed to be reached with the Good News of the Gospel....

Neither climate nor weather in New Guinea was conducive to "thinking Christmas," even for Californians. Also, there were no decorations around town to remind us. We hadn't yet bought a radio, and flights were routine. But after one flight into the highlands, Charlie surprised us by coming home with an honest-to-goodness Christmas tree. It wasn't large, but it looked authentic.

Our whole family was excited, and the boys were eager to help carry it into the house. Even though Charlie warned them to be careful when taking hold of it, we all had to learn the hard way to respect the character of that tree; its needles were real "needles"—in fact, very sharp needles—which made the tree extremely hard to handle and decorate. The Papuan helpers unloading it at the airport had used the expression, "Igat nels!" (Pidgin for "It's got nails!")—a very apt description! Once it was trimmed with our home-made decorations, we all agreed that, despite the weather, this tree really helped make it seem more like previous Christmas seasons.

The boys participated in a Sunday school Christmas program which was fun. But probably the most unusual and impressive Christmas program we ever saw was the pageant at Baitabag presented by the men of the technical school. Charlie described it in a letter to our parents.

> Baitabag spreads out over a pretty fair sized piece of ground; it's also quite rolling. There were some benches set up on one rise in the center, and there were different "sets" scattered around a quarter circle on the adjoining hill and on down into a valley. The set farthest away from the audience was Nazareth, where they had the Annunciation scene. It was so far away that all I could make out was the angel. But then the lights went out on that set, they lit up a real oriental looking palace with torches. (It was however made of bush materials so that it looked indigenous.) This was Herod's palace.

> Then, way off in the distance a runner came over the hill with a flaming torch—bringing the decree from Augustus. Then a group of runners went from Herod's palace with torches, relaying the decree. It was really impressive.

> After that, a not-too-bright spotlight played on Nazareth and followed Joseph and Mary clear across the hill, behind Herod's palace and in front of one of the mission buildings that was fixed up to represent the temple, and on down into a

vale to another school building that represented the inn. There they got turned away and went to the stable made of bush materials.

At first they went behind the stable. Then they came out in front with Mary carrying the baby—a bundle with a light inside.

The shepherd scene was the best. They had a real bonfire out on the ground and were milling around it. It looked very natural. Then, all of a sudden, the spotlight focused just above the gable of another mission building nearby, and there was the angel with his arms outspread and his flowing white robes flapping in the breeze. The person operating the spotlight was clever enough to keep the light off the building so that it looked like he was standing there in mid-air. The shepherds really put on a realistic display of fright; it was startling enough all right. Then the spotlight broadened and a lot of people came walking across the roof to join him. This was followed by the shepherds' adoration, the presentation in the temple, and the wisemen coming first to Herod's palace and then to Bethlehem.

On their way back, the wisemen were told by an angel on the temple not to go back to Herod.

The whole production was of course in Pidgin English, and was quite impressive and meaningful.

A secular celebration of Christmas was held on the athletic field in Madang. Papuans living in Madang joined together for a sing-sing that lasted all night. It was quite an affair. Although it is called a "sing-sing," it is primarily dancing accompanied by chanting and rhythmic drumbeating. Those participating gathered with others from their particular home area (*one-talks*) and formed separate groups to do their own traditional dances. There must have been 15-20 groups performing on the athletic field all at once, many with very distinctive and elaborate headdresses.

Spectators weren't relegated to sitting in bleachers, but could wander around among the dancing groups. We thought Gordon (now nine months) might be frightened by all the drums and chanting, but he wasn't. He just bounced up and down in his stroller trying to keep time with the music. The older boys (John and Jim) weren't shy either. When we joined the onlookers surrounding one group of dancers, we lost track of Jim. But in looking for him, we spotted him near the front of the circle where he had edged up to see better. A few minutes later John disappeared. It turned out he was tired and had found a place to sit among the New Guineans at the edge of the circle.

For the most part, the field was dimly lit by lanterns scattered here and there, although over at one end of the field there was a big fire. As we wandered closer we saw they were cooking their food in a huge kettle over that fire. The kettle was filled to the brim with a variety of foods. We could identify (or smell!) papaya, taro, pig meat, yams, and bananas among other things. I'm sure cultural differences played a part in our agreeing that the appearance of the combination in that kettle, along with the aroma, made us glad we had already eaten.

December had nearly ended—along with the year 1952. But what an eventful year it had been! The aviation program for the Lutherans had grown to the point of needing a second plane, and another Cessna had been ordered. Additional pilots were being sought, to free us to move ahead with developmental work, particularly in Dutch New Guinea. That was the plan, although we were already realizing the target date for moving to DNG in February of 1953 was unrealistic. Charlie was now hoping for an April move instead. But little did we know, as 1953 began, that our actual move to Sentani (DNG) was well over a year away, with a good many frustrations and creeping delays in between. Nor did we know that the anticipated visit of an Australian MAF leader was part of God's plan to fulfill the primary objective for MAF-US's involvement in New Guinea—that of assisting AMAF back into being a contributing partner in mission aviation worldwide.

9
We Meet Vic

The January (1953) flight schedule was all but impossible. In addition to the usual loads of supplies, there were many people to move around—missionaries going to and from the Mission's annual conference; school children returning to school at Wau, or going to Madang or Lae to catch a flight south to Australia for high school; and Papuan teachers traveling to their assignments following graduation. A DC-3 took the teachers to highland locations that had adequate-length airstrips, and the fellows shuttled them to shorter airstrips from there, which saved countless trips by the Cessna to inland stations from the coast.

All of us looked forward to the arrival of the second Cessna, once the decision to order it was made. Grady Parrott had located a good buy in Los Angeles—a new plane, but a previous year's model with a lower price tag. (The newest model had few design changes, but its cost was considerably higher.) Although modifications and shipment were expected to take several months, just the thought of the program's growing to the point of needing two planes was exciting.

Meanwhile, the weapons carrier broke down completely, and we were told it would be out of service for some time. The hospital loaned the aviation department a *Blitz*—another aged vehicle left over from the war. Charlie described its "features" by saying:

> It's a British army truck, snub-nosed, with the engine between the front seats. The engine cover is gone, so the fan blows the hot air right in your face. This is counteracted by the cool air blowing in where the windshield once was. With the engine cover off, you have to be careful when you reach for the hand brake (its hydraulic brakes don't work) that you don't get your knuckles against the sparkplug leads—quite shocking. But it's really quite a vehicle—the mechanism that adjusts the seats back and forth still works!

That January everyone in Madang had houseguests. We added a fourth bed in our boys' room to accommodate a missionary on his way to the western highlands. He stayed with us a week, until the plane's schedule allowed a trip to take him into the interior. Then we had another guest the following week.

Those of us in the aviation department eagerly looked forward to a special visitor from Australia. Vic Ambrose, recently appointed deputation secretary for Australian MAF, wanted to become acquainted with the Cessna program in New Guinea before settling into his administrative duties in Melbourne. Although he was new to AMAF, he had been interested in that organization for several years. Charlie was especially eager to meet him because Vic was to be AMAF's key technical person. The relationship the two men would establish was highly important because of its potential for affecting the relationship of the two MAF organizations represented.

Their discussions were expected to focus on the development of mission aviation in the Territory and the anticipated service in Dutch New Guinea. Charlie and I believed Vic's coming was a specific answer to prayer. We were aware of certain tensions existing between AMAF and MAF-US and were hopeful that this opportunity for building personal relationships would help resolve them.

The more we learned about Vic, the more we realized how similar his background was to Charlie's. They were nearly the same age, married, and each had three children. He had served in his country's Air Force in the European theater during WWII, and had spent a few years in his family's business. Having that much in common increased Charlie's optimism about what they might accomplish jointly. (In fact, they became close friends. They developed a strong mutual trust and their ideas meshed well when it came to planning and strategy. They even approached a number of theological issues similarly.)

Even before Vic arrived in Madang, Charlie began to involve him in planning a survey in southwestern Papua. Several mission groups were already at work there and Charlie hoped air service could somehow be extended to them.

During Vic's visit, he and Charlie spent many hours in discussion, and he accompanied Charlie on some of the flights. Of mutual concern was the projected move to Dutch New Guinea. One morning Vic shared an idea with Charlie. Might it work, he wondered aloud, to begin serving DNG by operating from a base halfway between Madang and Hollandia—for example, at Wewak? Hmmm. They began to think through the ramifications of such a move and realized the idea had merit. For one thing, it would no doubt be easier to obtain permission to bring another plane into the Territory than it would a first plane in DNG. Current needs out of Hollandia could be met, temporarily at least, by periodic trips from Wewak. That led to thinking about the Sepik area west of Wewak. In their preoccupation with DNG, they had somehow not taken into account that the whole Sepik area was actually ripe for service.

Other thoughts emerged as they began to consider Wewak as an intermediate base location. Probably the most compelling consideration was that it would more quickly enable MAF-US to help AMAF launch a program of its own. The longer Vic and Charlie talked, the more convinced they became that this was the approach to recommend to the two home offices. In a letter to our parents about Vic's visit, Charlie went into a little greater detail:

> In the early part of our discussions we tried to view the field of New Guinea as a whole. Besides the need in Hollandia, there's a possible need down in southwestern Papua where UFM is working on the Fly River, and in the Lake Kutubu region (the latter, farther north, can be reached from Madang, but it's a long haul).

> But there's also another area we haven't given too much attention to—the Sepik area—between Wau and Hollandia. It is supplied from Wewak, which is located on the coast about mid-way between Madang and Hollandia. All of the Sepik area lies within the Australian Territory. ... Catholics have had work there, but evangelical missions have only recently entered that area: Brethren, Assemblies of God and South Seas Evangelical Mission. At the northern end, up near the DNG border is Telefomin (a really tough place to get to—planes turn back 50% of the time due to bad weather), where the Australian Baptists have begun a work....

> We drafted a joint letter for both our offices proposing this plan of attack. Then Vic spent 10 days in the Sepik visiting the missionaries and discussing the possibility. When we arrived at Wau for the Conference, both offices cabled us their enthusiastic approval of the plan. So we spent our last few days together working out the details of planning our first moves.

> As we talked, a schedule for the Mellises evolved, which looked like this: We'll stay in Wau through February. In March we'll go back to Madang to attack the accumulated correspondence, and I'll make a familiarization trip into the Kutubu-Tari region. (DCA has specified that I must be "pilot-in-command" on the first flight.) I'll also be able to get some building materials shipped to Wewak.

> In April I'll spend a few weeks in Wewak helping put up a guest house—which Rasmussens will move into in early May so they can help build the main house. (Our chief builder however will be Kay Liddle, a young Brethren missionary with building experience. We met him when he first arrived in TNG a month ago and stayed with us briefly in Madang. We're sure glad for his offer.) Then I'll return to Madang for May through July, though I may possibly slip up to Hollandia for a few more contacts and to hold the door open first.

By May we expect a Lutheran pilot from Australia will arrive and possibly also another pilot and his family from the States. (The second plane should arrive about June or July so we'll need three men by then.) I can see to their checkout during this three-month period.

By August the house in Wewak should be finished and our family will move up there for three or four months while I check out Charles R. on the routes and establish standard procedures. As soon as that's completed, we'll move on across to Hollandia to oversee its transition from a sub-base to a full base....

Vic is thinking in terms of possibly bringing his family up to Wewak to take over the leadership there to free us to move on to Hollandia in the fall. A lot of supervision will still be needed in Wewak, but probably not much technical supervision. AMAF expects to establish more than just air service there. For since there's no evangelical mission work on the coast (in the Wewak area), the missions inland need an agent on the coast to receive their shipments, and a place for their people to stay when they pass through Wewak. MAF therefore can provide these kinds of essential services. This will of course involve a lot of keeping of accounts. Vic thought I might be able to do all this, but I insisted that this was really their responsibility—and besides, they'd have to take over on this if we were ever going to get the job done in Hollandia. Beyond that, I knew that the longer we stuck around, the greater the risks of developing Yankee-Aussie personality conflicts.

Charlie continued to develop the scenario in his mind. Once our family moved to Hollandia, he thought, he and Vic could begin to plan the next aerial surveys for the missions' advance. And when this was pretty well completed, he thought he could then get away long enough to briefly investigate needs in the Philippines before planning further program expansion in New Guinea.

But wait! He was getting carried away with his projections. Actually, planning that far ahead was unrealistic; there were too many unknowns in between. Our progress toward DNG already seemed incredibly slow and now it would be slowed even further by a decision to postpone establishing a base there. Still, the more he reviewed his discussions with Vic, the more convinced he was of the wisdom of setting up an intermediate base at Wewak, especially when taking into account that our biggest assignment—and original objective—was to help AMAF get back on its feet. The Wewak-base plan certainly had the potential for seeing that earlier objective accomplished far faster than Charlie had originally thought possible. Earlier, he had seen no way to help them establish their own program until *after* our move to DNG—that is, until after the DNG program was underway. But the Wewak-base idea changed all that. If MAF-US bought a plane and loaned it to AMAF (with MAF-US maintaining technical control until AMAF could purchase the plane as their own), AMAF could more quickly begin operations with their own personnel. It would be their program! That prospect was both exciting and encouraging.

On top of seeing part of God's plan unfold before our eyes during Vic's visit, our family anticipated a vacation in the highlands after he left. MAFers often joked about change being normative in MAF, so we were in a sense prepared for adjustments to the schedule. But a number of unexpected developments threw us somewhat off balance.

10

A Temporary Task

Near the end of Vic's visit, the Cessna's schedule tightened up again with the addition of flights to the Lutherans' annual conference. Bob and Charles R. shuttled delegates from Madang and from highland stations to the conference site at Wau. Since Charlie had to be there to present the report on the aviation program, Vic went along so they could finish their discussions before he returned in Melbourne.

Delegates from Lae made the 90-mile trip south to Wau by road—over the one road in the Territory that linked an interior location with the coast. That road, constructed to transport lumber and gold from Wau and nearby Bulolo down to the port city of Lae, was a narrow mountain highway much like the early roads in our own Rocky Mountains; many of the grades and curves required four-wheel-drive vehicles.

Before the war, Wau had been the Territory's capitol and largest city, and was the site of its biggest and best airport. But by 1953, Port Moresby (and probably Lae as well) had superseded Wau in both size and prominence.

Surrounded by mountains, and with an altitude of 3,500 ft., Wau had a scenic beauty and a delightful climate that reminded us of Colorado. Temperatures ranged from very warm in the daytime to chilly—even cold—at night. The town itself lay in a small round valley which sloped up on all sides. Its airstrip was situated on a slope that rose one foot for every 12 feet in length; takeoffs and landings there produced quite a sensation.

Across the small valley from the airstrip and up on a little ridge, yet within the valley, was the Lutheran Mission's property. There they had a schoolhouse (for grades one through eight), a dormitory with two wings, a dining hall, laundry, an infirmary and eight little vacation cottages. The annual field conference, held there during the school's vacation period, taxed the available space to capacity.

Arrangements were made for our family to join Charlie for a couple weeks of vacation at the end of the conference week, when the Cessna went to take some of the conferees home. (About 50 of them returned to Lae by road.) Technically, our vacation began when we arrived, but until Vic left a couple of days later, he and Charlie continued to discuss MAF's future in New Guinea.

Shortly after the boys and I got there, the Cessna began bringing the children back to school for the new term. Normally, two teachers (an American and an Australian) shared the teaching load. However, the teacher from Australia had resigned just before Christmas and her replacement's arrival was delayed. That meant the American teacher had to assume the full responsibility for teaching all 25 children (in all eight grades!) until the new teacher got there. That was a big enough job in itself, even apart from the complicating factor of having to teach both American and Australian curricula.

Since I had majored in elementary education at the university and had taught second grade, I knew how overwhelmed I would feel in this kind of situation. So, vacation or not, I offered to help while we were there. I could at least work with reading groups, or do whatever else might be helpful. My offer was accepted and I began to work with seven of the children in the lower grades who could benefit from individual attention. More specifically, I helped two second-grade girls read Australian texts, two second-grade boys (our John being one) read American texts and a third-grade boy—whose family was new to New Guinea from Germany—with beginning English. (He picked it up quickly and soon joined his classmates in the Australian texts.) I also helped two other girls who arrived after the school term was already underway. But these two needed more than catch-up assistance since they were the school's first mixed-race students. It was important that they experience caring, acceptance, and encouragement as well—from teachers and children alike. A mission family had taken a special interest in these girls and was determined to see them given an opportunity for education. Neither of the girls knew any English, although one could speak a little Pidgin English. Obviously at square one, they needed help with basic English words, phrases and sentences. Everyone was eager to see them do well.

Meanwhile, the Wau climate was having a rejuvenating effect on our limp, energy-less bodies. What a wonderfully refreshing change this was after the heat and humidity in Madang. Jim's sores healed. (He had had four sieges of these small, ulcerous sores—the most recent count was more than 40 that we treated daily.) We were happy that Charlie's appetite improved somewhat, which helped slow his weight loss. (Not only had he lost 14 pounds since we arrived, but he seemed more susceptible than the rest of us to attacks of malaria, despite taking anti-malarial drugs regularly.)

Rarely, if ever, did I succeed in divorcing Charlie from MAF concerns or MAF-oriented projects during a vacation. This time he was thinking through and planning the next stage—the move to Wewak. He and Vic had discussed the move quite thoroughly, but Charlie had to work out all the details and implement the plans. Even though he loved this kind of challenge, he was already feeling some of the pressures. It wouldn't be easy to estimate schedules when he didn't know how much time to allow for potential shipping delays (of materials and supplies ordered from Australia) or delays related to availability of local labor. Beyond that, I don't think he was realistic about his own physical limitations in the tropics; he was apt to push just as hard as always to get things done in the least amount of time.

Neither of us looked forward to the inevitable separation involved when he first went to Wewak alone to initiate the building project. He wasn't eager to be away from the family for a month or more at a time, and I began wondering just where our family could stay while he was gone. With our personal attention beginning to shift away from the Lutheran program (except for supervision), I feared our family would become a burden to the Lutherans housing-wise—though Charlie tried to convince me I was overly sensitive about this. But I knew mission housing always was tight, so I really struggled with alternative options. I realized that with Charlie away, the boys and I had a greater flexibility to live wherever seemed appropriate—maybe even at Wau, since the Australian teacher wasn't due yet for a couple of months. The idea of staying at Wau temporarily appealed to me for three reasons: first, because I saw a way I could contribute to a need there; second, I thought maybe we'd be less in the way there in Wau (from a housing standpoint); and third, because the boys seemed to enjoy being with the school children.

By the time our vacation was over at the end of February (1953), a decision was made that the boys and I could remain at Wau, and my offer to help with teaching was accepted. We saw Charlie off, first for Port Moresby where he planned a courtesy contact with DCA officials. He planned to tell them of the Wewak plans, and he hoped to make arrangements for a survey of southwestern Papua. However, since air service in that direction was known to be sketchy, being able to conduct such a survey was by no means a certainty. If it didn't work out, he would spend the extra time in Madang ordering supplies and building materials he knew were unavailable in Wewak.

After he left Wau, the boys and I moved to a cottage across the road from the dining hall, which was more convenient. My work with the children went quite smoothly; I found myself enjoying them and the challenge of teaching. I was especially pleased with the considerable progress made in only a few weeks' time by the German boy and one of the mixed-race girls. The other girl needed much more help and encouragement. She tried so hard; but for her, everything came so slowly. Words that our five-year-olds know so readily with picture clues meant nothing to her. She not only used different words, but because her experiences were so different, the pictured items were unfamiliar. For example, one lesson included amusement parks with a merry-go-round. Another lesson had pictures of tall buildings, an elevator and an escalator. These things had no meaning to her, so I had to look for other ways to adapt to her situation. (Some years later I was thrilled to hear that both girls had not only completed school in Wau but had gone on to do well in high school in Australia.) Along the way I added sessions in third-grade arithmetic with eight children, using American texts with four of them and Australian texts with the other four.

At school in Wau, the children also enjoyed a variety of extra-curricular activities, from team sports like soccer to outings: picnics, swimming, hiking, and occasional field trips. On one occasion arrangements were made for them to take a field trip to a gold mine operation on the far side of the valley. At this particular mine, the rain water at higher mountain elevations was collected and channeled to flow down through pipes and eventually out through hoses with nozzles. It was amazing how much power the water had built up just from the flow of gravity. Workers aimed the nozzles at the hillsides in several places (we saw four) to wash dirt and rocks down into a stream where the muddy water traveled over several sluice boxes and then over some big rocks. If any gold washed beyond the sluice boxes, it tended to settle beneath the rocks. So every little while the rocks were moved aside and the dirt collected from under them to be passed over the sluice boxes again.

Each day the Papuan workmen carried the big rocks that washed down on one side of the stream across to the other side, so that in effect they rebuilt the mountain on the far side of the wash with stones and rocks that had washed down on the near side. In the previous two years this operation had not only leveled a mountain, but had washed away as much dirt below the average ground level as had originally been above it. Since there was no way to turn off the hoses at night, the whole operation went on 24 hours a day, seven days a week—with no holidays! The men worked in three or four shifts. Only a relatively few of them worked at night (to aim the hoses); the majority of them worked all day hauling rocks. The whole mining operation was fascinating!

Many children are very creative at play, and those at Wau were no exception. They discovered it was fun to slide down the hills near the dorm on corrugated cardboard "sleds." If a sled got away, they just slid down without it—to retrieve it, of course. The slopes were covered with tall, tough and stiff kunai grass which, when bent over, made a terrific slide. It wasn't even too bad a slide when the grass eventually got worn down to almost nothing but dirt.

But kunai grass also made super tunnels. Some of the older boys would crawl through first to separate the grasses near the ground. These then held their new shape while the tops remained where they were—even though the grass got pushed around near the bottom. It was great fun, especially since a regular maze of these tunnels now existed all over one side of a hill.

March was the month for our boys' birthdays, and Charlie missed all three that year. The school's staff, however, kept track of every child's birthday and each child's birthday was celebrated with a party and a special cake. The rest of the children were encouraged to prepare birthday cards or, in some other way, help make the birthday child feel important.

Probably my most memorable experience came when I discovered rats had invaded our cottage. I saw evidence of their presence before I first caught a glimpse of one in the bathroom. I decided to take action. But what could I use as a weapon? Ah, I remembered there was a broom in an adjacent room. Keeping my eye on the good-sized rat, I backed out of the room, squeezing through the barely open bathroom door, and quickly closed it behind me. I grabbed the broom and returned for the battle. My heart was beating furiously. I was conscious of goose bumps all up and down my legs. And I was trembling from head to toe. It took several blows, but I did it! I had won! Actually, that victory gave me fresh courage along with a determination to strike again if necessary. That incident happened to be my most dramatic encounter, but I eventually succeeded in tracking down and eliminating all their points of entry. My perseverance paid off. I could finally relax—but only for the moment. For this wasn't the end of my experiences with rats in New Guinea. They were to plague me again, in both Wewak and Hollandia.

After the boys and I had been at Wau for nearly two months, the new teacher arrived and promptly settled into her routine. My temporary duties came to an end. Over those weeks I had heard from Charlie fairly regularly, but now I was more eager than ever to have our family back together again. How soon could this happen? How much progress had Charlie actually made in Wewak during those eight weeks? I want to tell about that in the next chapter.

11

Pilot / Builder

When Charlie left the family in Wau, he flew first to Port Moresby where he intended to talk over the new Wewak-Hollandia plans with the Regional Director of Civil Aviation—first, as a matter of courtesy (to let him know what was planned); and second, to ask for some special concessions. But he was hardly prepared for the almost red-carpet treatment he received, which incidentally contrasted sharply with the reception he got eight months earlier. Their half-hour contact at that time gave Charlie the feeling of being addressed by a "Dutch uncle." This time the Director graciously gave his whole morning; and, in the course of their conversation, granted one concession after another. Charlie wrote of that office visit:

> I had a proposal to make concerning radio (both for Madang and Wewak) and he granted it. (He has still to work out the details, but he's obviously "on our side," so we can go ahead and install a radio in the plane that's coming.) There was a question whether my pilot's license was properly endorsed to cover the Piper Pacer. A subordinate didn't think so, but after a few questions, he handed back my license saying, "You're endorsed."
>
> I asked about getting licensed on floats. (I haven't had a lick of water time, but neither has anyone else around here. And even in the States that requires special rating.) He actually suggested that they could authorize me to teach myself, "and when you're satisfied you can handle it, let us know and we'll endorse your license." That is just not usual in Australia; the usual line is, "The regulation says, … " (I do not however plan to use his flattering permission to teach myself—we plan to have our next man coming out get his float rating, and then he can check me out.)

Charlie tried to analyze the reasons for such good rapport. It seemed obvious to him that, first of all, the Lord was answering prayer. He also believed the DCA officials had probably satisfied themselves that MAF's safety standards were as high as their own, so that they were now willing to allow greater leeway for the fellows' own judgment. Beside that, the Director was a very practical man; he knew he couldn't build a hedge around himself and at the same time oversee the development of a Territory like New Guinea. He spoke, as did

MAFers, in terms of calculated risks. But no one doubted he would be hard as nails if anyone was caught taking unwarranted risks. Charlie found him a most interesting person to talk to, and felt comfortable with him—probably because his theories and MAF's theories of bush flying ran so parallel.

One other item on Charlie's agenda for the Regional Director involved MAF's plans to utilize the same plane for work on both sides of the border. This included not only the general formalities of border crossings but also the activities requiring special permissions, such as initiating service to newly constructed airstrips and flying over unexplored areas. To operate in Dutch New Guinea the plane would of course be subject to Dutch regulations, but its Australian registration would require adherence to Australian regulations of the Territory as well.

The Regional Director assured Charlie of his full cooperation, which all but eliminated concern about difficulties on the Australian side of the border. His next step was to get to Hollandia so that he could talk over the same thing with the officials there, particularly since the subject of border crossings had not come up in earlier conversations. Charlie had begun to believe it would be wise to renew contacts in DNG in any case, if only to keep interest alive.

When he mentioned he hoped to get to DNG soon to talk to the aviation authorities, the director indicated he had been thinking of sending a man up there to confer with them, but he hoped to do it unofficially. He then asked when Charlie would like to go, and said he would send one of his chief assistants up in the MAL (Mandated Air Lines) Auster who would take Charlie along as his guest. It sounded almost too good to be true! Not only a gift flight, but a chance to be in discussions with officials from both sides of the border at the same time. He was sure that together they could easily iron out any potential border-crossing problem. They agreed the Hollandia trip could be made at the end of March (1953), and Charlie scribed out about five days on his calendar.

The hoped-for survey of the Fly River and Lake Kutubu areas that Charlie had planned did not materialize because transportation did not work out. However, in gaining additional information about the area while in Port Moresby, he came to the conclusion that timing for such a survey wasn't "right" anyway. In fact, he had the feeling that development of that area might not be any time soon.

Also, while in Moresby, Charlie learned that the grant to one of the missions of a piece of land in Wewak—that was, in turn, offered to MAF for use as its base—had been cancelled. This meant he had to rethink the situation in Wewak. He wrote immediately to Vic who replied by saying he should use his own judgment. Both realized that if a piece of property could be obtained fairly quickly, building could yet be underway in April. Most of the building materials that had been ordered were already in Madang, with the rest due to be shipped on the next boat.

On his arrival in Wewak, Charlie became discouraged when the officials he needed to see were unavailable—one didn't show up, and the other was tied up with a U.N. delegation that was conducting some kind of inspection. (The Territory of New Guinea was a Trust Territory, mandated to Australia under a United Nations charter.) Then there was the message from DCA in Moresby that the Hollandia trip had been cancelled—with no explanation. He had been so keyed up about the many things that seemed to be falling into place that this news was probably his greatest disappointment. He was, however, able to make arrangements for another piece of land. A few days later they had permission in hand to go ahead with the building, once they put the pegs defining the lot in place.

It was now time to send a couple of wires: one to Kay Liddle, the Brethren missionary standing by at his station at Lumi awaiting word to come help with the building. The other wire went to the Lutheran store manager in Madang who was waiting for instructions about sending the building materials that had been stored there. Charlie hoped these supplies could yet be loaded aboard the ship leaving Madang that night, but thought he could keep busy temporarily pre-cutting the lumber he had obtained locally. Besides, if it took Kay a few days to arrange a ride to Wewak, that would give him time to work out any extra details.

Because no Protestant missionaries lived in Wewak at the time (although Catholics had work there), the idea was that MAF would provide an added service of receiving shipments for the Protestant missionaries inland, along with the flying service. Until now they had been dependent upon the charter services of commercial operators.

Just before Kay arrived, Charlie's preparations were slowed by having to treat some bad sores that had developed on his legs by soaking them with salt water and painting them with what he called a "triple dye"—measures that proved ineffective. He had to resort to aureomycin from the hospital to clear them up. His activities were then halted altogether by his having to spend a couple of days in bed with malaria.

When Kay arrived, he and Charlie were invited to live with John Newnham, a school teacher from Australia and fellow Christian. John had been in Wewak only a couple months, so it seemed the Lord had timed his arrival to coincide with the needs of the building program. The government school where John taught was several miles out of Wewak, up on a hill at Boram Point—a considerable distance from MAF's building site in town. The fellows realized they needed some kind of vehicle not only to transport them to and from town but to haul building materials.

Authorization to buy a jeep came from AMAF just in time for the arrival of the coastal vessel from Madang that brought the building materials (nails, hardware, corrugated roofing iron, fibrolite/asbestos sheets for outside walls, cement, etc.). Unlike Madang's harbor, Wewak's had no dock. Ships anchored out in the bay and cargo was brought ashore by small surf boats—a tricky operation in Wewak's unsheltered bay. From the beach, the cargo had to be loaded aboard the jeep and hauled up the hill to the building site. After several trips, everything was on hand to begin building.

The first project was a small (4 ft. x 4 ft.) shed with fibrolite walls and iron roofing, which they managed to put together that same day. It could than serve as a lockable storage facility for smaller building supplies.

After finishing the shed they pre-cut the wall lumber for the workers' house. They decided to build this before starting on the main houses for a couple of reasons. They knew the alternative local housing for their carpenter workers was totally unsatisfactory (and usually referred to as "a hole.") In addition to building the laborers' house first—to provide them a better place to stay—this project would give the inexperienced workers carpentry practice on a simpler structure where precision didn't matter quite so much. (Charlie had noted some of their cuts were far from "square" when they began.)

Along with arranging for additional lumber to complete the laborers' house, they began to set stakes and dig post holes for one of the main houses. The posts they ordered were made from a special hard native timber which ants (termites) reportedly wouldn't touch. While waiting for the posts, they pre-cut timber for joists and rafters and oiled all of it with a light motor oil (an additional ant deterrent).

Near the end of April (1953) they completed the workers' house. It was a simple 10 ft. x 16 ft. one-room box-like structure with a gabled roof of corrugated iron. Although its sides were eight feet high, its fibro-cement walls extended upward only six feet, which left open a two-foot section at the top for circulation of air. (Houses for all workers in the Territory at that time were constructed in similar fashion.)

Charlie's letter home included construction details which he knew would interest his father, a builder of small homes in St. Louis. (Charlie's building experience, working with his father before going to college, turned out to be one of the Lord's preparatory experiences for his assignment in New Guinea.) He wrote,

> In Madang they use concrete pillars, but that's not exactly the best because it can be cracked in the many minor earthquakes that they have around New Guinea. So where it is available, the best material is a very hard native timber called quila. The ants feed on the outside sap wood, but won't touch the heartwood.
>
> You buy the logs direct from the Papuans (that's a task in itself—took quite a bit of chasing around), and they trim off the bulk of the sap wood. We sink them about two feet in the ground which means they're usually resting on solid coral. Before you put them in, you soak them with common motor oil (light grade—#10— so it soaks in well) to keep down the dry rot. On top of each post you put a galvanized iron ant cap—similar to the termite shield FHA used to require. Then all the rest of the timbers in the house are also soaked with this oil.
>
> On the first (workers' house), we soaked them as soon as we pre-cut them. But this turned out to be awfully messy. So now I think we'll do the frame-up first and then douse it all at once. Also, we plan to go over it and soak the inside timbers once a month for several months so it really soaks in thoroughly. (We don't plan to finish off the inside for a while.)
>
> On the quila posts, we also bore three holes at an angle (and at different heights) in each post. Every month you squirt these full of oil and let it soak right down through the entire log.
>
> But it isn't just ants that give us extra building problems. The local timber mill has pretty primitive equipment and the lumber isn't gauged very accurately. Of course, nothing is planed. A 2' x 4' (always listed here as a 4' x 2'!) might be anywhere from 1¾ to 2¼ inches thick. And the only way you can pre-cut your studs is to gauge your top and bottom plates to 1¾ inch and then notch out where each stud falls. We've got the men checked out on this and also on cutting the studs, so that saves us a very time-consuming job.
>
> One of our big problems has been getting the lumber. At first we had a time getting the posts from the local people. We got a little other lumber, so we spent our time pre-cutting. Now we've got enough posts for the guest house, but the saw mill is plumb out of lumber. They can't get any logs in because the roads into the bush are all wet. (This rainy season has been long and wet! We'll sure be glad to see the end of it ... pretty soon now.) But with this lumber shortage, we just

get a few sticks at a time. Of course, there are a lot of other buildings being built around here also, so the mill owner is trying to keep everyone happy, and going. It's really been a hand-to-mouth existence. We seldom have more than a day or two of work ahead. About every other morning we stop by the mill on the way in. If he has a few sticks, we put them on the jeep and head for town.

There were also other problems. The jeep tires weren't much to start with, and two soon became unusable. Although the former owner had thrown in two extra tires, they weren't much better. The spare was borrowed! It was a great day when two new tires available in Madang finally arrived in Wewak. Two more had to be ordered from Australia and were expected the end of May—hopefully!

Life in Wewak had one particular attraction which the fellows could not resist once they got the jeep—a nice beach nearby. Their four-mile trip home to Boram Point each evening took them along the beach at one point, and they soon made it a habit to stop there for a relaxing swim after the day's work. (Before they had the jeep, they had walked the four miles out to Boram one day when they couldn't find a ride after working all day!)

The building was only just underway, it seemed, when near the end of April they had to pause for a holiday. ANZAC Day commemorated Australia's and New Zealand's first day of combat in the WWII. Quite a memorial ceremony took place around the town's flagpole that day. Charlie described the celebration, the participants, and other war-related activities in characteristic detail.

All the veterans (which included practically all the male [Australian and New Zealand] residents) lined up on one side of the flagpole, the Papuan veterans on another, the local police detachment on a third side, and we spectators on the fourth.... Most [of the veterans] wore their medals—including the Papuans, who had collected quite a few.... The fellow who directed the column had four medals and is quite a character. He really stands out from the crowd. We had previous dealings with him in trying to secure quila posts for our houses. He wears a full-blown beard (most unusual among Papuans) and an eye patch over the eye he lost during the war. He also lost one hand just above the wrist. He looked like a "veteran true"! Apparently he's quite a smart fellow for he dabbles in several other enterprises besides cutting timber. He collects scrap, for example. And there's plenty of scrap to collect. Wewak was the scene of quite an action during the war, and they've been a lot slower cleaning it up here than in Madang because it's a much smaller community. At places, the beaches are literally crowded with wrecked landing barges. There are several heavy army tanks standing around, and also loads of unexploded ammunition.

A couple of Aussie soldiers are assigned here for bomb demolition. They hunt up unexploded bombs until they've found about 15 or 20 of them, and then let them go all at once. Usually the word gets passed around when they're detonating a lot of them, so people are forewarned. But when I first came, I got caught by surprise once when they let go a bunch of them right near Boram Point. It sure made me jump. Last week they let go another bunch on the beach just north of town. One of the soldiers said that near that site they had stumbled onto a skeleton of a Japanese soldier in a sitting position, with his hand out like he was aiming a pistol—quite an eerie sight.

Then, this morning, they let go another lot of 20 bombs that they had carefully placed on the reef in the harbor—to blow out a passage that the launches could get through even at low tide. It really sent up a stream of spray. All the local inhabitants were planning to be on hand with boats to rush out and scoop up the fish. But the unexploded bombs are less plentiful than small arms ammunition, much of which was left in abandoned gun positions. This is really sought after because the brass of the cartridges is worth a fair amount of money as scrap metal.

One trader has bought the rights for the non-ferrous scrap, and others collect it to sell to him at a lower price. He prepares it for shipment ... by heating it in big drums until it explodes—then he keeps just the brass casings and throws the lead slugs away. The local men try to get into the act too, and often it results in disaster. They put the bullets in their cooking fires, and then when the bullets explode, they hit someone sitting around the fire. When I first came up here and was staying with the medical orderly, two fellows were brought in who had been "shot" that way. One of them had gotten hit right next to his eye. I never did find out whether he lost that eye.

Another interesting fellow is one we also bought some quila wood from. He's one of three Papuans on the territorial legislative council. After we'd asked him about getting this quila, he drove by the job on his bike one day to tell us that he had to go to Rabaul—then to Port Moresby—so we should settle up with his kuskus (clerk [employee]) when the posts were delivered! His village owns a couple of trucks which they hire out to the government. (Private enterprise is coming to N.G., though on a co-op basis.) One of the trucks is "grounded" right now because they got caught driving it without brakes, and I believe it hit something. They got fined a pound or two, and can't use the truck for a month. It's really not a very stiff penalty, but it is to them, I guess.

It's really interesting to work with Papuans who are sharp and interested in getting ahead. Our own Somu is pretty much that way, and I wouldn't be surprised that he goes far. He's one of our hangar helpers in Madang, but we sent him up here to help out during the time I'm here.... Some carpentry jobs I hesitate to tackle when he's around for fear they'll look inferior to his work.

Of course he's not that good at everything, but he is a fairly careful workman. Best of all, he goes ahead and does things on his own initiative. You tell him what you want done, and he figures out the "how" himself—that's most unusual.

Our other two helpers are right out of the bush—Kay brought them out from his station. They're doing very well, but they don't have Somu's know-how and self-assurance of course. But the encouraging thing about these other two is that they've shown fairly good spiritual progress, considering how recently the Gospel has been introduced into their area (less than two years, I believe), and the fact that the work has thus far been mostly in Pidgin (... which is native to neither preacher nor listener)....

It was nearing the end of April, 1953. Although Charlie and Kay were grateful for the progress on the Wewak housing project, they were obviously behind schedule. In assessing the situation, Charlie realized he ought to return to Madang to tend to administrative duties neglected during his weeks in Wewak. Recent events seemed to confirm this decision. Charles R. had completed his orientation flying with Bob Hutchins in Madang and was now available to replace Charlie in Wewak by helping Kay Liddle with the building. At Wau, the new teacher for the mission's school had arrived, so my help there was no longer needed. Charlie was particularly eager to touch base with Bob and the Lutheran leaders—to be sure the program was moving along well and to discuss with them the plans and strategy for the days ahead.

Charlie also needed time to *think*! His correspondence (with the two MAF home offices, in L.A. and in Melbourne) had suffered during the strenuous weeks of building. He found it hard to compose carefully worded letters when fatigued physically. There was also the matter of Dutch New Guinea looming in the background. How could he get there again? When would that be possible? What should be the overall strategy? Or, even the next step?

In addition to his concerns for the various aspects of the work, there was his family to think about. After nearly eight weeks of separation, we were both realizing we needed each other—not only to be under the same roof, but to experience each other's love, encouragement, and support. Charlie needed to be with his family, the boys needed a father, and I needed a husband.

12
Together Again

"He's coming, Mom!" called Jim. "I'm sure it's the Cessna's engine I hear!"

Yes, it was the sound we were listening for. Charlie was coming for us! We rushed outside, Jim leading the way. I picked up Gordon to hurry along a little faster, and we eagerly searched the sky to locate the sound. Suddenly the plane's silver aluminum body caught the rays of the bright sun. We watched as it flew closer and then began the wide circle of the landing pattern. We all knew the sequence. Charlie then lined it up with the mission's airstrip, lowered the flaps for the final descent, and eased the plane onto the airstrip. The minutes dragged as we watched it slow down and taxi toward us. In those moments it began to dawn on me that our lengthy separation was really over and we'd be together—at least for a little while.

How wonderful to be reunited! Charlie had only just returned from Wewak, pausing in Madang only long enough to pick up a load for the highlands where he was to meet us. Jim, Gordon and I had flown by airline a day or so earlier from Wau to the mission's station at Asaroka, leaving John at Wau to complete the final few weeks of the school term with the other children. I'm sure the thrill we experienced that day gave us a better idea of how missionaries in isolated areas feel when the plane reunites them with family members or brings special visitors, mail or other eagerly awaited cargo. Needless to say, we filled the plane's cabin with continuous and animated chatter all the way back to Madang.

As we settled in Madang once more we noted that the quality of life on the mission field had further improved. For one thing, the Madang bakery now had two deliveries a day; we could buy fresh loaves of bread in the mornings and other items such as tarts, cupcakes, and meat pies in the afternoons. Another surprise came in the form of the brand new pickup truck that had been acquired for use by the mission's aviation department during our absence.

As for the daily flying routine, Charlie began to wonder if there might be a better approach to scheduling. Always striving to streamline tasks to promote greater efficiency, he thought maybe his newest idea could reduce pilot fatigue.

How would it work, he asked himself, if he and Bob were to alternate days, each flying both trips on those days, instead of both flying daily with each of them taking one trip. Bob thought the idea made a lot of sense in that there would be fewer interruptions. When they tried it, both agreed the new schedule made things considerably easier—the new schedule *was* less disruptive, and the days were not as fatiguing.

With this new flight schedule in place, Charlie began to spend his flight-free days tracking down supplies for Wewak, and he hoped time would be available to concentrate on overdue correspondence. However, the reality was that accumulating the needed supplies took more time than he had estimated—some items were hard to locate. Often when a list was almost complete, along came a letter (or urgent wire) requesting that one or two additional items be included in the pending shipment. It could get very frustrating.

As for the flying, up until 1953 the Cessna's deepest penetration inland had been Mendi. Then, in May of that year, a request was received for a flight to a place beyond Mendi called Tari. Tari was at that time in "uncontrolled" territory, which meant the plane's payload had to be reduced to include selected but mandatory survival gear (e.g., foodstuffs and blankets). Actually this particular request required the pilots to make several trips into Tari to shuttle supplies from Mendi needed by the men involved in their mission's pioneer advance into Tari. Mendi was considered a more secure location, so the pilots planned to overnight there where the plane would be safer. Charlie wrote about their first venture into Tari, saying,

> Bob and I ran into some weather problems the first day, so we stayed overnight first at the Mendi Methodist mission. That was an interesting experience. It was the first time I had opportunity to cross one of the vine suspension bridges so common in the highlands—a shaky experience.

> Mendi is still considered *restricted* territory, though things are pretty quiet around there just now. The Tari people are becoming quite friendly too. But the people in the three narrow valleys between Tari and Mendi are still pretty rough.

> The Tari people are quite interesting. They mold their fuzzy hair into a helmet-like headdress. If they haven't enough hair, they make a wig to fit on top (but don't ask me where they get that hair!). So far, all this is common to most highland peoples. But the Taris garnish theirs with neat rows of colorful flowers. (One old codger had a row of flowers around the top of his helmet, and centered above his forehead he had pinned on a label from some canned goods

with a homemade wooden hat pin.) We expect to go to Tari again next week; the government is allowing missionaries to bring their families in now.

Usually the pilots were quite preoccupied with their job and all that it involved; they didn't spend much time thinking about how isolated missionaries view the plane's coming in for the first time. So it was particularly gratifying to read a letter printed in *New Life* (a Christian weekly newsletter datelined Melbourne, April 23, 1953). The letter described in detail the excitement of MAF's initial landing at Pabarabuk on Wednesday, March 25th and reported that air service to this station would make it possible for the missionary's wife to be taken by plane to the hospital location when her baby was due, rather than have to face an arduous trek over difficult terrain.

Early in June (1953), everyone's schedule was disrupted for a whole week while the entire Territory took time to celebrate the Coronation of Queen Elizabeth II. It was referred to as "the day belong putim hat long Queen!"

In Madang, the celebration began on a Tuesday—a declared holiday. The day started with a short prayer service for the new Queen at church, and was followed by a big parade at 10:00 a.m. There were uniformed police, groups from various schools (Papuan, European, and Oriental), a large group of village chiefs (luluais), and children from the different mission schools throughout the area: Lutheran students from Baitabag and Amele, and Catholic students from Alexishaven.

That afternoon the schedule called for games for the Papuans on the athletic field. Later in the day the District Commissioner hosted a reception for administration personnel at his home. In the evening a large crowd again gathered at the field ("the oval") for the customary *sing-sing*.

Sing-sing festivities got underway soon after the afternoon games ended, and continued all night. In fact, they were only just coming to an end as Charlie left for the airport at 6:30 the next morning. (One of the young men who worked for us had stayed up all night and came to work that morning practically asleep on his feet.) In a letter to our parents, Charlie described the evening activities:

> Floodlights had been rigged for that occasion so we could see a lot more than we did last time when they had only pressure lanterns. We found the sing-sing more interesting for many reasons. In the first place we understood a lot more about the people and their customs. Then, the headdresses were more elaborate—both from a primitive and a civilized standpoint. There were a lot more people with bird of paradise plumes on the tops of their headdresses like they always have up

in the highlands. But a lot of them also had a civilized touch; one even had a crude model airplane on his headdress—a really huge affair. Some of the headdresses were about 12 feet high supported by a pole strapped to the fellow's back.

Most of the sing-sing participants were local workers who divided into their tribal groups for the dances. But this time the Administration had brought people out from the Ramu Valley who were considered *bush kanakas* [less "civilized"]. And there was another, similar group—I don't know where they were from. But both groups really threw themselves into it…as they chanted and danced.

We were watching these latter two groups and there wasn't much room between them and the next group (the oval was really crowded). When they came around to our side of their circle, they practically brushed their feathers right in our faces. And it was their custom to perform [wearing] their spears, bows and arrows. So here they were, brushing right up against us with their spears pointed down and out—right at our legs…. It kind of gave us the creeps.

Just a few feet away from these primitive groups was another group (just a small one) that was a marked contrast. They were the educated Papuans who hold the white collar jobs in the administration. To them the dance wasn't something to throw themselves into as warp and woof of their lives; rather, it seemed a reenactment, to show "how our fathers used to do it." It was really interesting to note this difference due to the changes coming to the different people groups.

Wednesday morning we watched a parade of about 15 floats. Most were trucks creatively decorated with flowers. Some had people aboard to help illustrate activities of schools in the Territory. Madang's inhabitants had certainly produced unique and descriptive floats.

That evening everyone assembled on the wharf for a different kind of parade. This time it was a parade of canoes beautifully decorated with native grasses and lit by lanterns. They resembled colorful Italian gondolas as they glided along.

The festivities were climaxed at the end of the week by a formal Coronation Ball at the Madang Hotel—probably the European cultural equivalent of the Papuan sing-sing. Once the Ball was over, it was time to put partying aside and return to normal routines.

By this time Charlie was swamped with correspondence. Everything was interrelated, but needed separate responses. One group of papers, related to the new Cessna, had to be passed along to DCA together with a specific request for registration. There was the Bill of Lading for a shipment of building materials (due the next day). However, because no invoice was enclosed,

Charlie would be unable to clear it through customs. Wires and letters had to be composed and sent to straighten out the matter. Other letters (from L.A. and Melbourne) dealt with DNG and reminded him that another trip to Hollandia should be made soon. He was conscious of expanded responsibilities, and summarized his concerns for the three locations:

MADANG: New plane coming, approaching annual inspection, plus more routine matters; also, we're expecting one new man this month, and there's another one in Los Angeles right now who is being "looked over."

WEWAK: Building program, and getting the plane registered soon (it's now being modified in L.A.). And we're trying to negotiate a temporary hanger rental to save building one.

HOLLANDIA: Mostly diplomatic problems both with the missionaries and the government.

As he sat down to write (dictate) one day, he realized he was currently wearing several "hats." Which is to say we used three different letterheads for his outgoing letters. If letters related to the Madang program, we used a "Lutheran Mission New Guinea, Aviation Department" letterhead which Charlie signed as "Chief Pilot." AMAF letterheads were used for correspondence related to the Wewak program. These he signed as "Chief Pilot, New Guinea." When writing to officials in Hollandia, or to mission representatives in the Philippines (in anticipation of an eventual survey), we used MAF-US stationery, which of course he signed as "Secretary-Treasurer." A good many other letters did not call for letterheads, such as "inside correspondence" with both the MAF-L.A. and Melbourne offices. All of this made us realize that the work in New Guinea was fast becoming a *field operation* rather than a single developing program.

In addition to the mounting correspondence, Charlie flew three days a week. It is no wonder he ran out of energy in the evenings! In fact, ever since he returned from Wewak, he had been bothered by a slight but continuous spinning in his head. He made inquiries at the hospital and the doctor there thought the condition might come from a toxic reaction to the anti-malarial drug he was taking. So a different drug was prescribed, along with some liver and iron medication. We hoped this change of prescription might help.

The wire to Melbourne about the lack of invoices apparently didn't communicate the shipment problem. Charlie scolded himself for probably trying too hard to save money by keeping the wire too brief. The resulting delay, however, meant we couldn't expect to receive the papers before the middle of the following week. And even if customs were cleared promptly in Madang, it would be the end of the next week before the papers could arrive in Wewak—a building delay of an entire week! Here again our western time-orientation added pressures to find an alternate solution.

It was during his flight home that Friday afternoon—while still preoccupied with the invoice situation—that Charlie believed the Lord gave him an idea:

> I remembered a list that one of the MAFers in Sydney (the one who had done most of the buying) had sent; it gave the prices of the things he had bought to date. I decided to "take a flyer" and see what the customs man would do for us. I knew British customs men could be mighty unbending fellows, concerned with "the regulation says…." But the Lord had [this custom official] in the right mood. He said he'd accept the list as far as it went. So I was able to clear about ⅔ of the stuff—the important items. Then I had to get the papers made up. The Lutheran store manager could do it, but I knew he was as busy as a cranberry merchant trying to get his stuff ready to ship out on the Bulolo tomorrow. And, of course, everything shuts up tight at noon on Saturday. But I found him in the right mood also. We got it all cleared before noon, and they'll be able to take immediate delivery when the Malekula gets to Wewak on Tuesday.

What a relief to have this knotty problem solved! The decks seemed cleared at last for Charlie to give his full attention to getting to Hollandia once more. As it turned out, he had only just made tentative plans to borrow the Cessna for a weekend in mid-June (1953) when he heard that Unevangelized Fields Mission (UFM) had an emergency at their new Sengge airstrip and had sent a wire to Mandated Air Lines (MAL) requesting a charter flight. It was doubtful at first that MAL could supply a plane, so Charlie offered to go. In the end, MAL decided to send its Dragon based at Wewak. Again, Charlie was terribly disappointed. This had seemed like a perfect opportunity for him to make the trip. He even made arrangements with the Lutherans to borrow the Cessna for the emergency. From a purely psychological standpoint, he knew that MAF's being ready and willing to respond to such an emergency could maybe help gain back some confidence he feared had been lost through various delays in our getting air service underway in DNG. His bag was packed, and he was on stand-by all day—in case the Dragon trip didn't materialize, for whatever reason. In the end, we had to trust that, despite our disappointment, the Lord—still in control of all things!—would somehow use this experience in the sequence of events that would make possible the evangelizing of those yet unreached in DNG.

Charlie's hopes rose once more the next week when he learned that a Beechcraft would be making the trip to Hollandia. He immediately wired the pilot to ask if he could ride along. But that didn't work out either. So he returned to the idea of borrowing the Cessna for the trip. The thought of using the Cessna appealed to him for a variety of reasons. Yet, he hesitated to pull it away from its busy program, especially when the schedule for the next weeks looked heavier than ever: the school children were almost ready to go home; Ray Jaensch, the new Lutheran pilot due to arrive from Australia (with his wife Betty), would need to be checked out; and, with that kind of schedule, Bob would need Charlie's help with routine flying. It seemed he really had no choice but to settle back into the flying routine. The trip to DNG would have to wait a little longer.

We were now into the so-called dry season in the Territory. Usually that only meant "less wet." But this had been the driest season we had experienced since our arrival in New Guinea. Moreover, the lack of rain extended throughout this part of the island. Missionaries at all the highland stations were out of rainwater, presenting a need to carry it up from nearby rivers. In Madang we too had a shortage of water, and had to transport it—in 50-gallon drums—from a well at the town's pump. However, from a flying standpoint, the dry spell was incredibly good. Charlie wrote,

> We were doing such unheard of things as making two trips per day over Bundi gap (the 9,000 footer that we use most regularly—it's right by 15,400 Mt. Wilhelm, the highest in TNG, and therefore usually fills up with clouds pretty early in the day). And we came home leisurely over this gap as late as 2:00 or 3:00 in the afternoon.

Of course that beautiful weather did come to an abrupt end with rains that replenished water supplies for everyone. As for flying, the New Guinea weather factory was once again in full production, although the break had been enjoyable while it lasted. Unfortunately, the weather change was so sudden and drastic that for three or four days the fellows couldn't begin to meet their schedules. One day it rained so hard they couldn't even fly locally.

At last, in mid-July, the flight schedule showed signs of leveling off. Ray Jaensch had arrived from Australia on schedule and Charlie had flown with him, first to check him out locally and then to help him learn the more distant routes. With that taken care of, Charlie again made plans to borrow the Cessna to go to Hollandia for a few days. He looked forward to the trip, planning to renew contacts he had made previously. But I know he was also a little appre-hensive—concerned about MAF's standing in the DNG mission community in light of so many delays and changes in plans for setting up a program there. Humanly speaking, our timetable for getting a program going in DNG had been very unrealistic. Yet we had to trust God—He knew the situation and would continue to order the sequence of events according to His timing. What we needed at the moment was patience. But it was so very hard to be patient when what we knew of the situation kept pressuring us to get there with a plane and personnel.

Arrangements for using the Cessna were completed, and Charlie took off for Sentani. While the boys and I waited in Madang, I prayed for him, for his contacts and discussions, and for any decisions that might need to be made. We both knew much was at stake, with as many unknowns as ever.

13

Pressures Mount

It was Saturday, July 18, 1953, when Charlie took off for Hollandia in the Lutheran Cessna. He had looked forward to the trip, expecting it to provide a break—or at least a change of pace—from the pressures of recent weeks. But as it turned out, he only exchanged one set of pressures for another. Not only were the discussions about air service intense, but he faced a demanding flight schedule. Time for sleep was minimal at best, reduced even further by the need to spend time alone thinking through the many facets of the job. Not surprisingly, his dizziness returned.

Suddenly everything seemed to be moving too fast. It was understandable, on the one hand, that the missions were eager to take full advantage of the government's allowing them access to the interior. In anticipation of our air support, they had begun assigning more and more families to Dutch New Guinea—all of which increased the pressure on MAF to get a program underway—SOON! On the other hand, the more he learned, the more Charlie realized that setting up a program in DNG was going to require an approach different from MAF's other programs. There were problems to overcome here that we had not faced in the Territory—some rarely encountered by MAF anywhere, in any of its operations to date. In that sense, DNG was an entirely new ballgame.

With no existing airstrips in the interior, landings would have to be made on rivers and lakes initially. The fellows discussed amphibious equipment, but decided it would make more sense in the long run to begin with a small plane— a "pathfinder" plane—that had float capabilities. This meant that loads would be somewhat limited since floats weighed considerably more than wheels. But, once suitable airstrip sites were located and built, the use of wheels could be emphasized while the floats would be available for special situations or for entering new areas. This approach sounded logical, and they prepared to make appropriate adjustments downtrack. Too much was at stake to rush a ready-made program (that is, one identical to MAF-US's Latin America programs) and assume all would go smoothly or routinely. To assure a safe operation here we had to begin by providing limited service with basic equipment, and study the needs as we went along. The type of plane that best met the above criteria was a four-place Piper Pacer—on wheels, but with fittings for floats, which were to be ordered separately.

Flying in Dutch New Guinea was being approached with increased caution, particularly as more became known about the conditions. The additional caution, together with the many delays, was not what mission leaders or missionaries expected, as Charlie soon discovered. In their excitement of moving into hitherto untouched areas with the Gospel—and possibly because they saw the aviation program develop so quickly in the Territory—they may have assumed that MAF's original proposal of a limited service with a pathfinder operation no longer applied—or was now unnecessary—for inaugurating air service in DNG. Almost despairingly Charlie commented to me: "They seem to be looking for perfected or flawless service as soon as the plane gets here. And that won't happen!"

He also wondered what would be expected of future pilots, in light of the potential for undue pressures that became apparent during his visit. He could appreciate the mission's concern for keeping its one inland station supplied, but believed overall safety could easily be jeopardized if pilots felt pressured to fly. He may have been especially sensitive because of his own fatigue build-up at the time. But all this was a reminder that pilot fatigue is considered a major contributing factor in air accidents. Yet these considerations did not keep him from thoroughly enjoying his flights into the one inland station, as is clear from a letter to our parents:

> In the first place, Sengge is a real missionary airstrip—nothing like the ones in the Territory [Papua] which are controlled by DCA standards. The biggest trouble is that it gets pretty boggy when it rains. And it did rain. I made three attempts to get in on Monday, but the weather stopped us the first two times. We finally got over the strip late that afternoon but it looked absolutely swampy, so we didn't land.
>
> We got in radio contact with them by evening and again the next morning. It didn't sound extra good to me, but I decided to give it a try. The Cessna is a very good *mudder*. I dragged it in low and slow, and dropped it right on the very near end of the strip so that I got stopped before I hit the boggy spot in the middle.
>
> I made three more trips that day and two the next morning. On the last trip, I took the Director of Civil Aviation [for Dutch New Guinea] with me to see the strip. I was afraid he'd turn thumbs down on it. But by then it had dried somewhat. (The previous day I had churned up the boggy spot by taxiing through it eight times.) I had told the fellows to get busy and smooth that spot. Well, it worked—the Director wasn't at all unhappy with the strip. This was encouraging,

not only in regard to that strip but also it means that we'll be able to build strips where we need them without having to comply with a lot of arbitrary, meaningless standards.

After his last two trips to Sengge (on Wednesday afternoon, July 22nd), Charlie prepared to return to Madang. He had agreed to take three missionaries bound for Australia back with him that far. But by the time he loaded them and their gear aboard and was ready for takeoff, it was late afternoon. He had planned a stop in Wewak on the way back to Madang anyway, to discuss the building program, but the late start meant that he and his three passengers spent the night in Wewak, with Rasmussens and Kay Liddle in AMAF's tiny (recently completed) guest house. The little house bulged with people, but he managed to find opportunity to talk about their progress in constructing the main house.

Although he was physically and emotionally drained by the events of the previous days, he was pleased when Kay suggested they take a walk after the main discussions ended. The two had built a strong relationship during the weeks they worked together, enjoying a real openness with each other. It was while walking that Charlie asked Kay to stay on in Wewak a while longer. He had praised the Lord for Kay's wonderful attitude, his abilities and gifted contribution, and knew that if Kay could manage to stay on for a while to handle the administrative and spiritual end of the work in Wewak, it would give greater flexibility to his own schedule. In agreeing to do so, Kay told Charlie the extra time would be helpful to him as well, since it would give him a chance to follow through personally on some exciting and significant things he saw happening in Wewak.

For one thing, John Newnham (the teacher Charlie and Kay had stayed with at Boram Point) had started a Sunday school for Wewak children in the town's school building. As Sunday school attendance grew, Kay made plans to piggyback on it by adding a church service each week. A couple of weeks before services got underway, a missionary had been rushed to the government hospital in Wewak from his inland station at Maprik following a heart attack. While in the hospital, he died, after suffering additional heart attacks. Just the Sunday before services were to begin, news of his death circulated through Wewak. Kay indicated the incident (which had aroused considerable sympathy among the townspeople) could conceivably be an icebreaker for the Gospel's penetration into that frontier-like community. Although no results were immediately evident, the application is not inconsistent with Scripture (John 12:24). Charlie pondered the significance of these conversations with Kay all the way back to Madang. Just what kind of impact would MAF's presence have in Wewak in the days ahead?

In Madang, meanwhile, a considerable amount of work was accumulating for the Cessna's return. Bob had been kept busy assembling the Lutheran's second Cessna—which had arrived while Charlie was in DNG. He hoped to have it ready to fly by Sunday, August 16th (1953), the date set for its dedication. Since Ray had not yet been cleared for solo flying to the more distant destinations, Charlie went immediately back to the flight line to finish Ray's checkout along with distributing accumulated loads. For several days the two of them logged flight time of at least five hours a day. But that schedule left little or no time for Charlie's detailed report to L.A. and Melbourne concerning recent developments in DNG.

Charlie had admitted to feeling somewhat rundown when he returned from Hollandia, and the pace of the program allowed no letup. The fatigue and mounting pressures began to have a cumulative effect. I'm sure it didn't help to have to postpone writing to L.A. and Melbourne about the status—and urgency—of the situation in DNG. After two more busy weeks of flying passed, he was completely frustrated, and, not surprisingly, felt even worse. But, at this rate, when would he ever find adequate time to write?

Today, as I think about that situation, with its crosscurrents of external and internal pressures, several questions come to mind. With the various disappointments and delays we experienced in getting to DNG for the preliminary spadework, should we perhaps have been more relaxed (realistic) about the schedule? In other words, was God's timetable perhaps more open-ended than we thought? On the other hand, was this the Enemy's way of trying to throw us off balance? If we believed that God placed Charlie in this job, were we right to conclude that God saw his particular gifts of temperament and drive as a "fit" for the assignment? Other questions: Did God intend for Charlie to learn something about handling pressures? Is there a way he could have done the job well without pushing himself so hard in the energy-sapping tropical environment? How does the issue of "burn-out" fit into the equation? And how concerned should we be, anyway, for our own physical and emotional health when it comes to working and accomplishing something for the Lord? And also, how does one make realistic assessments in the light of deadlines and schedules? These kinds of questions I still find difficult.

As I look again at our New Guinea assignment, I am aware that Charlie often felt cut off, isolated, from his decision-making colleagues because of distance. True, he knew he was authorized to represent MAF-US and make certain decisions on his own. But he also considered himself part of a team. Face to face consultation would have been so helpful. Unfortunately, communication at that time had to be exclusively by correspondence, with an exchange of correspondence taking weeks. Moreover, there was always the risk of somehow miscommunicating, whether through inept writing at one end or misinterpretations or misunderstanding at the other. For that reason, Charlie's letter-writing took time—time to think issues through and compose letters carefully, so that the meaning would come through clearly and be interpreted as intended.

In hindsight I am realizing our New Guinea experience was complicated by an additional factor. I'm sure neither Charlie nor I realized at the time (in the 50s) the extent to which our inherent presuppositions about cultural differences (our own inculturation as Americans—our basic worldview) influenced relationships; in this instance, with AMAF. For example, although AMAF invited MAF-US to assume responsibility and take leadership for restoring mission aviation in Papua New Guinea after their fatal accident, they saw this as a temporary measure and didn't want to be crowded out of the picture. Because MAF-US was accustomed to making decisions unilaterally in all its other programs, AMAF leaders may have feared we would take a "typical Yankee approach"—which would take their ball and run with it. International working relationships can be risky. From our point of view, we understood the intent to bring AMAF back into the work as soon as possible. To guard that objective, Charlie continually reminded himself to include AMAF leadership in all that was going on. Unfortunately, what appeared to be happening in New Guinea didn't always seem to fit those joint objectives—sometimes from AMAF's point of view, and occasionally from MAF-US's. This meant that Charlie often found himself in the middle. His actions or suggestions might be interpreted by AMAF as promoting MAF-US's agenda (and therefore not in the best interests of AMAF), or they might appear to the L.A. office as actions or suggestions which catered too much to AMAF's wishes—all of which necessitated extra diligence when preparing reports and correspondence. It helped considerably when he and Vic related directly, but the potential for misunderstanding was always in the background.

Another factor—primarily self-inflicted—no doubt contributed to Charlie's stress. He did not want to hide behind his administrative responsibilities by avoiding his share of the routine work load. Besides, he enjoyed flying and earnestly wanted to understand the entire aviation picture on that island first hand. As a result, he often hesitated to delegate. Unfortunately, it was also true that he was frequently tempted to do a job himself to be sure it was done the way he thought it should he done. Either way, he ended up spreading himself too thin.

Also, in recent years we learned more about the issue of loneliness that individuals in leadership experience. In the 50s, we were unaware of such a phenomenon. I've wondered whether some feelings of isolation that were stress producing may have come from Charlie's lack of opportunity for interpersonal interaction with a team in decision-making, as was customary at the L.A. office.

Whatever the cause of this extreme fatigue after returning from Hollandia, Charlie decided it might help to get away from Madang, even if only briefly. As if to underscore the wisdom of that idea, chills and fever of another malaria attack drove him to bed the same afternoon he made the decision to get away.

Arrangements were made for our family to spend a week in the Highlands at the guest facilities of the Lutheran missionaries (the Bergmanns) at Chimbu. Despite his fatigue, Charlie intended to spend the first four days of that week on urgent correspondence—preparing the delayed reports to both MAF offices about the recent Hollandia trip. Only after those were composed, typed, and ready to mail could he allow himself a few days to relax. As for me, although I hesitated to voice an objection, I wondered if those few days would be enough to put him on top again. He had decided he could spare only a week, and I knew he had made up his mind. Raising a question about it could precipitate an argument which—in turn, would only add to the frustrations and pressures he already felt. Rather, I decided a better response for our family would be to do everything we could to make the week as relaxing as possible. He would benefit most if all of us worked together to help him accomplish his objectives. Besides, we all looked forward to the rejuvenating effects of cooler temperatures. At the same time, I must admit that for me the very best thing about the week's break was that the family could spend it together.

14

Chimbu

The village of Chimbu was a beautiful garden spot. Surrounded by mountains and with lush green growth, it was among the most scenic areas in the Highlands. Gardens belonging to the local people dotted the hillsides, some even on the rather steep mountainous slopes nearby. Perhaps as many as 130,000 New Guineans lived in and around Chimbu (in 1953), which made it a strategic location for a mission station and an airstrip. The Australian government had an Assistant District Officer residing there, and operated a good-sized hospital with one or two resident doctors.

The Bergmanns, veteran Lutheran missionaries assigned to Chimbu, were our gracious hosts and saw to it that we had everything we needed to make the week a restful one. They had come to New Guinea from their native Germany well before World War II. When the fighting reached New Guinea, they were able to get to Australia—where they remained until the war ended and it was safe to return to their missionary activities in New Guinea. An adult daughter who had completed a teacher training course in Australia joined them and helped her father with teaching and translating.

As we wandered around the station we thought it seemed almost like a big farm. Besides the mission activities of teaching, translating and preaching, the family cared for cows (which provided meat, milk and butter), horses (for traveling to villages and to other mission stations in the area), pigs, goats, chickens and sheep, fruit trees and a large garden.

Much of the food that grew well in the Highlands was familiar to us: bananas, green beans, lima beans, beets, carrots, lettuce, mangos, mulberries, papaya, pineapple, pumpkin, radishes, raspberries, strawberries, tangerines and tomatoes. Gardens belonging to the Papuans also yielded a lot of food that was brought to an outdoor market at the mission station and sold to missionaries and other Europeans in Chimbu, as well as to each other. The Bergmanns bought vegetables to send out to the coast as backloads in the planes that serviced the station. Missionaries were especially appreciative of the fresh vegetables that did not grow and were otherwise unavailable in coastal areas. The boys and I were fascinated as we watched the buying and selling procedures, which included some bargaining and weighing.

Probably what we most appreciated during that week was Chimbu's cooler (and perhaps slightly less humid) climate. Temperatures dipped enough for us to enjoy sleeping under a couple of blankets each night. Days were warm and sunny. The local people wore very little clothing—often only a piece of cloth hung over a belt in front and a branch of leaves tucked under the belt in the back. Those who were well-to-do wore gold lip shells around their necks. The more numerous the shells, the greater their wealth. These shells served as money, enabling the purchase of pigs, and even of wives. (We were told a pig usually cost 3-6 gold lip shells at that time; and a wife, about 30). Some of the Papuans wore unusual (to us) decorations in their hair; some had one or two bones in their nose septums or a few little sticks inserted in the nostrils. We didn't learn whether these were distinctive tribal customs or just fashion.

On Sunday of the week we were there, Rev. Bergmann conducted a baptismal service for about 130 people at a village across the Chimbu River—an hour and a half hike from the mission station. The new believers had received instruction and, in addition to being baptized, were to be incorporated into the Christian community in their village. When asked if we would like to go along, we were delighted. We looked forward to being at the service where these new believers were to publicly acknowledge their faith in Jesus Christ. This, after all, was MAF's (and our own) ultimate purpose for being there.

It was quite a group of us who started out that Sunday morning. Included were Papuan teachers and helpers and others from the station who wanted to go. Setting out from the mission station, we first followed the trail on foot down a steep hill to the Chimbu River, which we crossed a few at a time on horseback. From there we began the climb up the steep mountain trail on the other side. It was not an easy hike; all of us were puffing and thoroughly out of breath by the time we reached the village. (Several of the young women who worked for Mrs. Bergmann made the trip with us and took turns carrying our one-year-old Gordon both ways on their shoulders. He obviously had a good time, and they seemed to enjoy him as well.)

Part way up the hill, where we paused to rest, we saw skeletons of pig jaws strung on branches of a tree. Apparently after eating the meat, the villagers save the jaws, which they hang on branches to dry. We were told that the jaw skeletons we saw represented about a year's accumulation.

Village houses in the Chimbu area were constructed differently from those on the coast. Although still built on stilts, they were not as high off the ground. Each house also had a place for a fire inside, to keep the house warm at night. Since there were few if any windows, smoke was trapped inside along with heat. But the smoke probably helped keep the mosquito population under control.

As was true of any outdoor activity in the Highlands, the church service attracted the curious. In this case the spectators were distinguishable by their customary attire of practically no clothes. The baptismal candidates on the other hand all wore white—women, white dresses; men white lap-laps (material wrapped around like a skirt and knotted around the waist) over white shorts. Their children also wore white. None wore ornaments of any kind: no gold lip shells around their necks, and no sticks or bones in their noses.

Just before the service began, some previously baptized church members led the candidates for baptism down a path from a little knoll where they had assembled, toward the outdoor church location. All sang and danced to drum accompaniment as they came. Benches of split logs were positioned so that the candidate congregation faced a platform with an elevated floor surrounded on three sides by walls made from the local pit-pit wood, and covered by a thatched roof. We visitors were invited to sit with Rev. Bergmann and the other pastors on the platform, out of the sun.

Church members accompanied the candidates down the path as far as a barrier that had been erected at the entrance to the "church." There they stepped aside. One of the baptismal candidates knocked on an imaginary door. "Inside" the barrier, an elder responded to the knock by inquiring who was there and asking what he wanted. Speaking on behalf of the 130 candidates, the spokesman told the elder that they wanted to be baptized into the new life. The elder then asked if they were willing to give up their old (heathen, evil) ways. The spokesman answered yes, and said all had brought their fetishes for burning. At that point the candidates demonstrated their decisions by throwing their charms, fetishes, etc. into a nearby fire. It was then that the elder handed the spokesman a hatchet with which to chop away the barrier. The symbolism representing putting away the old life was quite effective.

Once everyone was seated, the spectators (all who were outside the designated church area) continued to mill around until one of the Chimbu teachers stepped over to tell them to sit down. (Rev. Bergmann's daughter provided us with a running commentary so we could understand what was happening, and what was being said.) Evidently the teacher told them they weren't to just stand there and look around, but were to listen to the Gospel! The spectators seemed to understand, for they obediently sat down and appeared to be listening.

The entire service was conducted in the local language. It began with a number of hymns and the reading of Scripture portions. After Rev. Bergmann preached the sermon, the baptismal ceremony followed. Even though Rev. Bergman was assisted by another missionary, this part of the service took quite a while because of the large number being baptized. The service concluded with a couple more hymns. It had been a very solemn occasion. Still thinking about the significance of that event, we made our way thoughtfully back to Chimbu.

At the end of our week in Chimbu, Bob came for us in the Cessna. Although our family had arrived together, Bob could not take all of us out on the same trip because takeoffs at that altitude (5,000 ft.) required reduced loads. So he flew Charlie out to Madang first, and returned for the rest of us the next day.

As the two pilots flew together to Madang, they stopped briefly at the Bundi airstrip to try a few landings and takeoffs. They were particularly eager to check out this strip because they planned to use it when they delivered Rev. Bergmann there to begin his village visitation trek and work his way back home to Chimbu on foot. It wasn't far by plane from Chimbu but was quite a distance to cover on foot, because the terrain was so mountainous. Going one way by plane would save him four or perhaps five days of walking. Since the airstrip at Bundi was higher and shorter than the one at Chimbu, loading would be more restricted. So it made more sense to take him there to begin his village trek rather than to pick him up from there at the end of his village visitation. Landing the plane at that altitude, and on such a short strip, would be far less critical than taking off.

Charlie felt a little better after our week in Chimbu, probably in part because he had caught up (for the moment at least) with his most urgent correspondence. Unfortunately the benefits of that week didn't last. After two days of flying, Charlie had to give in again and spend much of the rest of the week in bed with headaches and fever. His energy level continued to be low. Then, because his fever persisted, he finally went to the doctor, who first thought it was only the flu that was going around. As a precaution he took a blood smear to check for malarial parasites. When the results of that test came back negative, he began to wonder if Charlie's problem might possibly be related to his ears, due to otosclerosis (a calcification of the three little bones in the inner ear). If this were the case, he advised Charlie to think in terms of having a fenestral operation. That was certainly the last thing we expected to hear, and it wasn't a pleasant prospect—especially if it meant interrupting our work in New Guinea.

Despite feeling a little better the following week, Charlie decided it might be wise to go easy on flying for a while—once Ray's checkout was completed, which took another two days.

It is no doubt obvious by this time that Charlie was, by nature, task-oriented. He particularly liked to check his progress toward a set goal: where was he in terms of where he expected (or hoped) to be at a certain point in time? All Christians are accountable to the Lord, but to him accountability extended to one's organization (MAF) and to one's constituency as well. He found it satisfying (and took a certain amount of pride in it) to reach goals within the time frame he had projected. So it is probably not surprising that he prepared, as a part of a form letter we mailed to interested friends and supporting churches, an abbreviated update of the activities and progress made during the previous six-month period.

March-April: I secured property at Wewak; with missionary volunteer, started the first house. Claire taught at Wau.

May: Became a family again at Madang: I took over half the flying so Charles Rasmussen could move to Wewak to help with the building.

June: First house finished at Wewak and the Rasmussen family was reunited there. Right after that, Ray and Bett Jaensch (Lutheran personnel from Australia for the program here at Madang) arrived.

July: Second Cessna arrived for Madang program—too busy for one plane. Wewak-Hollandia plane delayed. So I used the Cessna to move new missionary candidates and urgent supplies into a newly-opened airstrip at an interior station in DNG [Sengge].

July-August: Flight tests for Ray Jaensch, and familiarization for him with the special problems of missionary flying in New Guinea.

Reviewing first year: Original staff of two pilots doubled and will possibly triple by Christmas....Our one airplane is multiplying in the same proportion....The Madang program is well-established and growing. ...New base at Wewak well along. ... My pilot's log shows: practically 400 hours the first year (even though I did no flying at all for 10 weeks). Comparably, that's as much flying as our "full-time" pilots flying other MAF programs.

New Guinea is no longer a program, or two programs. It's a field! (More like Los Angeles every day.) My task now will call for concentration on the development of the new service (rather than just flying–though there will be the exploratory surveys in DNG).

We've had some health problems which resulted in slowing down to half speed. But even more than health and vigor we need wisdom in planning these air services. As work grows, problems increase but also become more complex and interrelated. Easy to be frustrated, especially when our physical strength hits bottom at the same time.

Despite disappointments here and there, Charlie was gratified and reassured about the progress thus far.

On the lighter side, we discovered our three boys all had worms and needed to take special medicine for a week. Reaction to the medicine varied. We never knew what to expect. Sometimes they threw it right back up; sometimes not. Sometimes they had accompanying stomach cramps, but not always. At least the condition was treatable, and the time finally came when that episode was behind us. What a relief! The older boys had made a game of swallowing all their pills each time in one gulp. John's dose was eight pills per meal; Jim's, six; and Gordon's, two. Gordon tried to imitate his big brothers in the swallowing feat, but it didn't work for him; he couldn't manage to swallow his two, even individually. Instead, he chewed them and ended up with the purplest mouth I ever saw. It was rather amusing, but also extremely messy!

Charlie was scheduled for further tests related to his headaches, but these were cancelled when it was concluded they probably wouldn't tell us anything new. The mission's doctors considered advising a return to the States for ear surgery, but then realized there was an alternative: he could consult a specialist in Australia. Both doctors agreed and firmly recommended he do something about the condition–soon–since they believed it would be unwise to let the matter drag on.

This new development forced a number of decisions. Charlie's first concern of course was the work load that was expected in the next two months (mid-October through mid-December). As he analyzed the situation he began to realize it was probably more important to be on hand for the arrival of the Pacer designated for Wewak (due the middle of December) than it was to help with routine flying during the intervening weeks. Beyond timing, another consideration was whether the family should accompany him to Australia. Or, should go alone? Neither alternative was appealing. If surgery was recommended, he would ask if it could be done in Australia. But what if he had to face a waiting period if a hospital bed was unavailable? We had heard that waits were customary in all but emergencies. Suppose it would involve a two- to three-month wait? We finally concluded we could not anticipate every potential question or decision at this point in time.

Both of us dreaded another separation, particularly of indefinite length and with so many unknowns. Yet I had the impression Charlie was more concerned about the work he was leaving behind than about what he might be facing when he saw the doctor in Australia. This was a situation neither of us chose; we could only pray for the Lord's wisdom as we went along, and wonder how He was going to work it all out. Ultimately, it would be a matter of day-by-day TRUST!

Charlie Mellis at the controls of the first New Guinea Cessna 170.

Mellis home in Los Angeles that housed the MAF office 1946-1948. (Office was moved to house in rear, 1948-1954.)

Charlie and Claire, John, Jim and Gordon, with rented Cessna 170 for cross-country trip just prior to departure for New Guinea.

The MAF dinner was also farewell to the Mellis family in June of 1952. In background at left are Daws and Lila Trotman. It was Daws, founder of the Navigators, who in 1945 first provided desk space at their downtown L.A. office to the fledgling CAMF group (which later became MAF).

Ready to board Pan American's Stratocruiser in Honolulu for the second leg of our flight to New Guinea, June 1952.

Control tower at Madang airport.

Wrecked WWII airplane adjacent
to Madang airport.

Hangars at Madang airport. (Lutheran
Mission's hangar at right.)

Bob Hutchins with first Cessna
170 in Lutheran Mission's hangar.
Inflammables were stored in "wire
cage" behind hangar. Right rear
corner housed the "shop" and the
left rear corner, the cargo shed—
which also doubled as the
"Flight Office" for all the
necessary paperwork.

At Home in Madang...

Above: First new house for aviation families in Madang completed, with the Mellis family as the first occupants.

At right: Laundry facilities. Washing machine in foreground.

The Mellises in the old weapons' carrier; surplus army equipment purchased by the Lutheran Mission for use by its aviation department.

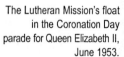

The Lutheran Mission's float in the Coronation Day parade for Queen Elizabeth II, June 1953.

Family holiday in the Highlands, at
Chimbu, 1953.

Candidates for baptism filing into the
specially prepared outdoor sanctuary.

Mining operation near Wau. Note the men carrying
rocks up the near side of the gulch which had been
washed down earlier on the far side.

Claire on the steps of school for missionary children
at Wau.

Aerial view of the Chimbu Gorge, in the Central Highlands.

Tari warriors beside one of their fighting ditches.

Spectacular three-way falls near Tari in Papua (eastern) New Guinea.

Charlie unloading first Cessna 170 at interior airstrip.

Charlie speaking at dedication of second Cessna in Madang, August 1953.

Flights across the border into DNG for Unevangelized Fields Mission. Shown here, Hans Veldhuis with daughter Susie who was bitten by a snake on their two-week trek into Sengge in Dutch New Guinea the previous year. Once the Sengge airstrip was built, the trip there by air took only 35 minutes.

Charlie (right) confers with Vic Ambrose of Australian MAF as they prepare for a Highland flight. Their discussions resulted in strategy for an intermediate program in Wewak (prior to establishing a base in Dutch New Guinea).

Construction of guest house for AMAF's first program in Wewak. Completed workers' house can be seen in background (at right).

Unloading AMAF's Pacer for the Wewak program from freighter at Madang harbor.

Uncrating Wewak Pacer at Madang hangar. Charlie (left) with Charles Rasmussen of AMAF. Lutheran Cessna in foreground.

Bob and Betty Hutchins host pilot families at Christmas dinner in Madang (our second year in New Guinea, 1953). Left to right: Claire and Charlie Mellis, Bett Jaensch, Betty Hutchins, Ray Jaensch, and Betty and Tom Johnson. (Bob Hutchins was behind the camera; the Mellis and Johnson sons ate on the veranda.)

The MAF-operated "fleet" together at an airstrip in the Highlands; two Cessnas and the Wewak Pacer.

Wewak...

The Mellises depart Madang to initiate air service in Wewak with newly assembled Piper Pacer.

The pilot's house, first occupied by the Mellises and Ambroses, with program's jeep at far left.

One Sunday's Lotu group in front of pilot's house in Wewak. Gordon Mellis (at left) is standing by Grongem (the man who requested the worship services). Brother of shark victim is third from right, front row.

With no wharf in Wewak, cargo was first unloaded onto surfboats and then carried ashore.

Charlie loading Pacer at Wewak airstrip for trip into Sepik area to the west.

Charlie and passenger loaded and ready for takeoff from Wewak.

Wewak Pacer airborne.

View of Lake Sentani (Dutch New Guinea) from Ifar, the site of Gen. Douglas MacArthur's headquarters during World War II.

Sentani landmark, Mt. Cyclops. Right foreground: surplus army mess hall purchased by Christian & Missionary Alliance for storage and guest rooms. Our Mellis family moved into the two rooms made available to us by C&MA.

A passenger boards the C&MA Sealand at Sentani, DNG.

Cement slab from WWII army installations, site of MAF's first house.

Jim, John, and Gordon Mellis sit on box containing the entire Kingstrand aluminum house shipped from England and delivered to the slab for construction.

Charlie opens the crate containing the aluminum panels for the Kingstrand house. Roof of the mess hall can be seen behind Charlie.

Gordon, John, and Jim (with hats) and friend (Rose Lenehan) help arrange individual planks for a section of the floor. The rest of the flooring came from a specially constructed truck crate we acquired made of Australian hardwood.

Bill Widbin (left) and Paul Gesswein help raise the walls in a giant Erector™set type of construction (over 5000 nuts and bolts).

Our house is finished, complete with shutter "windows" (extended at right).

Bird's Head survey pilots and Wewak Pacer, with Ambonese host on Noemfor Island. (L. to r., Vic Ambrose, Charlie Mellis, and Charles Rasmussen).

Survey team camps out with pup tents on Noemfor Island during Bird's Head survey.

Traveling by open-air bus for Philippine survey.

Passengers walk around one of 200 landslides caused by typhoon Ruby on road between Manila and Bontoc in the Philippines.

Wewak Pacer (left) with DNG Pacer outside Sealand hangar at Sentani airstrip.

Bob Hutchins steadying the Pacer as it is being towed from the hangar to the launch site at Lake Sentani.

Launching operations at Lake Sentani.

Taxiing for takeoff on Lake Sentani.

Float Service: Lake Archbold...

Trees were felled at one end of Lake Archbold to enable safe approaches by the Pacer on floats for landings and takeoffs.

Large tree stump at Lake Archbold.

Burning of stumps and debris at Lake Archbold.

Approaching Lake Archbold, DNG, for first landing since the original Archbold Expedition landed some 17 years earlier.

Beached Pacer on floats at Manokwari in the Bird's Head, DNG.

Crane lifts float plane for the change to wheels at Manokwari.

"On the step"—taking off from Anggi Gigi Lake.

Charlie checks out Dave Steiger (left) at Lake Anggi Gigi.

Left: Charlie, President of MAF (1970-1973), shakes hands with his newly appointed successor Chuck Bennett, MAF's President, 1973-1985.

Below: At the dedication of the new Redlands, California, facility, following the organizational move from Fullerton, in October of 1981. L to r: Grady Parrott, Betty Greene, Jim Truxton, and Charlie Mellis (MAF's original officers). This occasion marked Charlie's final public appearance before his death just 2 months later. Photo, courtesy MAF.

At left: Claire with their five children after Charlie's Memorial Service in December of 1981. (First row, l. to r., Gordon, Esther, and Gil; back row, John, Claire and Jim.)

15

While Waiting at Wau

I dreaded Charlie's going alone to Australia, but I was torn. I wanted to be with him, but I was concerned about leaving the children. Even apart from expense, we didn't want to impose on another family, especially for an indefinite length of time. With Charlie away, it was not necessary that the boys and I live in Madang. But where should we go? Might Wau once again be a possibility? We knew that various missionary wives had been filling in at the school while waiting for the new matron to arrive from Germany. It was now early October (1953). We subsequently learned she was not expected until November, which meant I could help out by offering to take a turn, even though such a responsibility was somewhat frightening to me. I tried to convince myself it could be a "growing experience," but my self-confidence was shaky at best. In fact, it was a time when my emotions about everything see-sawed. At times I even felt somewhat sorry for myself—which showed in a letter I wrote home the second of October.

> Charlie and I have already had 10 weeks apart this year, plus many, many other days—and nights. Now we're facing two months apart again, in addition to this coming four-day weekend when he goes to Hollandia. When he gets back from there, we'll have just one week together to get everything packed and moved before we'll be separated again.

> Besides planning the packing next week, I have been making curtains for the main house at Wewak. That's the house we expect to occupy, but it will be ready before long and will have to house a good many guests already before we arrive. With Betty Hutchins' help I hope to finish curtains for the four bedrooms and bathroom (curtains for 27 windows!) before we leave for Wau, but I can hold off making curtains for the livingroom and kitchen for now. Since houses here are mostly windows, and since curtains double as shades for privacy, we have to use nontransparent fabrics. So bedroom curtains are a necessity.

I can see from our letters that I spent a lot of time working through the whole idea of Charlie's going to Australia, for I continued by writing,

I realize Charlie has his hands quite full right now with the immediate crises here. A culmination of problems with programs and personnel makes it seem his trip to Melbourne is wonderfully timed. He has faced a number of discouragements lately. Yet the Lord has brought about a mutual confidence between MAF-US and AMAF through Vic and Charlie, and we do feel the support of the L.A. office. These facts thrill our hearts. We're trusting that as Charlie goes South primarily for his hearing problem that the Lord will further knit the two MAFs together and bring about a more complete confidence among the missions that will be served....But I surely hope there's a specialist down there that can handle his case so he can get back here quickly! ... It's wonderful to know you'll be sharing in the prayers about this.

Please pray too that I won't let [the Matron duties at Wau] get me "down." I'm afraid I haven't entirely overcome my fear of such situations. At least I know the children there. And Gordon is a bit older, which will help some. Even though the school children have had four other temporary matrons this year, at least some routine has been established. And I know it is much better for me to keep busy...the boys will have activities with the other children. So if I'm to be "left," Wau is probably the best place.

Meanwhile, Charlie accomplished the supply trips and everything else he set out to do in Hollandia that weekend (though his dizzy spells which had nearly disappeared returned). And I finished the curtains and sorted, aired out and repacked things—some for Wau, but most things went into a barrel to await our move to Wewak.

Charlie left from Wau on Thursday, October 15th (1953) to catch the Sunday flight from Moresby to Melbourne. His appointment with the specialist was set for Monday afternoon. In my letter home, written the day he left us at Wau, my apprehensions surfaced once more.

It's nice to be at Wau again. I start my matron duties tomorrow. I'm looking forward to its being a very good experience, and am trusting the Lord to give me whatever it is I need. In some ways I'm plain scared. And yet, to be defeated before one starts—when I have the Lord to go to for help and strength....well, I must trust and pray more—and worry less.

There are 20 other children (besides ours) in school....Johnny is all keyed up about being in a Christmas program. He will also be able to continue with piano lessons while we're here. I will continue to teach Jimmy, but have Johnny do his Calvert correspondence lessons mainly at the school. He needs contact with other children, and yet I hate to keep shifting to and from the Calvert Course each time we move.

In a sense, I started out with the hardest part of the week—since weekends were the matron's busiest days. John moved into the dorm with the boys, and I kept Jim and Gordon with me in my rooms. Gordon surely basked in the attention he got from the children—loving every minute of it! Two other children arrived after that first weekend. …A few weeks later I could write:

> The Lord has been very gracious to us here. So many times I've been particularly conscious of His presence. I've run into some situations that have been different from those I anticipated. And then again, the problems I anticipated haven't been as big as I expected (so far!). I don't think I'll ever apply for a job of matron—in case I should need to look for a job someday. And yet, I am enjoying the children.…

One Sunday we attended the dedication of the new little church in town. It was built to serve the Papuans who had left their villages to work in Wau (for gold companies, for the government, or as domestic workers). With a number of tribal groups represented, the service had to be in Pidgin English. In addition to the singing, Scripture reading and preaching, special music was provided by a conch shell band. Gifts were presented by various village congregations who had workers in Wau. The amounts given that day, together with larger gifts received earlier, nearly covered the total cost. I was surprised to learn that the building was actually a little more elaborate than originally planned because of building regulations (yes, building regulations exist even in Wau in the 50s!). Its location is ideal (close to the workers' living quarters), and the service drew a sizeable crowd. But it was the spirit of giving that made the greatest impression on me.

At the end of October I learned that the Johnson family had arrived from the States. With their arrival the Lutheran aviation program had now grown to three pilots: Bob Hutchins, Ray Jaensch and the newest pilot, Tom Johnson. (Interestingly, all had wives named Betty!) Bob remained the only licensed mechanic so the others apprenticed under him. It was hard for any of us to believe that this aviation program for the Lutherans had become MAF-US's largest program to date: two airplanes and three pilots under one man's supervision—an increased responsibility for Bob.

I was not unhappy to relinquish my task when the new matron arrived in mid-November. I had rather enjoyed it, although near the end of my responsibilities, I somehow contracted and suffered from the worst cold I'd had in a long time. Meanwhile, Charlie's time in Melbourne took an entirely different turn from what we had expected. His return to New Guinea was still a couple weeks off, but I was most eager for him to return and fill in all the details.

16
Contacts in Melbourne

Charlie's first letter to me was written in Port Moresby. In it he described his contact with the Acting Regional Director of Civil Aviation—the Director was out of town. The purpose of this visit was to inform the Director about his current health problem in case he might need to request special consideration related to his flight status. They also talked over a few program matters. The Acting Director was most helpful, and then volunteered, "We're really pleased with the way your organization maintains standards; we often hold you up as an example to the other smaller operators." He went on to say that when another mission had recently approached them with plans for a separate air operation, DCA had suggested that they drop these plans and ask MAF to do their flying for them. This unsolicited information was very gratifying in that it showed MAF had gained DCA's confidence. Charlie was also glad to know DCA's attitude before he engaged in conversations with AMAF Council members in Melbourne.

While in Moresby he was also able to finalize licensing for the Wewak Pacer. He made an appointment for Tom Johnson (the new Lutheran pilot) to take his medical exam in Moresby upon his arrival in New Guinea—before flying on to Madang.

Because everything in Moresby had gone so smoothly and he finished sooner than expected, he decided to inquire about an earlier flight South. He found a seat available on a flying boat—a plane he had not flown in before. He was impressed with the flight, but what he found particularly intriguing was the seating arrangement. The irregular shape of the hull made it necessary for seats in the passenger compartment to be placed on different levels. Noting there were tables between the seats which faced each other, he (typically) wished he had brought his typewriter.

His first concern upon arriving in Melbourne was his appointment with the specialist. Surprisingly, he wrote:

> The specialist has recommended no operation. He said such operations often cause dizzy spells. Apparently I'm one of the rare birds who gets them [dizzy spells]

94

before the operation. Not only does the specialist not recommend the operation (since I will continue flying) but he said he himself would not perform it. However, this does not mean there will never be an operation. In fact, the audiograph indicates that I should probably not wait too long to have one...once I get home. In light of this, I presume I carry on as before and plan my schedule on the basis of what I've learned from living with this condition....I am relatively certain that I can control them [the dizzy spells] by avoiding fatigue. They seem to be completely predictable, even if only partially controllable. Somehow I can tell in the morning whether it will be a "bad day." I do, however, feel obliged by DCA regulations to reveal my situation to them.

Soon after he saw the specialist, he learned that the Regional Director of Aviation for Papua was currently in Melbourne. (He had been away from Moresby when Charlie visited the DCA office there.) Charlie now considered him a good friend of MAF in that there was every indication he had gained confidence in the MAFers he had come to know. Might he have a suggestion for complying with DCA regulations, given the health situation involved? Charlie believed he would do what he could to help. At the same time Charlie was confident that the Lord's direction would soon become clear. As he thought about the ramifications of the medical report, he put some of those thoughts on paper in a letter home:

My one big concern is that in taking it easy to keep this thing in check, I may prove to be a bottleneck in the survey work ahead. But perhaps when that happens, the work will just have to be planned around a recognition of this fact while I am still needed here. Perhaps my flying days on the field are limited. I probably should be spending more time on the ground anyway since it's enough of a job to handle the planning and administrative matters. But there's always something coming up which leads me to fill in for the other fellows, and I hate to act like the big shot who's too busy to fill in for them.

Spending time in Melbourne seemed a time-consuming and expensive way to find out nothing could be done for his condition. But, apart from this seemingly urgent medical problem, he'd have never made this trip. Did the Lord maybe have a purpose for his being in Melbourne apart from the medical reason? As days went by, he began to realize that certain pieces of the puzzle were beginning to fit together. He wrote:

... the Lord's hand has so obviously been in everything. We needed time for profitable discussions with AMAF here. As we've met together so far we've all remarked that the timing just couldn't have been more perfect. I am utterly amazed at the quantity of material we have covered in the past 75 hours, much of it just in incidental discussion. But there's much ground yet to cover. The problems are really complex and interrelated.

During his appointment with the DCA's head doctor, he was told there was no need at the moment to change his pilot status—that it would be necessary only if the condition worsened. The doctor did take a couple of hearing tests for DCA's records; but beyond that, raised no question about Charlie's retaining his commercial license.

It was almost unbelievable how precise the timing appeared to be for conferences with AMAFers. As he reviewed the events, Charlie wrote,

> A year ago when the snarl between us developed, the Lord called out Vic at exactly the right time, and sent him on up to Papua for conference. Together we laid a groundwork for cooperation that resolved the problems and got AMAF well on the road to autonomy. We [MAF-US] in turn gained confidence because there was now both technical leadership and full-time leadership that had been lacking before. Since then we've been progressing beautifully in accord with the plans laid in January—with no new snarls developing. However, now that we've got our teeth into it, the picture is growing and becoming more complex. Our January plans were valid as far as they went, but we have now outgrown them. By correspondence we were merely adding patches to the quilt. We needed to restudy and redesign them....

True, Vic's visit the previous January (1953) had resolved many problems but did not immediately or entirely erase all Melbourne's concerns about MAF-US's role. And although the intervening eight months had seen some rather phenomenal strides in the building of a mutual trust relationship, this opportunity for additional personal contact was advantageous. The AMAF Council seized the moment to quiz Charlie in detail about his experience in New Guinea and about MAF-US's experiences generally. Evidently the Lord had prepared the way for their interaction. For as Charlie pondered his visit, he realized he hadn't expected the trip to be overly significant in this respect. He commented to our parents,

> I didn't feel under any pressure to "get something across." On the other hand, they've just peppered me with questions. Apart from either their questions or my intentions, I'm amazed at the way things kept coming up in the normal, natural conversations which tended to "impart" without any premeditation. If I've thought of this process of imparting at all, I tended to think of it as occurring when we would pass through here on our way home—at the end of our work here. But when you think of the advantage of sharing much of it this early in the game...it's not hard to see the Lord's hand in it.

Other openings to share came as well. The home Council of one of the missions working in Dutch New Guinea, concerned because they felt they had no clear picture of what was happening up there, invited Charlie to meet with them. They hoped for input regarding aerial advance from MAF's viewpoint to aid their own planned entry into DNG. Charlie commented on this by saying,

We really appreciate this because we have, on occasion, had to bail missions out when they hit snags by planning their work without technical consultations. On the other hand, I realized we must be careful not to go beyond the air transport and technical matters to matters involving mission affairs and field leadership.

From his perspective, his time in Melbourne flew. One evening the discussion about operational costs for the plane and program took more than three hours. They were diverted time and again by matters that needed to be addressed before specific figures could evolve. It was a long evening—but it would have taken much longer by correspondence.

In addition to being invited to speak a number of times at churches (and he was so rusty that preparation seemed to take an inordinate amount of time; besides, he was always more comfortable writing than speaking), Vic suggested a trip to Adelaide. He was eager for Charlie to meet Max Flavel and his family. Max was AMAF's next available pilot-mechanic assigned to New Guinea. The Flavel family was impressive. "They really sacrificed for the past five years in preparing for this work," Charlie wrote me. They were scheduled to arrive in Madang soon after the turn of the year. Initially, Max would help Bob with the mechanical work and do some of the flying, but he'd also be in position for an available subsequent assignment.

Discussions about equipment for the guest house in Wewak led to a firm decision that the Ambrose family would move to New Guinea in a few months to take over management of the newly inaugurated Wewak program. Once Vic and family arrived in Wewak, he and Charlie would conduct a few joint surveys together before our family moved across the border to finally launch the Dutch New Guinea program, to be based in Sentani.

Charlie's dizziness continued to lurk in the background while he was in Australia. It was a nuisance particularly when he was under pressure, or tense before a meeting. But he remained convinced that he could plan around those dizzy spells and continue working.

The return trip to New Guinea held further surprises: Dr. Talbot of BIOLA was aboard the same plane as far as Moresby; a DCA radio man, waiting at the

Moresby airport to meet another passenger, was the very person he had brought a radio manual for; and another radio official sat across from Charlie on the flight between Moresby and Lae. In Lae, the planned session at the Lutheran headquarters proved highly profitable; and on the flight between Lae and Wau he discovered that a fellow passenger was the head inspector of TNG (Papua) radio. In fact, this latter individual was the man Charlie planned to see in Moresby on the return trip, but an epidemic there prevented that contact. How could all of these events and timely contacts be purely coincidental?

At the Wau airport, John, Jim, Gordon, and I were eagerly awaiting his arrival. By this time we were nearing the end of November. A couple days later, Bob arrived in the Cessna to pick us up and take us to Madang. He told us we would be able to stay in a recently vacated house at Nagada—located at the mission's plantation a short distance outside of Madang—until our soon anticipated move to Wewak. Charlie, of course, went immediately back on the flight line to help check out Tom Johnson. And our family made preparations to spend our second Christmas in New Guinea.

17

A Second Christmas
. . . and More

The narrow road into the plantation grounds at Nagada wound around and in between tall coconut palm trees and led to the vacated house we were to occupy near the mission's print shop. From there it continued about a half a mile to another house where the plantation manager lived with his family. What a beautiful setting! We loved the view of the picturesque bay from our front porch. In fact, we were delighted with our temporary home. It was especially good to be independent as a family after our time apart, while Charlie was in Australia.

Its half-hour distance from Madang, however, posed a bit of a problem for Charlie's getting to and from Madang (or the airport). Sharing a vehicle, as the aviation families did, worked fine when all of us were clustered in Madang. But special arrangements had to be made—and extra time allowed—whenever Charlie needed to be picked up, or if an occasion arose when our family needed to go somewhere. Fortunately, these special scheduling arrangements were expected to be temporary—we were to be moving to Wewak soon.

Charlie's time in Melbourne coincided (intentionally) with the annual inspection of the first Cessna, which meant that flying slacked off while it was out of service. But now that both Cessnas were on the flight line once again, and the Pacer's arrival in Madang for assembly was imminent, everyone anticipated the resumption of a considerably tighter schedule.

For me, homemaking at Nagada was a challenge. That was evident from the moment I walked into the kitchen and noticed the wood-burning stove. The newer houses were equipped with three-burner kerosene stoves that had detachable ovens. These were not only easier to manage but they produced far less heat in that hot and humid tropical climate; meal preparation took less time, as did heating water for dishes, laundry, and bathing.

At first we wondered if it would be worthwhile to think in terms of hiring household help for what we perceived to be a relatively short stay. But when the Pacer's arrival by ship was delayed until after Christmas, we sent word to Marin, the young man who had worked so well for us previously, asking that he come back to help us. How thankful we were the day he appeared in answer to our request!

Yes, December (1953) had arrived. Once again we found it difficult to "think Christmas" without the familiar cultural indicators—that is, until we began to hear faint singing in the evenings. The music was coming from the small church on the plantation grounds where local Papuans were practicing for their annual Christmas program. We were delighted when we were invited to attend this special event.

The church was festively decorated with greenery, and candles provided the only lighting. I particularly remember holding my breath at one point while watching several men light candles on the boughs of the Christmas tree. Sure enough, a little flame did ignite a few nearby needles. But there was no panic. Someone just calmly stepped up and put it out; they had no doubt had this happen before. I was nervous, but realized that the greenery was fresh and moist and that, together with the high humidity, helped keep the situation under control. Once I was able to concentrate on the program, I found it especially meaningful. The message of Christmas expressed by those Papuan Christians that night in Pidgin English had a freshness I will never forget.

On Christmas day, the aviation families gathered at the Hutchins' house for dinner. We suddenly realized that our numbers had more than doubled over the past year. Instead of only two aviation families a year earlier, we in Madang were now joined by two additional families (Jaensches and Johnsons), and the third new aviation family (the Rasmussens) had already moved on to Wewak. We all wondered what the aviation family count would be in another year.

During the week between Christmas and New Year's Day, Charlie and Ray made a trip to Tari, which took a couple of days. Since that trip was especially interesting from several standpoints, Charlie wrote quite a detailed account of it to our parents:

> Yesterday [Dec. 29, 1953], Ray and I headed for Tari ... which has also been our greatest headache because of weather; we've had twice as many turnbacks from there as we've had on any other trip. So Ray and I planned to stay overnight. It was just as well we had our pajamas along, because we'd never have gotten back out yesterday. In fact, we barely got in.

The amazing thing is how fast the weather got that way [deteriorated]. As we approached Ogelbeng, a little over an hour inland, Mt. Giluwe was scot clear, and everything beyond it looked fairly clear too. We landed at Ogelbeng to refuel. There we ran into a bit of grief because one drum went empty and it took a bit of time to get the tap in the second one. We were on the ground nearly an hour.

By the time we got off, Giluwe was one huge billow of clouds which spilled all over the north side of it where we had to fly. We managed to pick our way over the ridge just beyond Ogelbeng, and then found it broken enough that we could keep going to the ridges nearer Tari.

About the time we landed at Ogelbeng (when everything looked so clear still), they made a weather observation at Tari which we picked up by radio after leaving Ogelbeng; they only had scattered clouds there, 5,000 feet off the ground. It sounded beautiful!

But when we crossed (with much difficulty!) the Rentoul Gap into the Tari Valley—one hour after leaving Ogelbeng, and only two hours after the report—we found it covered by what looked like a solid cloud cover. We climbed on up to 12,000 ft. to have a look. We saw one pretty big hole. I wasn't satisfied about coming down through it, though, for there is high ground between there and where the Tari strip is—even though it is in the same general valley. But we did fly over to it, using it as a stepping stone. It was then that we saw another (bigger) hole in a better location. We started down through it, but it wasn't the right place—it took us over the Tari River. We had only started down through it (it was a big hole, with plenty of room to climb back up again) when we saw the strip off to the right—a most welcome sight!

We stayed overnight in order to make a survey today—just a short one—over the ridge that borders on the south side of the valley. Mr. Len Twyman of the UFM [Unevangelized Fields Mission] had asked us to do this. (He was one of the pioneers of UFM's work on the Fly River in southwestern Papua, and is now pioneering all over again in Tari. He had gone in just a year ago along with two young fellows, and about seven months later his wife and their three boys went in to join him.)

We made the survey, but we didn't get where we wanted to go. The ridge we wanted to cross had clouds right down on it. We'll have to go back in February to try again, with the Pacer. However, while we were in the air, we went on up to another part of the Tari Valley to have a look at an area that the ADO (Assistant District Officer who had gone along on the survey) wanted to see. As we were flying from the cloud-covered ridge to this upper part of the Tari Valley, we flew right over a huge waterfall—the most impressive one I've seen in New Guinea. It wasn't so terribly high, but it really had some water tumbling over it. It billowed and foamed at the bottom like a small-scale Niagara. Then, to top all that, only about half the water plunged over the fall. A fourth of it rushed through a tunnel on one side. The other fourth just oozed through the limestone on the other side and shot out like a couple dozen fire hoses...It was really something!...

Staying overnight at Tari was really interesting too. We learned a little more about the people there. I guess things aren't quite as "quiet" there yet as I thought. Normally they are, but they've had a number of fights break out. The people near the airstrip know better than to bother the white man (they all know what a gun can do), but they still have their fights among themselves occasionally.

One day a big brawl broke out right on the UFM mission station grounds. There were about 800 people around and arrows were flying everywhere, I gather—as well as clubs and spears. The missionaries grabbed three of the people as hostages and locked them in the dispensary. Then they sent a tribesman for the government officers a mile away. The patrol officers view such things pretty calmly—hardly ever fire a shot unless fired upon. They just strode up to the mission and spotted the fight leader of one group. (The fight leader of each of the three groups involved was equivalent to a chief, but not exactly the same, since his jurisdiction is mainly over the art of fighting—[which amounts to] half their life.) They told him that this was enough of this foolishness; he was to call off his group. He obeyed almost immediately, and upon his signal about a third of the people just dropped back to the edge of the fight area and became spectators.

After a bit they spotted the other two fight leaders and called them over. With a bit of convincing, they finally obeyed and the fight was over, practically instantaneously. The two fight leaders most responsible were hauled off to the caliboose where they'll probably be kept for two or three months while they are assigned work on the airstrip.

That may seem a bit lenient punishment. But you have to consider that fighting is to them what football is to us—only it affects the whole community; and it is their consuming passion. You can't expect them to gain a moral consciousness about these things overnight. I don't mean that it's just a game and that no one gets hurt. Most of these Taris have a piece of arrow stuck in them somewhere. In fact, some will work with a shovel but won't act as carriers because they get a jab from a piece of arrow inside now and then.

In the fight mentioned above, I believe one woman got shot in the leg. And of course, sometimes someone gets killed. They really don't like that though. The group that loses a man is supposed to be reimbursed with pigs or something. If not, they're apt to get pretty treacherous and unsportsmanlike about getting revenge.

A lot of these facts of why they fight are true of other tribes in New Guinea too. But the really distinctive thing about the Taris is their "fighting ditches." They remind me of the subterranean tunnels we kids used to make all over our back yards. These ditches are something like that, only the stakes in their "game" are higher. And the ditches are deeper. They also vary. Some may be only four feet deep, but one right by the airstrip is about 12-14 feet deep. This extra good specimen has straight cut walls gradually slanting to make a "v" effect, and is wide enough at the top that they can't jump across. (The Taris are actually very small people, smaller than the Chimbus and Hagens in the Wahgi Valley, but not quite as small as the Pigmy of the Bismark Range area. And none of these pigmies are as small as the African Pigmy.) The bottom of the ditch is only the width of a man's foot.

I didn't completely understand how they use these ditches. Apparently sometimes they'll fight right in the ditches, but more often they attack on top, then drop down into the ditches to run through them, threading through their maze-like channels until they can encircle the enemy and come up to attack him on an unexpected flank. I assume this happens when they are on their home ground, and are attacked by strangers. Another technique they use is to drive sharp sticks in the bottom of the ditch just below where they have a bridge (just a split log). During the fight, one of the women will pull the bridge away. As the strangers start losing out, they back up toward the bridge, firing arrows as they retreat. They feel for the bridge with their feet without looking back, and end up impaling themselves on the spikes. Gruesome! … So far the mission is very restricted in its movements. At first they could only go a mile from the government strip. (They built their station at that limit.) Now they may go a mile from their station in any direction. They would like to establish another station five miles away, but the Administration will probably be pretty slow about opening new territories for a while after what happened at Telefomin, even though the latter was not just routine native fighting. (It was a deliberately planned bit of treachery—apparently to keep the government from interfering with their planned initiation rites.)

Of course, the Taris are not all so respectful of the white man yet either. The patrols have not yet covered the entire valley, so some have never seen a white man. When we were out on the survey—not far from the waterfall, and only about eight minutes flying time from the airstrip—the ADO [Administrative District Officer] said, "That spot right underneath us is where I got an arrow through my hat.".…

The people's houses are the poorest I've seen in New Guinea. They build them out of grass, very low, under the trees, and just over the brow of a hill where they have all the natural camouflage possible. The patrol officers say that they can walk for days without seeing a house. Yet it is one of the most thickly populated areas in New Guinea.…

The day following the Tari trip was a real RED LETTER day—the day we had eagerly awaited. It was the day the Malekula (freighter) finally arrived in Madang from Australia with the new Wewak Pacer aboard. Excitement filled the air as all the aviation families gathered at the wharf. We loved watching the docking activity as that big ship was being directed into place. Then we heard the rumors: they weren't going to unload anything until the next day, probably because it was New Year's Eve. However, later we were promised that the ship's cargo would be unloaded in the morning—holiday or not. Before leaving the wharf all of us took turns peering anxiously down into the hold, each hoping to get a glimpse of the plane's crate. We thought we located the edges of the crate, but it was hard to be certain because those edges were only barely visible—the entire crate was almost completely hidden by all the burlap sacks of rice that had been piled on top of it.

Early the next morning all the pilots were on hand to watch the unloading process. When the crate finally became accessible, a large crane lifted it out from the hold and set it down (quite gently, actually) on a waiting truck's flatbed for transport to the airport. Everyone breathed a sigh of relief, for the crate had looked so vulnerable; first, as it sat exposed in the middle of the open hatch, and again when it was hoisted in the air. Rather ironically, it was then that we noticed large signs all over it (in English, however) that practically shouted out the message: "Load nothing on top!"

18
Coping Difficulties

The fellows had estimated they'd have the Pacer ready to fly within two weeks of its arrival. But they bettered that estimate, getting it airborne in just nine days. It took a few more days to replace the U.S. registration numbers with the assigned Australian letter registration and to make the necessary test flights. All of this meant our family's departure date for Wewak was imminent—planned for Thursday, January 21, 1954.

The Hutchins and Jaensches came to see us off at Madang's airport, where Charlie had loaded our belongings into the Pacer and tied everything down. The boys were eager for the chance to fly with their dad. No one had to tell them to fasten their seat belts. Once airborne, our two-hour flight took us north and west along the jungle coastline. A number of scattered villages lay below us; and off to our right, a short distance from shore, was a very small docile-looking island. Charlie told us it was, in fact, an active volcano.

Nearing Wewak we spotted what looked like a couple of half-submerged ship skeletons in the harbor. Not far away a few rusty landing barges lay abandoned on the sandy beach. All had obviously been left behind after the war's activity ceased. As we descended to land, we flew over a number of bomb craters all but concealed by jungle growth over the nine intervening years. I found myself thinking about the cost in lives represented by all these remnants of war and was glad we were on a different kind of mission—one of helping to bring the Good News of God's love to the many people in this war-scarred and remote part of the world.

Wewak's European inhabitants, for the most part, lived atop a hill on an island adjacent to the coast—which was also the location of AMAF's property. A narrow causeway (often flooded during heavy rains) connected the island with the mainland where the airstrip was located. Only a few roads existed in or around Wewak in 1954, and none of them extended more than a few miles in any direction. However, such a limited network of roads was quite adequate for the needs of the local population at that time.

Living "up top" (on the hill) had certain advantages in that its relatively slight elevation, together with the way the houses were positioned, allowed the residents optimum access to any prevailing breezes. In the hot humid coastal climate, any moving air was most welcome.

Rasmussens were already occupying the recently completed guest house on AMAF's property, and we were to move into the main house situated between their house and a government hospital. The main house lacked a number of finishing touches, such as completion of electrical wiring. As a result, we were not yet hooked up to the city's power source. Having to use kerosene lamps and pressure lanterns presented no particular problem—we were accustomed to that. Rather, it was the lack of ceilings (dependent on the completion of the wiring) that concerned me the most; for without ceilings, I knew it would be impossible to prevent intrusion into the house by those pests I had encountered earlier: those awful and inevitable rats!

We did have running water in the kitchen, piped in from a large tank on a platform outside, as in Madang. Runoff rainwater from the roof, directed to the tank by means of guttering, flowed by gravity through pipes near the bottom of the tank to the kitchen faucets. Water for the bathroom (at the far end of the house) was supposed to come from the city's system—which at the moment was shut down for repairs. Despite the lack of city water, we managed quite well, especially since the bathroom was constructed to utilize a "bush" shower, (This consisted of a bucket with a spray attachment screwed into the bottom of it to regulate the flow of water. So one just filled the bucket with water of the desired temperature and raised or lowered it into position by means of a rope and pulley. As for flush toilets, there were few if any of those in town anyway. Townspeople were accustomed to the "waste buckets" that were replaced daily with disinfected empty ones by Papuan city employees. The exchange was made through small doors on the outsides of the houses. It was a step toward indoor plumbing but with more outhouse-type equipment.

We also had the use of two new appliances that I considered luxury items: a kerosene refrigerator and a kerosene stove. Both were purchased by AMAF as equipment for the house. Once the wiring of the house was complete and we were connected to the city power supply, electricity for me would become the third luxury item (available between 7 am and 11 pm). Meanwhile, we managed with pressure lanterns, kerosene lamps and flashlights.

Because MAF families were the first Protestant mission families in town, the main house was built with four bedrooms so as to accommodate overnight guests as well as the resident MAF family. Two of the four bedrooms were already in use as guest rooms when we arrived.

Furniture was sparse, consisting of beds, one table and a few chairs. We knew early settlers and pioneers (including missionaries) fashioned furniture and shelves out of assorted packing boxes and crates so we had planned our own packing with that objective in mind. In fact, it became a kind of family joke that this experience would qualify us as "pioneer" missionaries.

Moving is sometimes seen as an adventure. But for me, there was one aspect of moving I had come to dread. A pattern had seemed to emerge in our family moves that led me to expect that within a day or two of our arrival at each new location, Charlie would leave on an extended trip. His routine flights presented no problem; it was only when he scheduled a trip that was to last from several days to a few weeks—right on top of a fresh move—that I found it especially hard to cope. Somehow, no matter how well I understood the reasons (and the reasons were usually very legitimate), I always tended to feel sort of dumped and abandoned—despite the fact that Charlie inevitably tried hard for the first few hours (or maybe a day) to help us get settled. After that, he expected the family to take everything in stride and get on with working things out. We managed most of the time—one can do more than he or she thinks is possible (even when there is lack of motivation) if the necessity arises. But this seemingly consistent pattern didn't make moving something I eagerly anticipated—except that it meant we were one step closer to getting the overall job done.

I do not mean to give the impression that Charlie never took time for family fun. He did. But accommodating to MAF business usually had top priority. We spent occasional afternoons in Madang playing badminton, and went swimming a number of times at the beach in Wewak (with Ambroses and Rasmussens). In Sentani, we made very few trips to the beach near Hollandia (due to distance), but we did go a number of times to a small, cold water "swimmin' hole" not too far from Sentani that servicemen during WWII had constructed by damming up a stream descending from Mt. Cyclops (behind Sentani). Charlie's presence and whole-hearted participation with the family during these times made them very special.

With the plane's arrival in Wewak, flying began immediately—to take accumulated supplies into mission locations in the Sepik area. During this time I kept busy unpacking and getting the family settled. The flight schedule was unusually demanding: the two guests who were in the house when we arrived were taken to their station at Lumi to make room for two other, rather special, guests—mission leaders Charlie was scheduled to take from Wewak to Hollandia to attend their mission's field conference. Charlie (accompanied by Charles R.) expected to be away from Wewak a week or longer, depending on whether they received government permission to do some mission-requested surveys while there.

Always, when Charlie expected to be away for a period of time, he presented me with a list of things to do for him while he was gone. This time he needed a 25-page maintenance manual typed (with four carbon copies), along with an aviation report to type—all for the Lutherans' upcoming annual conference at Wau. Needless to say, I felt overwhelmed. We had scarcely unpacked, and I didn't yet feel settled in these new surroundings. My coping level seemed woefully inadequate. I felt frustrated and disorganized. With so little in the way of furnishings, there were very few places to put anything I unpacked. We had house guests and I wanted to be a gracious hostess. I was also under pressure to get the boys back into their schoolwork routine. I saw myself trying to respond to too many different demands all at once. However, as I look at that situation these many years later, I believe that underneath these frustrations lay feelings of inadequacy and feelings of aloneness in trying to assume the accumulated responsibilities. Everything came to a head when I looked at Charlie's imminent departure and indefinite return schedule.

There was a sense in which all separations were difficult for me. I don't believe I ever really got used to them—even with lots of practice! More often than not it was the final day (or hours!) before Charlie left on a trip of a week or more that seemed the hardest. Emotionally, I didn't want the separation. Yet in those final hours before the unwanted separation—with the accompanying buildup of negative and guilt feelings—I felt I was expected to "cheerfully" receive the inevitable barrage of instructions on what to do after he had gone. Each time, his lists seemed interminable, which only served to increase the strain on already frayed nerves. Here I was helping him leave while fighting my reluctance to see him go. Intellectually, I could nearly always support his going. In fact, I rarely questioned the wisdom, the reasons, or the objectives of his trips. But my feelings inevitably ran counter to all such reason.

I realized later that, for any husband leaving on a business trip, he must of necessity focus on what lies ahead. He should be concerned about business matters, schedule demands, and about how to coordinate the various components. Admittedly, at the time, I tended to interpret his attention to these things as a lack of concern—perhaps an indifference, or not caring—about what I was feeling. The result? Frustration (and occasionally tears) on my part, and impatience on his—all of which produced a scrambled combination of unintentional miscommunication and imagined, if not real, misunderstandings. When that happened, our "goodbyes" were highly unsatisfactory. Often, Charlie's attempts to "understand" did not help. I remember being almost angry a couple of times with his seemingly flip comment, "I'll pray for you," as he said his goodbyes. In my frustration at that particular moment, such a phrase seemed totally inadequate for all I was feeling. Yet, in my more rational moments, I knew he meant well and that I could count on his earnest prayers for me in the midst of whatever I was facing.

Some years ago I heard a prominent Christian speaker—a man—share his experience of similar frustrations each time he prepared to leave his family to make needed business trips. He, too, found the tension-filled hours prior to his departures particularly difficult. I found myself saying inside, "He's describing from a man's perspective exactly what I have experienced!" He suggested these kinds of feelings are common to both husbands and wives—that it's normal to feel reluctant about separations. He further suggested that while we need to deal with our emotions and not give in to them, we should recognize that they probably indicate a deep caring for one another. I think I needed to hear this. It surely helped me put my own experience into a better perspective.

Back to Charlie's departure from Wewak. Once he was gone, I set to work. Most of my fears turned out to be manageable—except where the rats were concerned. Without ceilings in place it was useless to try to keep them out of the house. In fact, those critters seemed to be having a field day. They teased me every day by scampering along the rafters and playing tag anywhere they pleased. At night I was never sure what they'd find to get into while the boys and I were asleep. I did try to fight them—I had to do something!—by faithfully putting out poison each night. But in the mornings, although every morsel of the bait had disappeared, there was no sign of a diminished rat population. There must have been an army of them!

We had only token protection at night—mosquito nets. But I remember two incidents that were especially traumatic. One happened one night when I heard Gordon cry. I grabbed my flashlight and dashed into the boys' room. I found a tiny spot of blood and a couple of teeth marks on one of Gordon's ears, but saw no sign of the culprit. The next morning I took two-year-old Gordon to the hospital next door, where he was pronounced OK. But that incident made me more determined than ever to somehow triumph over those pesky rats.

The second incident happened another night while Charlie was away. Awakened by a strange noise, I reached for the flashlight I always kept next to my pillow, and sent a beam of light around the room. Everything seemed in order until, as the beam came close to the wall by the head of the bed, I suddenly realized that just on the other side of the mosquito net from where my head had rested on the pillow just moments before, a large rat had paused to return my stare. In another instant, of course, it scampered off and was gone. I sank back down onto the bed and lay there feeling terribly helpless. It would have been useless to go looking for it. I knew that. But my heart continued to pound furiously and my imagination ran wild. It took quite a while before I could settle down enough to get back to sleep. I told myself to be grateful for the mosquito net. But I could hardly wait for the fellows to return—and hoped they'd find time soon to finish the electrical wiring so that the protective ceilings could be installed.

19
Contact with Government Officials

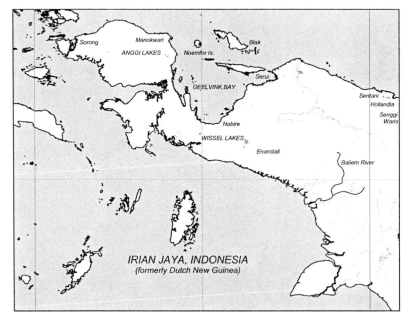

Sorong
Manokwari
ANGGI LAKES
Noemfor Is.
Biak
Serui
GEELVINK BAY
Sentani
Hollandia
Senggi
Nabire
Waris
WISSEL LAKES
Enarotali
Baliem River

IRIAN JAYA, INDONESIA
(formerly Dutch New Guinea)

The first trip to Dutch New Guinea in the Wewak Pacer went well. After arriving at Sentani, the pilots' most urgent task was to take supplies to the missionary family at Sengge whose food supply was nearly exhausted. The Veldhuis family at Sengge was the same family Charlie had talked with by radio a year earlier—the morning after their little girl was bitten by a snake during their two-week, 65-mile, trek from Hollandia. During that intervening year an airstrip was laid out and prepared for use. Charlie landed on it for the first time when he took supplies to them in the Lutheran's Cessna during his previous trip to DNG. At that time he calculated that in 2½ minutes the plane could cover the distance of *an entire day's* walk. This meant that their earlier two-week trek on foot was now reduced to a mere 35 minutes by air.

Charlie decided to fly the first load into Sengge himself, to check on the current condition of the airstrip before turning over the remainder of the supply trips to Charles R. He was then free to turn his attention to making additional contacts with government officials. Most of these contacts had to be made in Hollandia, which was about an hour's drive from Sentani.

Since my last visit they have completely paved (black-topped) the road. But what a difference it makes! It's quite a mountain road in spots, with beautiful scenery. First it winds through the foothills of Cyclops Mountain along the edge of huge Lake Sentani. Then, after you pass Hollandia Stad, the small city about half way to Hollandia, you climb over a small pass and break out onto the scenery of the Bay. Here you wind along for another five or six miles through the hills until you descend a steep slope to the Haven [harbor] itself. Quite a setting!

There is also a bus service now. In fact, I went in one day by bus. They have good equipment, and the drivers are excellent. But the schedules from the Haven out as far as Sentani aren't too frequent. I lost about two hours just waiting on buses. But I did get a driver's license and we made another trip in the UFM jeep. (One of their workers had to go in to get her papers validated.)

Charlie particularly wanted to see DNG's Director of Civil Aviation to seek permission to follow certain technical procedures he had in mind once survey authorization was given for the Bird's Head area (the northwestern portion of New Guinea). He wrote,

I planned (if I got his approval right away) to wire the Mission in the Bird's Head that we'd be over in about a week to do the [requested] flying there. Things seemed to be going well in the interview, but then he [the director] excused himself to talk to his boss, the Director of Technical Services. I was then told that, although everything was all right from a technical viewpoint, it would have to be cleared with the government's political branches. (It seems that for those deeper penetrations these men have to be concerned primarily with the rescue part of "search & rescue" operations. They have the facilities to look for a plane that is down in the bush, but it's a lot harder to get people out.)

He suggested I get an appointment with the Governor's secretary and lay the whole thing before him. The Director of Civil Aviation offered to make the appointment for me and to come along to the interview to advise on technical questions. I knew this was obviously going to take a lot more time than we anticipated, but there was also plenty to rejoice about. (The Director of Technical Services was voluntarily stepping out of the situation, and the Director of Civil Aviation had all along been a real friend. I was glad he was going along.) He got the appointment for Monday morning. But I was to write a letter addressed to the Governor and have it with me as we went to the interview. This letter was to outline exactly what we proposed to do, in 1-2-3 order.

During the interview I was very conscious of the Lord's presence. The Secretary was very friendly, and the Director of Civil Aviation did a lot to help matters along.

The subject of single-engine planes came up indirectly. I told the Secretary how MAF had been operating for eight years, that we were now operating eight planes with only one light-plane engine failure—and that one was due to accidental damage rather than to mechanical failure. He seemed impressed.

From there I swung into a positive approach: I told him we considered the possibility of engine failure negligible (even though we make full preparation for such a possibility with shoulder harnesses, emergency survival equipment, etc.), but said we considered the real danger in this operation to be getting trapped by weather. I then emphasized why I wanted the surveys to be made in the order listed in the letter, because that way we would gain route familiarization as we proceeded, moving progressively deeper in stages. I told him that we intended to make additional route familiarization trips if necessary. That is, we would not just barge into an area in order to have a look at it. I let him know we planned to know at least two, and preferably three, ways out of each area before making our final thrusts.

I had reason to believe, once again, that he was favorably impressed, though he tried to cover it by reminding me about the international complications, their limited facilities, their responsibilities as a government, etc. I assured him profusely that we understood and appreciated that. I told him we would appreciate rescue facilities if [they were] needed, but were also prepared to look after ourselves. At the same time we recognized that even though we were prepared to go it alone, such operations could automatically involve others, especially responsible governments.

Before I walked out the door, I was fairly sure we'd get all we wanted. I was more sure after the temporary field leader of UFM [Unevangelized Fields Mission] (Hans Veldhuis, a Dutch Canadian equally at home in both [Dutch and English] languages) reported the exchange between the Secretary and the Director of Civil Aviation in Dutch. For one thing, they had said that our first survey area request could be granted without study by the Governor (it now has been—we'll probably make the trip on Tuesday, weather permitting) since it was a comparatively short thrust.

They also had commented to each other that the fourth area we asked for was one they themselves wanted to know more about. In English, he asked me if they could send an observer along. I told them that load-wise we were limited to two pilots and only one missionary, but I said we'd be glad to repeat any survey. All this makes me fairly sure that they'll come through. But it will probably take time. If the Dutch are noted for anything besides good pastry and cleanliness, it's super-caution. I'm trying my dead-level best to play the game their way, and to be the exact opposite of the "typical" impetuous American tourist (as well as some of the American missionaries with whom these same men have had to deal). But even with all these hopeful signs, we're making it a definite matter of prayer.

It was becoming obvious to Charlie that his contact work had only just begun—there was much more work ahead. At the time he wondered if it would be necessary to work out a contract with the Dutch government similar to the ones MAF had made with the governments in South America. Then, in reference to another concern, he added,

Along with my other contacts I've been trying to line up housing for our family so we can move up here as early as May if things work out to do so. So far, nothing is definite, but I have some prospects. I've also been working on getting Claire's visa extended, but I doubt that I can complete that until my next trip.

It was the weather that forced Charlie to abandon his plans for the hoped-for survey during this trip. So, with the mission's conference over, the two pilots and their two passengers returned to Wewak. Charlie had planned to spend a few days in Wewak with the family before leaving again to take the UFM men on to Tari where he had agreed to do a few surveys for them. But as so often happens, those plans had to be altered—as we shall see.

20
Some Incredible Timing

Back in Wewak, Charlie consulted his calendar. If he was to be back from Tari in time for the Ambrose family's arrival, he should move the Tari survey schedule up a few days—which allowed for only a day or two in Wewak.

I must admit I prayed for rain—heavy enough to cancel the flight. I knew Charlie was very weary. Still, I understood his decision was based on the good of the work, so he would be deterred only if the Lord intervened. The weather, however, was good, and became even better—almost perfect, according to Charlie—once they were on their way.

That whole trip included a number of unexpected events and some incredible timing. It's quite a long story, but a fascinating one. The following is Charlie's account:

Our first stop was at Baiyer River to talk with Gilbert McArthur of the Baptist Mission about the flights he wanted us to make the following week.

When we saw how good the weather was [at takeoff from Baiyer River], I thought of the passage about Paul's voyage to Rome, "...supposing that they had obtained their purpose...they sailed..." No, we didn't end in shipwreck, but we soon saw our beautiful weather going to waste. For when we took off from Baiyer, the radio was dead. We stopped at Ogelbeng for fuel where Charles R. worked on it a while, but without result. We lost a couple of hours there—fueling, working on the radio, eating, and buzzing over to Mt. Hagen (5 minutes away) to get a message out on their radio.

We finally decided to give it away and go to Madang to get our spare power supply (parts were waiting there for trans-shipment to Wewak). Had we been going anywhere but Tari, we could have gone on without radio, but radio is required for that area.

The amazing thing about it all is this: the only spare parts for the engine, airplane or radio that were sent with the airplane were a spare propeller and a spare radio vibrator. The rest [of the spare parts] were sent separately and were in the box that was waiting in Madang. We had carried that spare vibrator with us on the trip to Dutch New Guinea, but had forgotten it this time. If we had taken it along, our troubles would have been over. As it turned out, we didn't even replace the vibrator on that trip. For we weren't 10 minutes out from Ogelbeng on our way to Madang when I gave the radio a try (just for fun!) and it came good. We called Madang and those voices boomed in. They asked for our position and I had to stall them off while we huddled over whether we should continue to the coast or go back to Ogelbeng. It was too late by that time to get to Tari anymore that day, so we decided to go to Madang for the weekend, pick up the spare parts and then continue.

Meanwhile, we decided to stop in Goroka en route, to ask the operator of air services there to stop at Hagen for our passengers since he was going into Tari the next day (Sunday morning) anyway. We knew too that both Cessnas were on the ground at Goroka, waiting for a DC-3 load of Lutheran missionaries to arrive from Wau. As soon as we got to Goroka, we began to see why the Lord had delayed us.

In the first place, the DC-3 was really late. It had been due at 10 in the morning but finally turned up at close to 5 pm. With no accommodations [available] in Goroka, the missionaries were going to have to be taken to other stations. The two Cessnas would have had trouble trying to get everyone settled by sundown. So we pitched in to help. Ray took one load of men up the Wahgi Valley and stayed the night there himself. Bob shuttled loads over to Asaroka, five minutes away. I took one load over there, and another load to Kainantu—25 minutes in the other direction. Both Bob and I ended up at Rintebe for the night. Besides being able to help out the Lutheran Mission in return for our "borrowing" the Cessna for Hollandia trips and the like, here was an excellent opportunity to talk over with Bob the decisions made at the Lutmis [Lutheran Mission] conference just concluded. This was particularly important in relation to the work just ahead with the Baptists.

We really made the most of our time together. And it was thrilling to hear how the Lutherans had been so completely in agreement with the suggestions I had written—even though my writing was a bit "stiff" in spots. Furthermore, we had the opportunity to do "all in one crack" what I had hoped to do over a longer period—that is, give the Lutheran Highland missionaries a chance to see the Pacer (in case they later decided to consider using Pacers instead of Cessnas). We found we had buzzed into the place where the whole Highland staff was congregated, which gave them a chance to see the Pacer in action. At the same time, we had our first chance to test the Pacer on high altitude strips—with loads.

All of this still was not the end of what the Lord had in store for us on this trip. The next morning we shuttled the missionaries from Asaroka to their homes. (It was our policy to return home on Sunday, though we do not originate work on Sunday normally. So we felt we should take all these folk on home instead of leaving them crowded up at Asaroka.) Most of them were on their way to Madang, so Bob and I then spent the rest of the day there, which gave us further opportunity to go over things together.

Instead of rushing out to Tari the next morning—since I was in Madang anyway—I was eager to take care of a radio shipment personally for a mission in DNG which had been shipped to Madang under bond for trans-shipment. I was even more eager to follow through on it when I learned that the business manager of Lutmis had gone ahead and paid duty on it by mistake (a whopping amount, too!). I knew that if we took time for this business though, we'd not get an early start and would probably have little chance to get into Tari the same day.

But the Lord had the schedule all worked out, and all my stomach tensions were pointless—as usual...[for] as we walked into the customs office, the Collector of Customs greeted me with, "Just got your letter five minutes ago!" (I had sent him some of the new Bird of Paradise stamps from DNG because I knew he was a stamp fancier.) The timing was perfect. Needless to say, we breezed through the business at hand.

The fellows had a chance to do another big favor for Lutmis (Lutheran Mission) that day. They picked up a load destined for Tari, but just before take-off they found out an incoming passenger on the Qantas flight that morning was headed for Tari. If they could take her, it would save a Cessna trip. (Both Cessnas were already booked for urgent flights.) By rearranging the Pacer's load—to make room and allow for her weight—they were able to take her. But it gave them a very late start (10 am). In fact, Charlie prepared himself mentally for the possibility of not even getting to Tari that afternoon.

Refueling at Banz, they noticed the weather appeared marginal in the direction of Tari, but they decided to give it a try. They found a path alongside a ridge behind Mt. Hagen and then flew through a little very light rain before the weather opened up a bit. Charlie reported:

> Before passing Mendi, we could see the gap ahead very plainly. (This is unusual even earlier in the day.) But we still couldn't tell if the Tari Valley would be covered [by clouds]. However, we could see the Valley before we even got to the gap—about ten minutes away. It was obviously going to be beautiful. Considering there had been no high overcast that morning, it was practically a miracle to fly into Tari at 1 pm. But that's what we did. And more than that, we even did a very brief survey around the Tari Valley yet that afternoon. Yet, when we landed, it was only about half an hour until it began to rain, and rain continued the rest of the day.

> Still, despite this unusual help, we seemed to be running a day behind schedule. We should have flown the two UFM leaders out of Tari to Goroka on Tuesday in order to be sure they'd get the Thursday morning (early) plane for Port Moresby. But they decided to stay until Wednesday and take a chance. That meant only Tuesday was left for the survey.

> Just then one of the men from the Methodist mission in Mendi popped in. He wanted us to do a short survey for them also—on the other side of the Tari Valley

where they hope to work. Imagine! Two surveys in one day (though both were short). Usually we allow up to a week for one survey—especially in a weather trap like Tari, and even more during the wet season.

Tuesday morning, when we got up, there were the usual fog patches—so we couldn't tell what to expect. As we got to the airstrip and the patches began to clear, it looked a bit dark to the south where the longest survey was to be made. So we buzzed off on the one for the Methodists. We had hardly gotten airborne when I realized that the weather to the south was perfect for our purposes—high overcast with a drizzly rain, but no cumulus activity or fog. The mountain we wanted to have a look around stood out like a sentinel, as did a mountain behind that range out on the Papua flats. (We had tried this survey once before, at the end of December, and failed because we couldn't get over the ridge at any point.) This time we buzzed on around, did the short survey for the Methodists, refueled and headed south. It was well worthwhile; the mission folk were thrilled to have all the information they gained…on all three flights.

As could be expected, after all the evidences of the Lord's leading, the weather Wednesday morning was beautiful again. I was aware of how different the weather had been for each of the three days' flying, but yet it was incredible how ideally suited each day's weather was for that day's job.

Leaving Tari, we flew straight to Goroka, refueled, and then went on to Wewak via Baiyer River where we picked up Gilbert McArthur. I had my doubts about getting from Baiyer to Wewak in the afternoon on a day without any high clouds. But the cumulus buildups were quite broken; it turned out to be what we'd consider an easy trip. Furthermore, the radio worked beautifully all the way without our replacing the vibrator. It was all rather ironic. But in looking back, I wouldn't wish any change in the order of events.

Back in Wewak, Charlie spent time in discussion with Gil McArthur. He hoped the Baptists would choose to participate at least for the next couple of years (perhaps longer) in a plan he had devised. The plan called for basing one of the Madang Cessnas in the Highlands (at Banz), where it could serve the Baptists along with the Lutherans. At first Charlie didn't feel overly optimistic about a positive response, but the Lord seemed to prompt him to make the proposal. This new approach seemed a far more practical answer for the Baptists than establishing their own air service. So as discussions with Gil began to move in that direction, it became a special thrill to anticipate the results.

Although this much was encouraging, Charlie also received a different kind of news: The Wewak Land Board notified him, that despite the fact that they had approved our leasing of two lots (including one we had already built on following verbal permission), they were turning down our request to build a temporary hangar at the Wewak airstrip. Almost at that same moment we, got word from Melbourne asking that we hold off on the hangar-building project, for financial reasons. Charlie realized that such a delay would be difficult, for he had already ordered the lumber in anticipation of the supplier's going on leave. Not only that, but delivery was expected within a few days. He needed to go see him immediately to find out what could be done.

Interestingly, when he asked about the status of the lumber order, the man apologized profusely, saying he had had saw trouble and hadn't been able to cut any lumber. Incredible! Charlie then learned that the local operator at the airstrip was apparently happy to allow MAF continued use of his hangar—indefinitely. This whole set of circumstances served to remind us that the Lord very often brings good out of seemingly hopeless situations.

Within a week of Charlie's returning Gil McArthur to his Baiyer River home (and making some surveys for the Baptists while there), the Ambrose family arrived. We were now two families (with seven children between us) sharing the main house; it was a beehive of activity. There was scarcely time to get acquainted in the midst of the hectic schedule. Joan did most of their unpacking and getting their family settled (just as I had done when we arrived), for Vic began going along with Charlie almost immediately to deliver supplies and move mission personnel around in the Sepik area. Going along was the best way for him to become familiar with the plane and learn the routes.

But there was another reason for the almost frantic pace. The three pilots (Charlie, Vic, and Charles R.) were scheduled to leave the week after Ambroses' arrival for a survey in Dutch New Guinea; and, since they anticipated being gone a month, they wanted to be sure all the missions in the Sepik area served from Wewak were adequately supplied.

Preparations for their leaving were hampered somewhat by the lack of rain in Wewak. Our household water supply ran so low that it was necessary to take time to haul water from a creek behind the Catholic mission station on the mainland. Since all three of the men were going to DNG, we wives had to be checked out in this matter of getting water ourselves. Neither Joan Ambrose nor Dorothy Rasmussen drove, so Charlie took me along in the jeep one day to show me where the creek was and how to handle the jeep. Our three Papuan helpers and sons John and Jim went with us.

Hoping to avoid having to make the trip, I prayed it would rain. But no rain came, and I ended up having to make that trip for water eight times while the men were away. The road to the creek had a number of sharp turns and deep ruts. There was no way we could arrive home with the three or four 44-gallon drums full of water because of the inevitable sloshing on the way. Furthermore, I had never driven a four-wheel-drive vehicle before and didn't have the slightest idea of what "double-reduction" meant. (It referred to the gears.) I just knew I had to use it to get the jeep out of the creek bed, then over the ruts, and finally up the steep hill to our house. John and Jim thought the trips were great adventures, while I focused primarily on getting us all home safely—*with* water and *without* vehicle problems. I was especially grateful for the help of our three Papuan employees!

Before leaving, Charlie and Vic arranged with a European contractor in town to put guttering along the front edge of the roof and to install a second tank to collect additional water. Once that tank was in place, a decent rain would provide plenty of water for both tanks. But until the rains came, we had no choice but to haul water—and to be thankful there was water to haul.

There was one other matter we wives were left in charge of while the fellows were away. Shortly before Ambroses arrived, we had a visitor one day—a Papuan who came to ask if we would help start a "Lotu" (church service) for Papuan workers in Wewak. We learned that the inquirer (Grongem) had had some training by the Lutherans and apparently was aware of our ties with the Lutheran Mission in Madang. He indicated he knew a number of Protestant workers in Wewak who would be interested in attending church services. This seemed a wonderful way to serve, so we told him we'd be glad to do it.

The first Sunday only Grongem came; the others, he said (mainly policemen) had to work. Naturally we were a little disappointed, but Grongem, along with our family and the Rasmussens went ahead anyway with a worship service conducted in Pidgin English. The next week twelve came. But then our husbands left, and we wondered what would happen to the Lotu idea. My letter home began,

> We were excited that we had 16 show up for Lotu last Sunday. I had planned to do the little talk ("liklik toktok"), and then read other parts of the service from our [Lutheran] Lotu book. But when Grongem, the fellow who asked to have the Lotu in the first place, came a few days before to discuss with me the songs we could choose, we started talking about the story I was planning to use.

I was so impressed with the way he began talking about the story and the applications he made that I impulsively asked him to do it on Sunday since his Pidgin was so much better than mine. He agreed but suggested he'd come back on Saturday to share what he wanted to say for any last-minute suggestions from me.

It turned out to be a good decision because Dorothy R. was in the hospital that day for a minor problem, and Joan and I had eight children to look after between us. Under the circumstances I asked Grongem to do the reading as well. He agreed and did a very commendable job. I was particularly impressed by the way he prayed for the fellows in DNG at the close of his final prayer. My letter continued,

> This Sunday another chap is to take the talk, so he will come over tomorrow to go over it with us. This man has been quite well educated. He understands English and speaks it some too. He's a teacher at the government medical school out from Wewak. He had been asking us to get him an English Bible. We are so thrilled with the Lotu—it is giving us a chance at a bit of spiritual ministry…I wasn't especially looking forward to this job here in Wewak, but I'm thrilled at the way it is turning out—particularly meeting and working with Joan and Vic, and the Lotu….

> Another Sunday we had only eight Papuans at the Lotu. I took the service that day (in Pidgin)…The next Sunday we also had eight…I began to realize then how much I am going to miss this service when we leave Wewak for Sentani.

The fellows wired us that the DNG government had denied permission for two of their hoped-for surveys. We realized that meant they'd return sooner than they originally thought. But we also wondered how much they were able to accomplish. How had they fared sleeping in tents on that island? What proposals would they now make, and what would be the time frame? How would their recommendations affect the various families? We were full of questions as we eagerly awaited their return.

21
Pioneering Pilots

The most important survey Charlie and Vic hoped to complete on their joint trip to DNG was in the northwestern tip called the Bird's Head. A description of their planning and of the survey itself gives a pretty good idea of what was involved in attempting to launch a new MAF program.

If we visualize the shape of New Guinea—the side view of a large bird—we can identify the area to be surveyed as the upper back of the bird's head. Unfortunately there was no usable airstrip in the whole of that area since all the wartime airstrips had been pretty thoroughly bombed. For this reason the fellows planned to use an existing airstrip on Noemfor Island, about 40 miles to the east in Geelvink Bay. Noemfor, a tiny island with a reef most of the way around it, was about 15 miles across at its widest point. To get there from Sentani, the pilots first had to island-hop to Biak. There they could contact the tower at Biak's International Airport about weather briefings for their surveys.

Because so much of the flight from Sentani was over water, they planned to fly at a high enough altitude so they could glide to one shore or another if the engine should quit between islands. As a double precaution, all wore life jackets which Charlie had purchased earlier in Australia in anticipation of this trip. He had also ordered gasoline for the plane while in Australia, since no fuel was available on Noemfor. He ordered the fuel shipped to the Evangelical Alliance Mission head-quarters at Manokwari, located at the northeastern tip of the Bird's Head. The TEAM missionaries there, who expected to participate in the survey, were to trans-ship it to Noemfor about the time they left to rendezvous with the Pacer and its crew. Both missionaries and fuel arrived in Noemfor a week before the plane. As it turned out, however, the camping experience of the pilots-turned-pioneers ended up providing more to write home about than did the survey. The following was Charlie's account:

> When we dropped into this field on Saturday afternoon, there was no one around. We had spotted a village a little way away, so we had buzzed that first. About 20 minutes after we landed, the TEAM missionaries appeared. They had hoofed it

from the village. While we fueled the plane for an early start on Monday, we worked out our accommodations: one fellow was to camp out by the plane, and the rest of us were to sleep in town—the local controller (an Ambonese) had turned one room of his house over to us.

The first night there we had quite an experience, even more so for Vic than for me since he had left Australia just 10 days before. We weren't used to the kind of evening meal we were served—incidentally, served at 9:30 pm, which was the customary hour for the local Ambonese. The meal itself was a huge colander of rice, topped with vegetables, meat, etc. We had quite a variety of meat that night: chicken, boiled fish, smoked fish, etc.

We were there all day Sunday, and then moved Sunday evening out to the campsite, figuring we'd probably get an earlier start from there on Monday morning. That was the first time I had slept in a pup tent since my Boy Scout days. It was sorta fun. The frankfurters (canned) and beans were a real treat after the very different fare of the previous 24 hours.

Our campsite was in a narrow grove of scrubby trees between the beach and the airstrip. The airplane was only 50 feet away in one direction; and the beach, 30 feet in the other. There was quite a breeze in the evenings.

We enjoyed this open-air living for two days. Then about 2 am Wednesday the rains came. Vic and I were now sharing one pup tent so that two of the other fellows could also move out to the campsite. With one of us touching each side of a poorly-waterproofed tent, the rain really rolled in. After about 15 minutes of wishful thinking, we fished our rain coats out of our bags and "abandoned ship." We hurriedly made for the airplane and spent the rest of the night there. I curled up on the front seat and Vic on the back. It's not as roomy as a car, but it was dry. We told each other, "If you're going to play pioneer missionary, it's nice to have a plane to fall back on."

The next day we moved back into town. And how we enjoyed it! Even the meals! They had killed a pig, and the taste of fresh pork was wonderful. One night they even roasted it on sticks like "city chicken legs," and was it ever good! I could have enjoyed living another week on that fare.

But, getting back to the survey flights, the weather was beautiful for our first flight on Monday; "stinko" on Tuesday, Wednesday was fair—and we got in a short hop. Thursday we tried it, but gave it away before we even left the island. (Each day we climbed for 30 minutes over the island to get enough altitude so we could cross the water with the proper gliding range to shore.) Friday was beautiful again, and we finished the job.

That same afternoon we left for Biak and stayed in the KLM hotel. What a place, stuck way off in the south sea isles. And what a contrast to our camping out! We really basked in wonderful food, foam rubber mattresses and private showers (hadn't had a decent bath in a week). We knew it would cost a lot, but were not quite prepared for the shock we got the next morning—$10 each (supper, bed and breakfast). Ouch!

The weather wasn't much good Saturday morning, but we fought our way back to Sentani. Had a short survey there on Monday, spent Tuesday in town seeing officials and headed back to Wewak on Wednesday....

Though we were denied permission to do two of the four anticipated surveys in DNG, I somehow feel it is the Lord's way of giving us a much-needed breathing spell to catch up on our work a bit. And there may be other less tangible factors involved. The Lord will open the way in His time....

Charlie really did believe this; but, as he reflected on the whole DNG situation when he returned to Wewak, he had to admit there were some puzzling aspects. The whole picture somehow seemed a bit more confused than before. He felt it would be easy to be discouraged if he looked only at the surface picture. But he reminded himself that with all the good things we had experienced in recent weeks, we should probably expect some testing of our faith along the way. Characteristically, Charlie determined to keep plugging away doing what there was to do while waiting to see things "break" in the Lord's time.

In turning his attention to the program at hand, he was gratified to realize that our Wewak operation was now generally accepted by the local commercial operators who had been somewhat standoffish at first. This was understandable; they no doubt saw the MAF operation as competition, small though it was.

Interestingly, within a one-week period, a couple of unforeseen events brought about some positive attitude changes. For during that one week these two operators each had a plane down unexpectedly for maintenance, and neither had a spare plane available to take a mechanic to the sites of their disabled planes. In both cases MAF was able to help.

One of the operators had an additional problem; his downed plane had left the District Commissioner stranded at a place called Telefomin. The airstrip there was one our fellows had been eager to visit, but they lacked the loan of an experienced pilot to accompany them for the first landing. Now, with the District Commissioner stranded there, MAF was asked to go in and bring him out from that very strip. Charlie wrote,

We had to turn back the first day, so one of their pilots flew with us on our two tries. We ended up buying good will by the ton that week. We were even asked for a charter flight on a couple of occasions, but had to decline. Nonetheless, things have changed considerably around here as a result of our help.

The improved relationships at the airstrip were most welcome. But on the home front all of us were getting additional practice in coping with multi-family life in a single dwelling. It had its challenges at times, but also included fun and humor. Our ceilings were finally installed in early April (1954), which meant we could now hopefully begin to control the rat population! Along with the ceilings, the completed wiring also made possible our hookup to the city's electricity. Even that wasn't the end of the good news. We had rain—enough so that both storage tanks were completely filled. Such luxury!!

Our double-family setup was working exceptionally well, although we did make one minor adjustment. Instead of both families eating together at one large table (actually, two tables put together), we decided to try eating as separate families; Joan and I had discovered it was too easy for the daddies to continue their shop talk right through mealtimes if we all sat together at one table. Our strategy worked. Eating at separate tables gave each family unit time for some special attention from dad—and helped bring him back into his family's orbit. Joan and I made another rather interesting observation: in taking turns preparing the dinners (with the other assisting), we noticed that the children of the one in charge of the menu had the better appetites—an interesting illustration of our culturally different backgrounds.

One further observation about our combined household, it seemed to me, was that each of the children at one time or another showed signs of emotional stress that might have been due to one or more of the following factors: more complicated relationships, along with the continual presence of more people, an elevated noise level, and fewer opportunities to be alone. It was perhaps just as well that the two-family arrangement was temporary. Yet that "togetherness" experience most assuredly resulted in close and long-lasting ties between our two families—and undoubtedly contributed positively toward the relationships between the two MAF s.

22
A Sad Event Mars the Transition

About the end of April (1954), we got word that Betty Hutchins was ill and probably needed to go to the Highlands for a few weeks' rest. For this reason our family moved back to Madang for a month so that Charlie could help with flying, which also allowed Bob a bit of a vacation break. While in Madang, in addition to making routine flights from the coast into the interior, Charlie checked Bob out in the Pacer and helped with Max Flavel's checkouts in both Cessna and Pacer. All month long, the Pacer shuttled back and forth on flights from both Madang and Wewak. Also during this period, Charlie and Vic managed to make another survey flight together—this time in the Tari area where they flew over the Strickland River Gorge, a particularly spectacular sight to behold because of the altitude variations. The altitude at the river bed was less than 1500 ft. while the mountains all around rose to heights of 10,000 ft.

I used the month in Madang to get John and Jim back into their school books since we had gotten behind in the press of "just living" in Wewak. It was a difficult time for me in that I was feeling especially unsettled—Charlie was away flying nearly all the time, and for me everything seemed so temporary. In the midst of these feelings, I was looking forward to a weekend when Charlie was expected to be home with the family. However, that afternoon, I heard via our shortwave radio that he had had to turn back to Wewak on account of weather. I was so keenly disappointed that I vented all my pent-up emotions in a letter home—something I rarely did.

> Now I don't know when he will be coming. I'm getting to the point where I'd trade this schedule for most anyone else's. I'm getting eager too to be settled down with my own things again. This time here in New Guinea has been a wonderful experience and I'm so glad we were given the opportunity of actually living here for a while, but I have had enough of living with other people, and living in other people's houses, with their things. I won't be sorry when it is time for us to turn this over to others. Don't misunderstand. I'm happy over here. I wouldn't mind even settling down over here for a full term, but I'd sure like a house to ourselves and our own things from home to use—and my husband home more!

I'm probably feeling down more because it's seemed longer than normal this time. Gordon came down with dysentery last Wednesday night and it continued all day Thursday, with fever. Thursday and Friday he could keep nothing down either. By Saturday he had lost the fever, but still ate almost nothing. Even yesterday and today he has not been himself. It's his longest sickness to date, and he wanders around like a lost sheep. And now tonight Jimmy has a bit of fever. Wonder if he's next. Charlie had it so badly just before he left last Tuesday—he had it really for a couple of weeks, but not severe enough to keep him in bed. But neither has he had time, or a letup in tension, to relax enough to rest and get over it. I wish his schedule would let up just a little bit to enable him to really get rested this time.

When Charlie returned from Wewak the middle of the following week, I learned his weekend had been difficult too, for he had been asked to conduct a funeral service. He was finalizing his revised flight schedule as he returned to Wewak because of weather (the report I had heard on the radio that Saturday) when he heard about a death. One of the young men who had been coming quite regularly to our Lotu services had been killed very suddenly. All of Wewak was stunned. How had it happened? Charlie recorded the details of that awful accident in a letter to our parents dated May 16, 1954.

As you know, we've been using the Pacer part-time in Madang to get Max checked out. And we've returned to Wewak periodically to take care of needs here....The plan was for me to go back [to Madang] yesterday. The government had a patrol officer that needed transportation direct from here to the Central Highlands, and there is no regular plane service from here—the Central Highlands are served from Madang. But I'm familiar with the route, having made it several times for mission societies. So I was to fly him to the Highlands, and from there go on to Madang....We might have made it, but the rain was fairly heavy in the valley we follow—so we gave it away...and made arrangements to repeat the trip on Monday morning.

We soon learned that weather was not the main reason for the turnback. In the afternoon, some of the policemen were spear-fishing out on the reef near the police barracks—like they do almost every day. One of them saw some blood on the surface. They investigated by diving and found the headless body of one of the policemen lying on the bottom. Apparently they saw the shark that got him, and even had a couple of shots at it. They said it was a monstrous thing! It must have been, to get a whole head in its mouth. I didn't see the body, but was told that it was cut off as clean as if it had been done by a surgeon—no sign of tearing or of a fight. The shark apparently got him from behind so that he probably never saw it or knew what hit him.

The first we knew about it was when the police master came by our place and asked us if we would take the service since he was a Protestant. It turned out he was one of the policemen who had been attending the Lotu services quite regularly. He was here two weeks ago when Liwa [the Lutheran pastor from Madang] gave his excellent message. The policeman was from New Ireland Island—a product of the Methodist mission. We trust that the Word spoken both previously and recently had found root in his heart.

The police master suggested that we could conduct the service in English; then the District Officer would turn the talk into Pidgin. But we didn't like that idea; it's hard enough to express Christian truth in Pidgin after studying it carefully. So Vic felt I should take the service, for I've begun to get the swing of it after conducting the Lotu here.

It was quite an experience for me. I don't suppose I've been to half a dozen funerals in my life—let alone conduct one. And then to do the first one in another language....I was very thankful for the Lutheran Lotu book, which has a funeral service in it. It's excellent—gives direct translations of several important verses: "I am the resurrection and the life ..." Job's "I know that my redeemer liveth...." [and others]. Following this they have a translation of Psalm 90 which is as good as a translation of a Psalm could be, I guess. But the Hebrew poetry is hard for us to understand in English without confusing the Papuans by giving it to them in a language that is not their own. So we skipped that, and I gave in place of it a very brief talk on Jesus as the Door (we'd had the lesson on John 10 twice in Lotu)—not just to the Church on earth but to the Kingdom in Heaven. I emphasized that for the believer, death was not the finish, but the beginning of something better. Then I went back to the written form: "Man that is born of woman is of few days...." followed by a prayer, rather typically liturgical, but not bad at all.

Then came the committal to the grave. Maybe you'd like to see it in Pidgin. Here it is: [In reading it, use phonetic pronunciation.]

"God yet itok na ipulim soul bilong disfela brata bilong yumi, igo long em; yumi plantim bodi bilong em long graun. Tru bodi bilong em itern bek long graun; tasol [however] long strong bilong Jesus Kristus [by the power of Jesus Christ] igirap gen long de bilong em [i.e., the day of Christ]. Long dis taim [here we made an insertion to get away from ... preaching universalism in a funeral service: 'ol man ibilif long Jesus'], Jesus ternim bodi bilong dai [body of death—I believe AV uses 'vile body'] long mifela bodi long strong bilong em."[1]

This is followed by the verse from Revelation: 'I heard a voice from heaven say to me, write....' Then the closing prayer, which is an excellent funeral sermon in

---

[1] Pidgin English quotations are from the *Lotu Buk*, compiled by E. Hanneman, 1950, Lutheran Mission Press, Territory of New Guinea.

itself. It emphasizes the antithesis of universalism without being offensive; and it brings the lesson of death right down to the practical application to each listener. I'll copy it with its translation. But actually, it's more effective and beautiful in Pidgin than in English.

O God, bel bilong yu sori tumas,

O God, Yours is a loving heart,

yu Papa bilong bigfela Helpim bilong mifela, Jesus Kristus, em bilong girap na laif.

You are the Father of our great Saviour, Jesus Christ, the resurrection and the life.

Em supos man i bilif long em, long idai tu i ken istap, ino lus,

When a man believes on Him, when he dies, he can remain; he doesn't lose [life],

Olsem man istap long graun na bilif long Jesus, ino ken idai tru long oltaim.

Likewise, men now on earth, and believing on Jesus, they'll not suffer eternal death.

Em tu i soim yumi long tok bilong apostle Paul ispik,

He [God] also shows us in the writing of the Apostle Paul, who says,

Yumi no bel bruk tumas long taim brata bilong yumi idai; no, haiden man i olsem— em ino save tok bilong God.

Our hearts shouldn't despair when our brethren die; no, sinful man is that way —he doesn't understand God's word.

Olsem na mifela prei long yu,

So be it, and we pray to you,

O Papa, yu lusim mifela long sin i strong long me olsem dai ikisim finis mifela, yu girapim mifela long gudfela fasin bilong yu.

O Father, you keep us from sin which binds us the same as death, you raise us to your good fashion [way].

Behain de bilong mifela ikamap idai, yu ken bringim mifela long gudfela ples bilong yu.

Later, when our day comes to die, you can bring us to your good place.

O Papa, yu redim mifela long taim nau long ples bilong yu. Yu holim strong mifela long tok bilong yu. Satan ilaik kisim bek mifela na yu fasim rod bilong em—holim mi.

O Father, you make us ready now for your place. You keep us by your word. Satan will try to take us back, you deter him— hold me.

The funeral was this morning. It rained steadily right through the service (this is the wettest part of the wet season—no water shortage now). Charlie R. held an umbrella over me so the book wouldn't get wet. Since this was a policemen, there was some military form to the service, too, but very little. Right after I finished, the District Officer said just a very few words—very well put. He principally called attention to my "gudfela tok" and exhorted them to hear it well; then he pointed out that this man had stepped out to help the government in its job, and that the government wouldn't forget him ("no lusim tingting") and his service. Then there was the volley and the bugle call.

Our little group was well represented (there was quite a group there). At least one of the firing party, and the bugler were "our" men. The bugler is not a confessed Christian [so far as we know]. He's the brother of a fellow that attends the Wunsches' missionary school out from Lumi. But this bugler left before that mission work was established. So,… " I'm sure praying earnestly that this incident will help bring conviction to his heart. Equally earnestly, I'm praying that it will challenge the mission-trained men to really give their lives to the Lord.… While I'm praying for them, I'm also praying that the Lord will give us one or two who really mean business—who can become the nucleus for a strong group here. This may come from one or both of the two chief mourners: the dead man's best buddy in the Police force, and his brother, Darius Nepal, who teaches out at the government school.… The latter is well-educated and speaks English. Both are bright fellows, and both have given "liklik toktoks" at Lotu.

I sure felt sorry for these fellows. Darius bore up under it better than the buddy, but both were deeply moved. I had short private talks with each of them—wish I had had more chance for that. The fellow was married (no children) but his wife isn't here—stayed at her place (which is quite customary).

Vic took Charlie as far as Ogelbeng, where he was to pick up some goats for Lumi. Since Ray also flew into Ogelbeng that day, Charlie rode back to Madang with him. As he reflected, Charlie came to believe this trip marked the conclusion of one phase of our New Guinea objectives. He wrote,

I feel like I've reached one more milestone—the Wewak program is more-or-less on its own now. That leaves DNG—plus the Philippine survey, and possibly a little more administrative work in Australia. We're "getting there!"

He began to focus his complete attention on DNG, knowing that paperwork for our move was incomplete, and housing had not yet been arranged. Beyond that, there were many questions: How was the periodic service from Wewak all the way to the Bird's Head going to work out (once the TEAM missionaries were moved into the surveyed area in early July)? And how long would it take to finalize permissions with the DNG government? All this was bound to evolve and become clearer soon, for our move to DNG was finally imminent.

After Bob and Betty Hutchins returned from vacation, we moved back to Wewak to finalize preparations for our move to Sentani, DNG. Charlie decided to make one more trip alone first, to find housing for the family and take some of our belongings over at the same time. He returned a few days later with news that we had a place to live temporarily, but he had run into a snag on my passport; it had to be sent to Sydney to have my visa inserted. This was expected to take about 10 days. To redeem the time while waiting, Charlie and Vic returned to Sentani for a week; Vic, to make flights into Sengge, and Charlie, to build some minimum furniture (a platform for our foam mattress and a couple of tables).

Word received from L.A. indicated that the office had concurred with Charlie's recommendation of the purchase of a pre-fab house for MAF Sentani. The order was placed from L.A. by cable to London, where the crate of unassembled parts would be put aboard a Dutch ship bound for Hollandia. If the order was processed quickly enough, Charlie estimated it might possibly make the ship leaving England early in July. If so, it could conceivably arrive in DNG as early as the end of August.

During the week that Vic and Charlie were in Sentani, the boys and I were invited to stay with the Newnhams at Boram Point (Brandi), since the MAF guest rooms were occupied. The Newnhams' house, up on a hill, was constructed of local materials, except for the floor, and it lacked indoor plumbing and electricity. The exterior woven walls had sections, in lieu of windows, that could be opened by raising and propping them up—which also provided air and light. The house had no screens, so everyone slept under mosquito nets.

Among the most vivid visual images of that week that come to mind are the unusually large-diameter spiders that quietly came and went on ceilings and walls. Although they helped by consuming mosquitos, I wasn't altogether comfortable being "watched." Another memory is of our two-year-old Gordon enjoying a piece of watermelon as he sat on the open window ledge blowing the seeds out of his mouth as far as he could into the yard below. How could anything be more fun?

As for John and Jim, it didn't take them long to become clock-watchers at Brandi. They could hardly wait until classes were over at about four o'clock every afternoon. That was when the boys (it was a boys' school) spilled out onto the adjacent level grassy field to play games. John and Jim were invited to join in the fun and eagerly raced down the hill to take part in the action.

Before the week was over, John Newnham arranged for a couple of his older students to take his wife Shirley, our three boys, and me for an outing in an outrigger canoe. They took us down the Brandi River to its mouth—to a point near where the river met the ocean. The river banks on both sides were densely covered with tropical foliage and in some places branches hung low over the river. The day was rather cloudy, which was perfect for our excursion. On one of the little muddy banks we saw jumping fish, and once heard a big splash—a baby crocodile entering the water. The canoe was really wide enough to sit in, but we sat up on a little platform built across its center that had a little fence around it. Two students paddled, one at each end of the outrigger. Each used a different shaped paddle—a somewhat blunt one in front to better propel the canoe and a more pointed one in back which doubled as a rudder. These particular paddles were very plain, but many had intricate carving and were quite fancy, as were many of the canoes.

The water was calm as we glided along. When we got to the beach near the ocean, we got out and spent a little time looking at shells. One of the students speared a crab about eight inches in diameter by hurling a slender bamboo pole with sharp prongs (shaped much like a badminton birdie) at it. Shirley told us the local people catch fish with those spears as well. She and John had enjoyed going on one of their night fishing expeditions when lanterns are used aboard the outriggers. On our return upriver, John and Jim begged for a turn at paddling and wanted me to try it too. It wasn't as easy as it looked!

After the good week with Newnhams, I wasn't prepared for the discouraging news Charlie shared with me when he and Vic returned from Sentani. In the first place, the Pacer ordered for DNG could not possibly reach Madang for assembly before November—at the earliest. On top of that news, the L.A. office indicated it would very likely be "next spring" before personnel could be assigned and ready to leave the States to join us. What did it all mean? We already seemed so far behind schedule in getting service underway in DNG. We found it hard to understand the "whys" of the many delays.

As it turned out, there was much more left to do than we had anticipated. In one sense, it was exciting to be at the point of actual entry into DNG. Yet we couldn't help feeling more than a little apprehensive about what lay ahead. True, DNG was our ultimate goal and challenge, but we were to feel, initially at least, an isolation in DNG that we hadn't experienced before—an isolation related not so much to the international border separating us geographically from the support of our MAF colleagues in Papua New Guinea as it was to the rather apparent indifference we encountered on the part of those in Dutch New Guinea who had previously been so enthusiastic and eager for MAF's arrival and service.

23

An Inauspicious Beginning

Vic flew our family across to Sentani in the Wewak Pacer in June of 1954. We had finally arrived in DNG—but without a plane, and no permission yet to operate a program, even if a plane was on site. And, our arrival was a year or more behind our original estimated target date. We seemed to be starting from scratch, despite all the preliminary legwork. Most missions had already been assigning more and more missionaries to New Guinea in anticipation of air support and were understandably restless—eager to move their personnel into the interior to begin work among those not yet reached with the Gospel. True, we had begun a limited service using the Wewak Pacer for survey trips and to supply one or two existing inland locations. But opportunities for mission outreach had far outdistanced MAF's progress in getting a full-fledged program underway.

Perhaps not surprisingly, the C&MA mission (Christian and Missionary Alliance) made a decision to move ahead with an aviation program of its own, complete with two pilots, a mechanic, and a twin-engine amphibious plane (a Sealand). Moreover, they offered to make their plane available to other missions—at least to some extent—by a charter arrangement. All this was most impressive; it was a hard act for MAF to follow! It was also understandable that the other missions, eager to move their waiting personnel into the interior, would turn to this opportunity as a more viable option, especially since MAF's plane and permanent pilot had not yet left the States. To all appearances, MAF had arrived too late with too little. We found ourselves asking the question we presumed everyone else was at least thinking: How can a tiny little single-engine Pacer on floats (with its very limited payload) compete with the roomy twin-engine amphibious Sealand? The thought was almost ludicrous.

Although no one voiced such thoughts to us, a variety of nonverbals were being communicated. It is probably small wonder that, from the outset, Sentani *felt* different. It's hard to share our feelings of embarrassment when C&MA leaders generously offered our family the use of a couple of rooms as living quarters, in an old army mess hall they had purchased. Much of it was being used for storage, but a section had been fixed up as temporary accommodations for housing their personnel while they waited to be flown into the Baliem—their one recently-opened inland station. It wasn't easy to be gracious recipients of such generosity when MAF's services seemed almost irrelevant. Nonetheless, we were most grateful for this temporary housing.

One of the two adjacent rooms we occupied was half the size of the other. Screens extended along the outer wall of both rooms. We put three cots (with mosquito nets) in the smaller room for the three boys, and the larger room with its built-in sink in a far corner became our multi-purpose room: that is, kitchen, dining room, livingroom, bedroom, school room, Charlie's study, and even laundry room.

Our furniture? Charlie built most of it—a platform for our foam mattress, a screened-in cupboard (to keep our dishes and perishables free of insects and rats), a set of shelves for our clothes, a table (for meals and to serve as Charlie's desk when we weren't eating), and a short-legged table for the boys to use for schoolwork. We purchased two canvas chairs, and the boys sat on crates. (Later we acquired four folding chairs.) Charlie arranged his files in one packing crate and turned another crate into a bookcase. Three cartons stacked on their sides held the boys' books. Talk about a *family room*! This togetherness, however, was a bit much for Charlie at times, especially when he tried to focus on composing business correspondence, or drafting important papers or documents for government officials.

Naturally, I was relieved to note we had ceilings in both rooms. What I failed to immediately realize was that the partitions dividing the rooms did not extend all the way from ceiling to floor—there was space between the partition and the floor, which meant that there would be no way to keep rats out. We learned the hard way to keep small things put away, or we'd find they were carried off during the night. (Even items like bars of soap disappeared if I forgot to put them in the cupboard overnight.) The rats' taste was rather indiscriminate in that they also chewed corners of Charlie's tough-hide briefcase and the edges of my wallet. We could never be sure what would appeal to them.

Still, our two-room accommodations had one big plus—we could be together as a family! I had calculated that we lived with other people 11 out of the first 24 months we had been in New Guinea. And Charlie had been away from the family for a total of six of the last 14 months. So, even though our accommodations were somewhat primitive, we enjoyed being about to live independently.

At that time (June 1954), about six other mission families lived on the hill which was almost a mile from Sentani's airstrip. The hill's slope continued its rise behind the houses up to a height of 7,000 feet, forming Mt. Cyclops. From the elevation where our houses stood (part way up the rise) we could see portions of Lake Sentani below, and on beyond to the ranges of mountains in the distance—a gorgeous panorama.

Languages used in this part of New Guinea (the western half) were different from those across the border in the Territory (TNG). Here in DNG (the Hollandia/Sentani area) the trade language was no longer Pidgin English, but Malay (or Bahasa Indonesia). Government officials and those operating businesses usually spoke some English in addition to Dutch. We knew neither Dutch nor Malay, but tried to pick up Malay phrases and words as best we could.

Once we became organized, Charlie began to dig into his administrative responsibilities. He outlined what he hoped to accomplish in the next few months and referred to our current situation in a letter home:

> As I see it now, our work in the next few months—until the plane arrives—consists of three main things: 1) preparing some written agreement with the government for the basis on which we'll work here. The Director of Technical Services told me that there is no present provision for an operation such as ours; it will require a special concession which can only be given by the Governor. That will take a lot of prayer along with a lot of work. 2) Working to improve the relationships with C&MA and to get the two aviation efforts on a cooperative, supplementary basis, so as to be worthy of the name of Christ we both bear. We need to show them that we are not interested in changing anything, but merely [want] to provide what may be lacking. We're perfectly happy to be the "second team," but for the Lord's sake we should not be competitive. This will take more grace than we could summon this past week, but the Lord is good to work with us gradually as we do His work. 3) Developing the relationship between aviation and mission work, particularly in organizing preparation of cargo and passengers for the inland flights. These are our goals and our prayer objectives, but we cannot share them with many.

Sunday evenings the mission community in Sentani gathered together for its own worship service in English. (Some of us tried visiting the Dutch and Malay services in Sentani on Sunday mornings, but it was hard to maintain interest when we didn't understand the language and when we had young children with us as well.) When Charlie was asked to take a turn one Sunday evening, he decided to base his talk on what he had been studying in his personal devotions from the book of Daniel. He shared some of his thoughts with our parents:

I'm supposed to speak for the [English] Fellowship meeting tonight....I'm enjoying my study—the prominence of the theme of wisdom in the first half of Daniel. It's particularly applicable to missionaries since we live under similar conditions (to Daniel): we're in a foreign country among people of a different culture, needing constantly to maintain good relationships with strange [to us] governments. Of course, Daniel had the additional problem of dealing with a completely irreligious government that went to the extreme of ruler-worship. So if he could gain such sweeping victories by the application of God-given wisdom, our victory is also assured.

I'm also struck by the fact that while we usually think of the first half of Daniel in terms of the unusual miracles that occurred, the more unusual thing really is the way Daniel and his three friends faced these trying experiences with calm, unabashed confidence: neither fear, nor the opposite extreme of fanatical, self-inflicted martyrdom. The three friends merely stood their ground; their deliverance was less remarkable than their assurance of deliverance, which in turn was less remarkable than their willingness to die if that was the Lord's will. It seems to me that the latter had a greater effect on the king than the miracle.

Then, when the other lords plotted against Daniel, the picture is again merely a calm adherence to principles—neither mealy-mouthed expediency nor I-dare-you boldness. It's good stuff—not nearly so remote from present-day experiences as we're inclined to believe.

One of Charlie's first concerns involved the purchase of a vehicle, specifically a ¾-ton Fargo truck that became available. He sought and gained approval from the L.A. office to buy it, but ran into a snag in transferring the registration. Once that red tape was unsnarled, the truck was a tremendous asset, especially with all the necessary trips to town. And sharing it made the trips less expensive for everyone. It was a rare occasion when the truck didn't return from town with a full load: kerosene, motor fuel, cement, lumber, supplies from Australia, foodstuffs, etc.

After an appointment with the Director of Transportation, Charlie commented:

It turned out to be a good opportunity to correct certain wrong impressions which were carry-overs from contacts with other missionaries. I think he was definitely impressed with our emphasis on supplementing existing transportation. He gave me more encouragement than I've had from him recently—said he felt that we'd get the concession, but that it would be limited. But that's OK; we've learned to move one step at a time.

A couple of weeks later, he had a follow-up comment.

The letter I've been drafting for the Governor (requesting a concession to operate on a near-private basis) has taken much more time than I had expected. And
a letter like that takes something out of you. For me, it's the toughest sort of
paperwork—especially when there is no one to hash it over with. But praise the
Lord, it is now finished. Claire typed the concession proposal last night and the
whole works goes in the mail tomorrow morning. Now I have to write a letter to
both [MAF] offices to go along with copies of it—explaining why I did what I did.
Some parts of it [the proposal] would not be very acceptable in Melbourne apart
from an explanation.

Once the proposal was in the mail, Charlie could turn his attention to other
matters, at least temporarily. He helped put a cement floor in a new C&MA
house (partly to communicate our thanks for being able to use the mess hall facilities). The truck needed repairs. And he was able to begin work on details related to setting up the pre-fab house—planning the basic construction, ordering
pipe and fittings for plumbing, locating suitable screen material, etc. To keep
things simple he limited plumbing fixtures to a kitchen sink, a shower head and
outside tap (faucet) fittings for the laundry, and arranged with two other families
living nearby to share one flush toilet between us—to be located in an outhouse-
type structure equidistant from all three houses.

After about a month in Sentani, we decided to take the plunge and buy a
kerosene refrigerator. We wrote about it to our parents:

This was our first attempt to live without one [a refrigerator]. It's by no means
impossible. Though we missed the cold water, that was not too drastic. The big
thing was that it limits one's diet. Either you can't fix certain things without a refrigerator, or things won't keep once they are open or started [partially used]. You find
yourself forced to eat things you can use up in one or two meals. All of us have lost
weight—and I [Charlie] am thinner than ever, so we need to do what we can to
regain some weight and try to stay healthy.

Not long after we got the refrigerator, we had an opportunity to buy a
kerosene pressure stove with a built-in oven. Charlie shepherded it through customs on a Friday, and Saturday night we had pie a la mode! We agreed we'd never
take either oven or refrigerator for granted again.

At the end of August we received a deluge of mail—seven letters from the L.A.
office arrived at once. Charlie reacted to their generally encouraging contents by
saying to our parents:

Some [contained] copies of our Articles of Incorporation and other things I
need to untangle the legal problems here…the office had confirmation from the

shipping company that the Fiji [ship] will sail to Lae on its next trip. It will also load at both L.A. and San Francisco, so we'll get our plane direct from L.A. to Lae [instead of its being routed through Australia]. That's really something! They have confirmed space on it for both the Pacer and the new replacement Cessna (the first Cessna is being sold). It also looks like there is some activity on the requests for personnel for DNG. And the floats are ready to ship. The cables involved information: I needed to get an import license here. There seems to be endless paperwork in this business. I made a special trip to town yesterday but didn't get the license, so I'll probably have to go again…I'm also working on getting visas for the Hutchins who will probably be coming here for a while.

Vic flew over in early September to resupply Sengge, and he and Charlie took that opportunity to bring each other up to date. The day after his visit (Thursday, Sept. 7th), Charlie left to accompany a group of missionaries from Sentani who were going by coastal vessel to spend a week with representatives of all the missions working in DNG. They were to assemble at Serui, on the island of Japen, not far from Noemfor—the island where Charlie, Vic, and Charles R. had stayed during their recent Bird's Head survey. If he could catch a ride from there after the conference with a government survey party, he thought he might be able to check several potential sub-base locations as they traveled by small motor launch along the coastal waters of the "neck" of DNG. He expected to be away about three weeks.

About the time he returned (early October, 1954), a news story broke. Some five Japanese soldiers, in hiding since WWII ended, were discovered living in a native village about 35 miles away. The story was of special interest to us, however, because MAF had been asked earlier (while we were in Wewak) to drop Japanese language leaflets urging any such soldiers to come out because the war was over. The request originated from a Christian couple in Japan concerned about their son. Charlie had begun working on the matter by going through channels to seek permission. But when newspapers in Sydney got ahold of the story and publicized it with a big splash, our request was firmly denied—and the idea dismissed as an absolute impossibility. So it was interesting to know that there actually were some Japanese soldiers still in hiding.

Also in early October a long flat box was delivered to us out at Sentani. It was our Kingstrand pre-fab house. As we eyed that box we could scarcely believe that all the necessary components for an entire 4-room house were packed inside. Assembling the house was rather like working with a giant-sized Erector™ set, with all its nuts and bolts. Surprisingly, in just two weeks' time—from when it was

delivered to the site, including two days Charlie spent in town on airplane matters and two afternoons spent at the swimming hole (when the fellows were too
tired to lift tools)—it was ready for us to move into. However, after feeling very
smug about spending only two weeks at it, we learned it was at least theoretical-
ly possible to erect such a house in just one day.

During the first week of construction, Charlie worked alone each morning laying the floor. When we bought the truck, we had also purchased its shipping
crate, which had been intentionally constructed (with re-use in mind) out of
Australian hardwood tongue-and-groove flooring. In measuring the panels,
Charlie found they could be arranged to fit almost exactly the width of the house;
and 2 x 4s from the crate's base would nicely fill the several remaining gaps. This
was a big job to tackle alone, but Charlie told himself it was easier than pouring
concrete. Afternoons, he had help from Bill Widbin and Paul Gesswein (of
Regions Beyond Missionary Union). Both Bill and Paul had erected Kingstrand
houses of their own so, in effect, served as technical consultants.

Additional help arrived at the end of the first week when Vic brought Bob
Hutchins along in the Wewak Pacer. These two were tied up with flights into
Sengge one day, but worked with Bill and Paul (who gave whole days the second week) and Charlie to get it to the point of being nearly finished by
Thursday. The roof was on, doors and windows hung (which had been assembled in the evenings down at our mess hall apartment), and odds and ends
were generally cleaned up for our move on Friday. Just before they left to
return to Wewak that Friday morning, Vic and Bob helped us move the refrigerator. It was too big to go through the doorway, but—no problem—it took only
about 10 minutes to remove a couple of aluminum panels, which allowed
room to spare. After moving the rest of our belongings, we slept in the new
house that night. Finishing touches like screens, remaining gussets (for rigidi-
ty), etc. had to wait until the following week—along with assembling the rest of
the pre-cut furniture, connecting the water, installing the kitchen sink, and a
few other details. We also had to finish putting the remaining nuts and bolts in
the centers of the wall panels—nuts and bolts that had been skipped temporarily since they weren't considered critical for strength. (Amazingly, a total of
over 5000 nuts and bolts held the house together!)

The rainy season couldn't have been more perfectly timed. Our first really
hard rain came shortly after we moved in. It was then that we discovered the roof
leaked! Charlie examined the roof and tightened all the bolts. When that didn't

entirely solve the problem, he spent nearly a whole day dabbing black roof cement around each bolt head. It worked—no more leaks!

Actually, Charlie had a reason for pushing hard to complete the finishing touches, for he had made reservations for the following Saturday's flight to the Philippines. He had decided it made sense to squeeze the Philippine survey trip into his schedule before the DNG Pacer arrived, since its arrival in Sentani had now been delayed until around Christmas. He reasoned that if he could gather data needed for considering service in the Philippines during November, he could be back in time to help Vic when he came to move UFM personnel into their new station in early December, near an airstrip the government was preparing for use. As the boys and I remained behind in Sentani, we wondered what he'd learn about the need for an MAF program in the Philippines. How might our schedule be affected as a result?

24
Time Out for the Philippines Survey

Manila seemed like "civilization" after living in New Guinea for a couple of years. Manila, however, was not Charlie's destination. Missions in two widely-separated areas had inquired about MAF's services. One was on the island of Luzon in the mountainous region north of Manila and the other on the southernmost island of Mindinao. In deciding to visit the area closest to Manila first, he and his missionary companion (from Far East Gospel Crusade, now SEND International) bought bus tickets to Baguio, the summer capitol of the Philippines.

At an elevation of 5,000 ft., Baguio's climate was considered perfect. The road from Manila to Baguio wound through a breathtaking canyon that, according to Charlie, made the Big Thompson Canyon in Colorado look as flat as Iowa (more or less!). From Baguio it was an eight-hour bus trip on to Bontoc. This particular leg of the trip proved to be quite an experience, as Charlie described it.

> The buses used beyond Baguio are all open on one side and have seats that extend the width. (I understand that on some routes both sides are open, which is very practical….) The roads are very narrow and buses have frequently gone over the sides. And what sides! Honestly, those roads hang onto the cliffs by their fingernails in some places.

The buses were built on truck chassis. There was some padding on the seats, but none for one's back. He continued,

> My hat is off to the drivers. I've heard some say that they are given to "Gillettes," but I couldn't say that. I rode in the front seat both to and from Bontoc. Those drivers really know, to the inch, where their wheels and fenders are. And they are not given to taking chances.…True, they seem to take the narrow corners pretty fast (where there is no chance to pass), while blaring their horns. But they're really not moving that fast; they're always in second or low gear, and the roar of the motor, coupled with the roughness and curving roads gives the illusion of speed. Several times when we did meet a truck right in the turn, both vehicles stopped

141

dead and had plenty of room to spare. I had the impression that the drivers are plenty sharp. Furthermore, they are doing a job I wouldn't care to tackle myself.

Headlines in the papers warned about a storm currently threatening Manila—typhoon Ruby, predicted to be the worst storm to hit Luzon in 10 years. Storms that severe inevitably affected travel conditions between Baguio and Bontoc by causing mudslides.

> We were not even half way to Bontoc when the cloudy weather became a drizzle and then the drizzle turned to rain. When we rounded a bend at the top of the 7,800 ft. pass (the highest in the Islands) the wind really howled. We pulled the curtains in the full-length "windows," but [the rain] still blew in around the edges.

> As we rounded the turn, we stopped dead. The sheer cliff rising on our left was not rock, but muddy shale. This is the place on the road that gives the most trouble. (A road is now being built "over the top" that will by-pass this bad spot.) We noticed that little bits of shale and mud were sliding, so the driver stopped to study the movement. Whenever it seemed to let up a bit, he would start to roll forward, then jam on the brake again as more broke loose. He must have repeated this at least a dozen times. It was a plenty "hard decision."

> Finally, when it seemed to settle down entirely, he jammed it into compound low and went roaring through. We all breathed easier. It was the only trouble we had with slides that day, though we did drive through a number of swollen waterfalls that spilled over the road. Still, we got to Bontoc pretty much on schedule....

Charlie and his missionary companion spent the night with Baptist missionaries in Bontoc. Next morning they were to leave there by bus for Banaue, ordinarily a trip that would have taken only 2½ hours. But weather continued to be a problem:

> ...when the rain turned to a drizzle by the next morning, we strolled to the bus station to inquire about the departure schedule. We learned that the bus hadn't come in the previous afternoon, apparently because of a slide. In fact, they had an unconfirmed report that there were three slides. So it wouldn't have been just a simple matter of having buses meet at the slide to transfer passengers. We decided to wait until the next day. A half an hour later someone came and told us that the maintenance truck (a nice new pickup) was following the bus to the first slide and would see that we got back if the bus couldn't get through....We got all our gear loaded on the bus again, and waited.

> Next we received an official report from the road engineer's office saying there were 22 slides between Bontoc and a certain town which was only half way to Banaue. (There were no reports beyond that town because the wires were down.) Of these 22 slides, three were not slides across the road; it was the road that was

sliding away! It looked hopeless, and we considered returning to Baguio right away since there was one bus that was yet to leave going in that direction.

We made one more attempt to call the fellow in Banaue to see if he could get to us in Bontoc by motorcycle (which is possible sometimes, even if buses can't get through). But the phone lines never opened, and we returned to Baguio on Wednesday morning, abundantly thankful for the way the Lord had led each step.

At the same time, we wondered about the other buses. During the first half of our trip back to Baguio, we saw few vehicles and no buses. The big question in our minds was: Where were the buses that left Baguio yesterday? (for none had arrived in Bontoc). Or, where were the ones that had left Bontoc but were turning back? Were they trapped between multiple slides? We had to wait for about a half-hour several times for a grader to clear a track through a small slide. Other slides covered only half the road, but there must have been a couple dozen of them. Then, about half way to Baguio we saw a lineup of vehicles waiting at a very muddy slide that had been opened, and where a truck had gotten stuck. While they were digging it out we noticed a bus on the other side headed this direction. When we talked to some of its passengers we found they had left Baguio just three hours after we left–on Monday. They had sat there in the bus all night Monday, all day Tuesday and all night Tuesday [night]. It was now 2 pm Wednesday, and they had the worst half of the trip ahead of them. Poor people! I'd have had double pneumonia by then with the sore throat I was developing.

Charlie continued to be impressed by the driver's ability. Wherever the roadbed was questionable–and there were several places–he asked the passengers to get out and walk across. He then drove the truck across. On one sharp curve Charlie's briefcase slid out of the bus–fortunately not on the side with the sheer drop! Despite the many delays–and the anxious moments that made their return to Manila seem interminable–they had made the return trip in ten hours, only two hours more than it normally took.

From Manila, Charlie went south by airline to Mindinao, the second largest (and southernmost) island of the Philippines. He visited missionaries in several cities–Davao, Cotabato and Zamboanga in particular–to assess with them the need for MAF's services. There was a lot of ground to cover in a short time. In the end, as he mulled over the situation, he came to the conclusion that needs there were not sufficient to warrant setting up a program–even when considering possible developments by the following summer. Apparently it was not yet the Lord's time for MAF to move ahead with planning a program in the Philippines.

Meanwhile, in Sentani, the boys and I tried to settle down to serious schoolwork each morning. It wasn't easy, with all the other time-consuming chores taking my attention. For example, it usually took me a whole afternoon (twice a week) to do our wash, even with a washing machine (of sorts). Our "washer" was a 44-gallon drum positioned on its side with two legs soldered at each end to provide stability. A section of its "up" side had been cut out so that a moveable paddle (attached to a pipe that was welded to the drum at each end) could be installed lengthwise. An upright pole connected to the paddle at one end served as a handle which one pushed and pulled to move the paddle to agitate the clothes in the drum. [This description is probably more complicated than was the simple "machine."] How long each load of clothes was agitated was determined arbitrarily. It could be decided by a tired arm, or by an impatient exclamation such as "Oh phooey, that's long enough!" Of course the water had to be changed for rinsing, and the wringing done by hand. By the time I had even a relatively small wash on the line (including time to heat the water in the first place, and cleaning up afterwards), three hours were gone.

The rainy season didn't make things easier, nor did it help that I was pregnant. At least in the Kingstrand we could close the shutters to keep the rain out. One of the missionaries who had lived for a time in the same mess hall rooms we had occupied told me that she had to wear a raincoat while preparing meals when it rained because the wind blew the rain crosswise through the screens "clear across the kitchen area!" Even if she stretched the account a little, I became fully aware of the effects of the wind this time of year.

November in the Baliem Valley was presenting a very different kind of weather problem—an unusually dry season. In fact, the missionaries living there began monitoring the river level very carefully, knowing that if it dropped below a certain level the Sealand would be unable to land safely. The plane was their lifeline; they depended on it for routine service, but also relied on it in case of emergencies. As a result, the lack of rain increased motivation for finding a place nearby where an airstrip could be built to accommodate wheel landings.

* * * * * * * * * *

Charlie returned from the Philippines at the end of November but had little time to relax. He finished the plumbing in our house, laid cement on the shower room floor, and accomplished a number of chores he had postponed until after his Philippines trip: cargo to clear through customs, including the floats for the Pacer, and a box containing a second (smaller) Kingstrand house. This smaller house was to be erected adjacent to our house, on the same cement slab, to house Bob and Betty Hutchins while they helped temporarily to get the DNG program underway. The plan was for them to ferry the Pacer to Sentani once its assembly in Madang was complete.

A "loose end" Charlie wanted to tie up during these few weeks before the Pacer's arrival involved a survey in southern Papua that had been put on hold for far too long. He suggested to Vic that they make that investigative trip together. As he considered the schedule, the timing seemed right, in that he would be able to rendezvous with the Hutchins in Madang once he and Vic finished the survey in southern Papua—which would, in turn, enable him to accompany the Hutchins on the flight to Sentani to deliver the new Pacer.

It was early in December that he got word that the DNG authorities had acted upon MAF's requested concession. So he scheduled a trip to Hollandia expecting to finalize that matter. Unfortunately, while in Hollandia, he learned another problem had surfaced that needed attention.

25
A Legal Snag

In mid-December (1954), when Charlie was granted an audience with the Governor of Dutch New Guinea, he found him agreeable to our operations. We were to receive a concession to operate for one year—provided we first cleared with KLM (the government owned airline) to make sure they had no plans to service the areas we expected to serve. Actually, this was only a formality, since we already knew that KLM had no such plans. Although the concession would carry the limitation of one year, we believed that by the end of that time we could prove our operations indispensable to the government. But to formalize our understanding, Charlie wrote a letter to KLM requesting clarification of their plans, and once again we settled down to wait.

During this waiting period, Vic flew in from Wewak accompanied by Doug McGraw from the AMAF office in Melbourne. Tensions between AMAF and MAF-US had surfaced again in recent months. Face to face discussions seemed the best solution. Along with routine supply trips to Sengge, the three fellows began their organizational discussions in Sentani and continued them as they set out together to conduct the frequently postponed survey of south Papua.

The trio got as far as Madang before they learned that the rainy season had created greater problems in the area of their destination than elsewhere, and therefore the survey once again had to be postponed. Disappointingly, earlier discussions in Sentani had left much to be desired, so the survey cancellation was beneficial in allowing additional time for further discussion toward a workable solution. Charlie commented,

> Doug, an Episcopalian, tends to see things in terms of "lines of authority," and Vic and I are knocking ourselves out trying to develop "teamwork." We find ourselves in agreement as to the need for authority, but we approach it differently, so there has been need for this kind of discussion.... Our aim all along has been to get AMAF on its feet to go it alone. But there are two limiting factors: Rome wasn't built in a day, and this field is growing so fast it's taking the resources of both organizations—so far—to keep up with it. Pressures for expansion are temptations, but quality growth is crucial in the first couple of years. AMAF is a smaller organization with fewer candidates than in the U.S. Field leadership will come

a bit slowly for them, and Vic (with his field experience) will be needed in the home office leadership. We have to plan realistically with all these things in mind. It may be a number of years before we can withdraw all our personnel. Yet, we've only committed two of our own couples here (Hutchins and Steigers). That's not bad juggling: to keep four planes going (some definitely requiring more than one pilot), process a constant stream of newcomers, and develop a new organization in the process.

In Madang, Charlie met Dave and Janet Steiger who, with their three children, had just arrived from the States. They were to join us in DNG after first helping in the Lutheran program for a few months.

Another piece of exciting news was the presence of the DNG Pacer. In fact, it was already assembled and ready for its flight from Madang to Sentani (DNG). This was quite a Christmas present—the Pacer together with its passengers (Charlie and the Hutchins). Incidentally, on this our third Christmas in New Guinea, our MAF families now numbered eight! We had grown from two MAF-US families our first Christmas in New Guinea to five families the second Christmas, which included one AMAF family, and now we were eight families—*three* of which were AMAF families!

During the two weeks that followed the plane's arrival in Sentani (while we waited for the final papers giving MAF official permission to operate) two emergencies arose that emphasized the need to be fully operational as soon as possible. The first incident involved the Sealand. It had hit something submerged while landing on the Baliem River. The men were able to beach the plane in order to examine the hull, and found only a good-sized dent—no hole or tear—which they were able to "bang out." It was then flown back safely to Sentani for more comprehensive repairs. Had the damage been worse, the folk in the Baliem could very well have been stranded—to say nothing of the repairs being more complicated in such a remote place.

We learned of the other incident by way of an emergency call from Sengge. A local policeman had fallen out of a tree at Waris and had been carried as far as Sengge (more than a day's walk), but he needed hospitalization. We were able to secure special permission for that evacuation flight and fly the injured man to the coast for treatment. Interestingly, this was not only the DNG Pacer's first flight, but it was our first opportunity to serve the Dutch government as well.

Not long after that flight, Charlie received the expected response from KLM. He immediately made an appointment to see the Government

Secretary, assuming the concession was practically in hand. But, believe it or not, we ran into another hurdle—a complicated legal matter this time. Before the concession could be granted, MAF in DNG needed to operate as a Dutch corporation!

Charlie hurriedly typed out a letter to the L.A. office, hoping for fast action. This requirement also produced a chain reaction. MAF not only had to choose a Dutch name: Zendings Luchtvaart Vereniging (Missionary Aviation Society), but also prepare incorporation papers in the Dutch language, and provide adequate translation. All this of course would take additional time. First of all, it sent Charlie digging for Dutch words. He also looked for some help.

While waiting to hear from L.A., there were a number of other things that could be undertaken. The smaller Kingstrand house had to be erected. (Bob and Betty were living temporarily in the old mess hall where we had lived when we first arrived.) Storage shelves needed to be built, for airplane parts and tools. Then, all those spare parts and tools had to be organized and arranged on the shelves. The floats waited at the dock to be transported to Sentani; and we needed some kind of rig—a platform with wheels, or some sort of "dolly"— to move the plane (when on floats) between the hangar and launching site at Lake Sentani, two miles away. A decision was made to have a trailer built for this purpose.

Bob began assembling the floats, and Charlie tackled the paperwork for Steigers' visas and began a search for housing for them. On a personal level, we needed to inquire about hospital arrangements for the birth of our fourth child due early in May. After some initial concern, we heard that the military hospital (formerly General MacArthur's headquarters during WWII) four miles away would be opening its facilities to civilians soon. This was wonderful news! Not only was it a newer facility, but it was much closer than the alternative hospital, 14 miles away.

❊ ❊ ❊ ❊ ❊ ❊ ❊ ❊ ❊ ❊ ❊

Some administrative responsibilities inevitably caused greater stress for Charlie than others. One sentence in a letter to our parents indicates the depth of his concern about AMAF/MAF-US relationships. He commented, "Sometimes it looks like this two years' work is sitting on the edge of the drain." Then he added, as if to remind himself, "But the Lord is still on the throne—I refuse to despair."

He noticed he was slowing down when it came to desk work, and spoke of this in a letter to our families:

> Jim Truxton was suggesting in a letter the other day that he thinks we should be getting a break again. He sensed from letters about our problems with AMAF that it was beginning to get us down. It's true that we get "down" a lot easier these days. And I don't have to overwork as much before I begin feeling my old problems (headaches, etc.) again. We're sure glad our return home isn't too far away anymore—not so much because of personal desire as in recognition of the fact that we cannot do a decent job of these delicate negotiations (with the government as well) when we are so tired.
>
> Still, there are some very touchy jobs yet left before we could possibly go home, so we can't just live for that day. I guess we'll have to take a break. The problem is where and how. The only answer to the first, I fear, is to stay right here. If I don't get something from the office on the corporation business tomorrow, we'll have a rather enforced vacation—for there can't be any more mail for 10 days after that....

We did see a slower pace over the next 10 days because the eagerly awaited mail did not come, and Charlie was able to accept the fact that the Lord no doubt intended the delay to allow for recuperative purposes.

The letter with the needed resolution finally arrived on February 23, 1955. (It had been mailed almost three weeks earlier, on February 4th!) Naturally, he immediately took it to the government lawyers, who assured him they would try to have a draft in English ready by the following Monday. He planned an additional trip into town so he could talk it over with them before they translated it into Dutch.

Once again we were hopeful. But, being realistic, we suspected the incorporation could still take about a week. The concession itself (dependent upon MAF's being incorporated) could take another week. That being the case, we would only have a one-week margin until the need to fly became critical. In the interim we submitted an application (laboriously prepared in Dutch), and subsequently gained permission to affix the new registration letters. Just before the U.S. registration numerals were deleted, one more previously permitted flight was made into Sengge (on wheels) before the masking was done for the new letters (JZ-PTB). Then it would be time to put the plane on floats. Charlie had estimated two weeks would be needed to practice water-landings since neither he nor Bob had yet flown a float plane. Both believed at least that much practice was mandatory before they were ready to make flights inland.

One day followed another and the schedule tightened. Our patience was wearing thin because we knew Hans Veldhuis (who had trekked in with the UFM missionary party to Archbold Lake) was having back problems and was eager to be brought out to Sentani for medical help. That small lake had been landed on for the first time in 1938 by members of the Archbold expedition, and no plane had landed there since. The UFM men, taken into the Baliem Valley in the Sealand some weeks earlier, had walked overland to a population center near Archbold Lake, where they set up camp. In preparation for establishing their new mission station there, the men began to fell trees at one end of the lake to clear an approach for a water landing by the Pacer. The Sealand had kept them supplied by air drops but was too large to land on the Lake.

Charlie continued consultations with the doctor. After a number of visits and tests, the doctor concluded his problem was not ulcers; and he found no evidence of amoeba. Charlie began to wonder whether it might be malaria after all. As a precaution, he decided to take maximum doses of anti-malarial drugs for a few days. This provided slight relief, but the daily stomach cramps continued and became quite severe at times. The doctor suggested a few other tests when the tests for malaria proved negative. However, without a definitive diagnosis, it was hard to know how to deal with the physical problems. They were a real nuisance when there was so much to do.

When visas for the Steigers were granted and housing arranged, Charlie wired them to come from Madang on the next Qantas flight, March 9th. (Qantas had only recently extended air service beyond Wewak with a bi-weekly flight to Sentani.) The Steigers had been assigned to take over the DNG program, which meant we would be relieved and our New Guinea assignment would be at an end. Charlie was determined to schedule a good overlap period with the Steigers. He commented,

> We originally planned a six-month overlap with Steigers, but that has been cut to four. But since this is a more difficult program than any so far, we can hardly cut it below that. There's so much invested here (sweat and tears, even more than money—plus the eternal fruit yet to be harvested) that we must not leave the job poorly done or we'd always regret it. A firm foundation means everything!

More trips to town followed: to check on the progress of the legal matters, and to follow-up on the building of the trailer to transport the float plane. It was increasingly hard to be patient. The men at Archbold Lake were growing restless, eager for the Pacer's arrival. By the time the trailer was ready, Bob and

Charlie had located and bought a surplus chain hoist ("for a mere $40"). It was a Yale & Towne hoist, in good condition. Charlie estimated it may have cost several hundred dollars originally. The fellows rigged the hoist, made their last trip on wheels to Sengge, and—finally—were ready to make the switch from wheels to floats.

Then, just as things seemed to be falling into place, we received an unexpected call from the immigration office: Steigers' arrival could be delayed because immigration needed clearance from the consul in Sydney first. If it wasn't received in time, the Steigers would be forced to wait for the next flight—two weeks later!

Charlie immediately began to explore alternative ways to get them to Sentani. He couldn't go get them—the plane would be on floats waiting to make that urgent Archbold trip. Should he perhaps ask Vic to bring them over in the Wewak Pacer? That would certainly have an added advantage of giving opportunity to confer with Vic. But…it would be far preferable if they could arrive as scheduled on the Qantas flight. Tension mounted for everyone. On March 6th, Charlie wrote,

> It seems so much is about to happen. But oh, the paperwork! We really made great strides this past week. First they made up the articles of incorporation in English. Then I went over them and found that they were very much to our liking—nice and simple. So they put them in Dutch and typed them up along with a letter to His Excellency (also in Dutch) asking for his approval. (That took a hundred guilder stamp—about $28.) It then went before the Governor. I'm supposed to call tomorrow to see if he signed it. I also submitted another letter to him asking for the concession (the former had been tentative—this is the formal request) and for exemptions from certain laws (one, that planes can only land on licensed airdromes—we'll have permission to land anywhere; the other, that local corporations must be made up of Dutch residents). It's all very interesting. But now it's only a matter of time—and process. We've been fairly well promised that we can make inland flights as soon as we're ready.…

When would that be?

26
The Float Plane Sees Action

Cause for rejoicing! Not only did the Steigers arrive on March 9th, 1995 (on schedule), but that date coincided almost exactly with our putting the Pacer on floats. On the 13th, Charlie was exuberant. He wrote,

In spite of many obstacles, we're on floats and flying! Monday morning we made our last trip [on wheels] to Sengge. Then we got everything ready for lifting the plane, and were going to do so Tuesday morning, but the surplus chain hoist I had purchased had the wrong chain on it. So I got up before dawn Tuesday and was in the Haven (an hour's drive) when things opened up at 7am. By 10:00 I was on my way home with the chain—got it at the least likely place, and they had only one size chain, but it was perfect! We had the plane lifted by 12 and had it completely on floats by 6pm. But not without further difficulty. The outside chain (the one you pull on) turned out to be slightly wrong size, too. We had to work it very carefully. It slipped once—dropping the plane about an inch and a half. But no damage was done, for which we praise the Lord. It was a gruelling day!

Wednesday we hooked up cables and generally got the plane ready for launching. Thursday morning I flew into the Baliem with Al [Lewis] in the Sealand. (Dick [Lenehan] couldn't go and Al prefers to fly with another crew member along. Actually, that was the least we could do when Al was giving his afternoons to check Bob and me out [on float flying].)

While we were gone, Bob, Dave (who arrived with his family the afternoon before—at 6:20pm!!!) and Bill [Widbin] hauled the plane down to the lake and launched it. They finished this just as we got back about 11:30am. By 1:30 we were underway with our practice flying [on floats]. I put in over two hours and Bob one hour (with Al) that afternoon. We each got another hour on Friday afternoon. Al had to leave for the Wissel Lakes this morning, so we'll be doing solo practice on Lake Sentani this week and then Al will check us out when he gets back.

We will have to give all the time possible to this practice. The fellows at Archbold are getting very eager to have a plane. They haven't called it an emergency yet, but they're getting jittery, so we must give full priority to this need....We'll have to make quite a few trips to get several of their carriers out. From our practice so far, and after seeing the Lake from the air, I'd say that we'll easily get out with one passenger—possibly two light carriers—at a time. They've cut the trees all the way to the river at the end we take off over. Then, as soon as we get these carriers out, we've got to dash up to Manokwari to take care of TEAM's needs—then back to put the plane back on wheels, both for drops out of Manokwari and for a probable few trips to Sengge.

In addition to the hours of practice on floats, Charlie drove to Hollandia to apply for residence papers for the Steigers and to check with the lawyer. He found the Governor had signed not only our corporation papers but also the necessary exemptions. Charlie was now the proud possessor of the official document, complete with government seal that affirmed MAF as a Dutch corporation. With this much in hand we were now free to begin operations, even though getting the formal approval for the concession might take a couple more weeks.

On top of all this good news, Charlie was praising the Lord for somewhat improved health; he felt better that week than he had in months. Although he was very tired by the end of the week, his aches seemed to have subsided, at least temporarily.

Because of the pressures to get the plane flying, the Steigers spent their first couple of nights with us. We borrowed five cots and managed to fit them all in our livingroom—after moving tables, chairs and everything else out into the kitchen or up against the side walls. We also worked in a celebration for three birthdays during those first few hectic days; for Miriam Steiger, and for two of our boys (John and Gordon). When things calmed down slightly, the Steiger family moved into the two rooms in the mess hall. Where else? Didn't all MAFers begin life in Sentani in that old mess hall?

Practicing on floats filled the morning hours—before the wind picked up and became too strong. Afternoons, the fellows did their airplane checks, fueling, etc. Alarms went off at 5am and the fellows took lunches and stayed through until 2pm, when they came home to rest briefly before returning to work until dark. After showers and the evening meal, they practically fell into bed.

Al Lewis returned from the Wissel Lakes at the end of the week and took time on Saturday morning to check out both Charlie and Bob. That same afternoon the two pilots headed for Hollandia to see the Director of Civil Aviation who gave them the go-ahead for their first flight to Archbold the next day (Sunday). Normally MAF did not originate flights on Sunday, but Hans' back trouble had been getting progressively worse the past weeks and he was more than eager for medical attention. For Charlie, this was an especially significant occasion; we had planned and waited so long for this day. The weather seemed to provide a serious note as I tried to describe it to our parents:

> It was quite a dark day to begin with—had been raining most of the night, and hadn't yet stopped altogether. From a radio conversation with the fellows at Archbold at 7am, we learned that the weather there was the same. It was decided they would have another radio contact at 8am before making the final decision about going ahead with the flight.
>
> After talking again with the fellows at Archbold, and talking to the folk in the Baliem and to Al Lewis who flies quite near Archbold on his frequent trips into the Baliem, Charlie and Bob decided to give it a try. Their plan was for Bob to stay at Archbold so Hans could come out. The float plane can't carry as much payload as the wheel plane, and the higher altitude limited it further.
>
> Charlie first tried a solo takeoff, then a takeoff with Bob before he brought Hans out. They made it fine, getting back to Lake Sentani at about 1:30pm. It was quite a thrill for Charlie to be in the second plane ever to land on Archbold Lake—and the first one in 17 years since the [original] Archbold Expedition.

On one of their initial flights into Archbold, Charlie and Bob spent an hour conducting a survey of the area and picked out an excellent airstrip site much closer than the lake to the population center. They hoped it wouldn't be too long until they could supply that area (and future areas) by wheel-plane since the weight of the floats considerably limited loading. (The floats alone weighed 245 lbs., compared with 80 lbs. for the wheels.) Of course once the procedures for switching between floats and wheels became routine, it would undoubtedly take less time. Still, the sooner airstrips were built, the better MAF could serve.

Flying with floats wasn't the kind of flying that allowed pilots to relax, as Charlie noted:

> You have to be on your toes every second during the takeoff, and until you've made your turn-around and are heading down the canyon. The last trip in, after making the survey, I was making the final takeoff about noon and a fairly strong crosswind had sprung up. It gave me a few anxious moments, but we made it with a good margin. The carrier I was taking out was pretty apprehensive about the whole proceeding.

Once supply flights at Archbold were cared for, Charlie and Dave left for Manokwari (in the Bird's Head). Missionaries from TEAM (The Evangelical Alliance Mission) had asked to be taken to one of the two interior Anggi Lakes. (This was another instance where there had been only one previous landing.) Since it would take several trips to transport the mission party and all their gear to the lake, the two pilots expected to spend a few days in Manokwari. And because the party had to trek from the lake to the site they had chosen for their base, the plane would be able to return to Sentani to work temporarily and make the switch to wheels before returning to Manokwari to drop supplies at the missionaries' destination.

Rather unexpectedly, Bob and Betty had to return to Madang in early April in response to a wire requesting his help in overseeing maintenance. At that point Bob became a permanent part of the Lutheran program, heading up their aviation department. And we concentrated on helping the Steigers get set to take over the DNG program responsibilities on their own.

This was MAF's first float plane operation—and flying a plane with floats was new to both Charlie and Dave. Charlie found it most interesting, often fun, sometimes frustrating, but always challenging.

27
Service to the Bird's Head

Charlie and Dave found the missionaries in Manokwari ready and waiting to be taken to Lake Anggi Gigi. Of the two Anggi lakes, Gigi's elevation was 6,100 ft.—somewhat higher than near-by Gita's. Charlie wondered how the Pacer would perform at that altitude. He wasn't concerned about landing the plane; the lake was plenty long. It was the takeoff that might present a problem. Perhaps after the first landing it would be wise to try a takeoff with the load he brought in before the plane was unloaded completely. However, when he tried a takeoff, it didn't work; he couldn't even get the plane up *on the step* (the preparatory stage for getting the floats to lift off the water).

For his second takeoff try, he unloaded 70 lbs. of baggage and took only one passenger. That time he got the plane airborne, but he said he had to "walk it up onto the step" to do it. There was no danger of running out of room—the lake was three to four miles long. So, once he managed to get the plane on the step, it lifted off easily.

It took several trips to deliver the missionaries and their gear to Anggi Gigi. From there the missionary party set out on foot for the site of their new station (Tistega). They expected the trek to take several days and arranged for the plane to drop supplies to them once they were situated. Those several days gave Dave and Charlie time to return to Sentani to restock the men at Archbold Lake before they switched from floats in order to make the supply drops from the plane on wheels.

The switch to wheels had only just been completed when a wire arrived from Manokwari with an urgent request. One of the women who had made the trek from Anggi Gigi to Tistega (the new station) had broken her ankle. Could MAF send the plane back to Manokwari immediately to fly a doctor to Anggi Lake? Responding to the emergency, the fellows hurriedly switched back to floats and prepared to leave early the next morning.

At first the weather for the flight that morning looked bad; but after it improved later in the morning, the fellows set out—about noon. Once they cleared the Sentani area, the weather gradually improved and eventually became beautiful. Despite a strong headwind they made the trip in good time (and with almost an hour's worth of fuel left). But there was not enough daylight to continue on to Anggi Gigi with the doctor.

The next morning they flew first to the new station (Tistega) to drop a few small medical parcels—plaster of paris for the cast and that sort of thing—before landing at the lake with the doctor. The fellows hated to think of his three- to four-day walk to get there. As for the patient, it must have been a frightfully long time to wait for a response to a medical emergency! Might there be a suitable place nearby that would lend itself to easy construction of a landing strip? The two pilots searched the area carefully on their way back to Manokwari, but found nothing that seemed right.

Back in Sentani, they were met with requests for additional flights to Archbold Lake. But they had to keep in mind that they'd be summoned back to Manokwari any day to bring the doctor back out—and perhaps the patient as well.

After a few days of hearing nothing, they went ahead with the change to wheels, thinking they could make some supply trips to Sengge while they waited. Wouldn't you know, once the wheels were on, the apparently-delayed wire arrived. Hurriedly, they switched back to floats, but decided to take the wheels along. If they could somehow arrange a switch to wheels in Manokwari (after first bringing the doctor out, using floats), this would enable them to make the planned drops at Tistega on the same trip (i.e., without first returning to Sentani to make the switch to wheels).

Due to the delayed wire, the trip back to Manokwari had become urgent. Supplies at Tistega were running low—they had counted on being resupplied earlier by the drops. Although we were unsure about the patient's need to be evacuated, we were aware that the doctor's wife (in Manokwari) was confined to bed in her final weeks of pregnancy. So he needed to get home. (I could empathize, because I was hoping Charlie would be in Sentani for the birth of our baby, due very soon. In fact, we had calculated that, if everything happened on schedule, Charlie's return would allow a margin of three days. At the same time, both of us knew MAF's schedules were unpredictable. But then, so too were babies' arrivals!)

On the lighter side, the fellows ran into a very embarrassing situation while refueling at Biak on this particular trip to Manokwari. Charlie's account:

> We pulled a dumb stunt in Biak … we got stuck while refueling. I had even taken the precaution of asking one of the sailors (you'd think they'd know) whether

the tide was going out or coming in. He said it was coming in. Well, he was dead wrong. Anyway, we did get planks under the keels and saved some scratches. Then, when we got to Manokwari, the tide was way out—in fact, it was one of the lowest tides of the year; we waded around in muck.

Although that blunder delayed their arrival in Manokwari, Charlie did take off for Anggi Gigi yet that afternoon. The weather in the Highlands, while not too promising, was within limits. But where was the doctor? Charlie glanced at his watch. Obviously, time was a factor. It getting late in the afternoon; they would need to load and take off quickly. He circled the area twice before spotting him, and then descended to land.

The doctor, however, in realizing the time, had given up on the plane's coming yet that afternoon; he was busy fixing his supper. So it took extra time to gather his belongings. By this time it was approaching six o'clock. Although official darkness was pegged at 6:40 p.m., Charlie knew they'd have sufficient light up until 7:00. He described his feelings as he looked first at the doctor and his belongings, and then at his watch as he started to load the plane:

> First came a tin box, then a bedroll. Many minutes later there came two more tin boxes. But the Doc is a swell understanding fellow. He knew it would probably be too much. He had already arranged to possibly leave one [box] that was mostly food. In the other one he had about 10 lbs. of potatoes to take home. We had to leave those. His jungle boots were just about shot, so he took them off and gave them to a carrier. In the end we weighed in at 230 lbs., for a gross of something over 1,780, which was getting up toward full gross.

> There was little or no wind, and what there was was indeterminate. In reflection, I'm quite sure we had a slight tailwind the first part of our run (trying to get on the step) but, just before breaking water we got a slight wind on the nose. In both cases, however, the wind was very slight.

The takeoff itself was a real thrill. Charlie said he doubted he'd ever forget that particular takeoff run. He was so thankful for plenty of room. They needed it! He recounted the experience in its entirety:

> At first the bows just wouldn't come up. Once I thought I felt them inch up just a bit, so I held on. They inched up just a bit more. But after several such small gains I looked down and saw that the spray was fairly far back, even though it didn't feel like it was ready to go on the step. I shoved the wheel forward. That didn't do it either, but neither did the plane squash back in the water. I knew we were getting somewhere.

By now we had probably run a quarter of a mile, but with miles ahead of us, that was no worry. I rocked it back and forth a few times and by then I felt the bows were fully up. Then I started walking the rudders. Quick strokes had no effect, so I made some strong, long yaws. On the second swing left, I was certain I felt the right float come up. So I swung really hard right, and there was no question but what we were on the step—though seemingly drawing more water than usual.

The planing was sloppy, but it was planing. At 40 mph it seemed to quit gaining, so I pulled full flaps and yanked. I didn't make it. But as I came back to planing position, I seemed to be riding on top of the water in normal planing position. From then on I knew we had it made. It was at that point I think we also picked up the slight headwind.

I had considered making a step-turn to try to take off the other way (there's gobs of room). But, in any case, I was not going to cut the throttle and let it down off the step. When I realized I was really planing, I kept straight ahead. So in just a few hundred feet more, when we had 43 mph, I jerked full flaps and we were off. We staggered to be sure but didn't touch the water again. There was another shout of praise! It was the most-fun takeoff that I ever hope to have—but I really had to work for it….We climbed up to 9,500 ft. and made our way to Manokwari.

The next day, everything clicked for the change to wheels. The tide was in—which was essential because of the big rocks. And because the sea was calm, the plane could be taxied to the beach on the step. Getting the plane out of the water, however, was not so easy. They finally managed to wedge it between some big chunks of coral that wouldn't budge. Chuck Preston (of TEAM) held the plane down firmly so it wouldn't lift with the rising tide, and Charlie took the fairings off so it would be ready to hoist.

Just then they spotted the mobile crane they had arranged for, though it was barely visible in the distance. Just behind the crane in an old Japanese truck was Dave, with Harold Lovestrand (another TEAM missionary), bringing the Pacer's wheels. The four men shared some anxious moments watching as the crane got stuck in the soft ground, with 100 yards to go. They could think of only two things: the charge per hour for the crane; and, more importantly, the possibility that the crane operators would become so discouraged on this occasion that they'd refuse to return when it came time to switch back to floats for the return to Sentani.

Thankfully, it took only about five minutes to free the crane. Ten minutes later the crane had the plane dangling from its hook—like a toothpick. The operators swung it around and, with Charlie and Dave guiding the wings, lowered it gently to within about an inch of the ground. It didn't take long to get the bolts out, put on the few fairings and fill the brakes. They pushed it over the soft ground, and from there Charlie taxied it slowly to the field while the others steadied the wings.

After lunch they fueled and loaded the plane, washed it down with fresh water to remove the salt residue, and brought the floats to store near the plane overnight. By then they were too tired to wash the salt from the floats, but a good hard all-night rain took care of that.

The next morning the fellows were up at 5am, hoping for a 6:30 takeoff for the first drop. But because it took longer than expected to load the truck with everything for the several drops, they weren't actually airborne until 7am. Both pilots thought making those drops was actually *fun*:

> Round trips took us only an hour and a quarter, including almost 15 minutes over the "target area." We averaged 17 minutes on the ground between trips for refueling and reloading. Although there were three of us doing the drops, we had to stack the stuff pretty carefully to be sure we could get back amongst the cargo and get the stuff out in the proper order. It was quite a trick. But to use Edison's words, "We didn't work today—it was all fun."

> I flew the first trip with Dave dropping; then we alternated the rest of the day. We didn't get down too low the first trip; we wanted to feel our way along for the best way to get at the target circle. It wasn't an easy place to drop—on a narrow, sloping ridge that also undulates. We had to keep losing altitude while cutting back our speed. (I took the turn at 80 and cut down to 70 for the drop proper.) But still we tried to keep some power on so that it would catch solidly when we "poured the coal to it" right after the release. If the release is too soon, the packages are apt to hit a mound, which gives them quite a shock. If the release is too late, the packages roll way down in the bush. I think we only hit the knoll with about three or four, and only about four rolled into the bush. Anyway, they let us know they got them all, and very little was broken. All in all, I guess we must have dropped about 40 packages today, averaging about 40 lbs. each.

> We did discover one occupational hazard of this business: cold! With the door off, it's pleasant just up to about 3,000 or 4,000 ft. Above 5,000 ft. it gets chilly, and above 7,000 ft. we shivered even with the cabin heat on (which doesn't really do much good—just gives you hot feet and leaves you shivering). Tomorrow we definitely take sweaters.

It turned out there were four more loads to drop than the fellows originally thought, which meant taking an extra day (Friday) to finish up—assuming everything went without a hitch. There was, however, one slight problem. The crane and its operators would not be available on Saturday (April 30th), because that was Queen Juliana's birthday—a holiday. Which meant that Charlie and Dave would have to spend the weekend in Manokwari and make the switch back to floats early Monday.

Accepting this fact, the two pilots began to relax after their Thursday drops and to reflect on the day. Both had noticed (though independently) that the TEAM fellows seemed to prefer that the pilots handle the drops. At first they weren't sure why, because they didn't seem afraid or unwilling. Then it dawned on them: the missionaries may have realized that the combined weight of the pilots came to 290 lbs. while the TEAM fellows weighted 185 pounds—each! So there was actually more payload available if the pilots made the drops. Understandable, but somewhat amusing.

As the two pilots drifted off to sleep anticipating another interesting and enjoyable day, they were unaware of the tragic event that had already occurred —an event that was going to sadden the entire missionary community and have a profound impact on MAF's future in Dutch New Guinea.

28
The Search

The date was Friday, April 29, 1955. Charlie took off for the first drop early that morning accompanied by one of the TEAM fellows. By then the procedure for shoving the cargo out the open door was almost routine. They watched, satisfied to see the supplies fall close to the target area. Then, with the first drop completed, Charlie turned to head back to Manokwari.

Suddenly, as he adjusted his earphones to listen to radio reports, the usual chatter was interrupted by a piece of unbelievable news. The Sealand was missing! It had left Sentani for the Baliem Valley the previous morning (Thursday), but failed to arrive. Apparently the last radio contact with the pilot, Al Lewis, came a half hour before his expected landing on the Baliem River. Since then—silence. The news report ended with an urgent request directed to the Pacer pilots. Would they please return to Sentani as soon as possible to join the search.

Actually, the search was already under way. The Dutch government responded immediately to first reports by ordering one of its Navy twin-engine Catalinas to begin searching. Although the Catalina and its crew took off as early as 2pm that Thursday, its flight from the naval base in Biak to the search area near the Sealand's Baliem destination took three hours. That meant only about an hour of daylight remained in which to search. Disappointingly, they found no sign of the Sealand in that short time. Then, instead of returning the long distance to Biak, the crew flew the plane to Sentani to base there for as long as the search continued.

Meanwhile, stunned by the grim news he just heard, Charlie instinctively grabbed the Pacer's microphone and pressed the button to radio Manokwari. He asked the operators there to contact Dave immediately—"ask him to get the crane in place and the floats ready for a quick switch."

Dave had everything in place when Charlie touched down in Manokwari. The switch to floats was made without incident, and, with the wheels stowed aboard, they were ready for takeoff shortly after noon. Normally the flight east from Manokwari to Sentani took 5-6 hours, but that day the Lord provided a tailwind that enabled them to get back to Sentani around 6pm, including the stop in Biak for fuel.

After landing on Lake Sentani, they taxied across to where the plane's transportation trailer waited. Charlie also spotted Mr. Troutman, head of C&MA's New Guinea field staff, who had arrived earlier in the day from his station at the Wissel Lakes. Together, he and Charlie rushed to the radio at the airstrip to talk to the missionaries in the Baliem, leaving Dave, with Bill Widbin's help, to get the plane out of the water and towed back to the hangar. There they installed the extra gas tank and refueled for the search that would begin the next morning (Saturday).

Although 6pm was not the regularly scheduled hour for radio communications with the Baliem folk, the Catalina—during its initial search that Friday afternoon—had dropped a note asking them to make radio contact with Sentani at that time. Static interference made communication very difficult. They didn't talk long, but it became obvious they did not yet know the Sealand was missing. They had assumed when Al didn't arrive on Thursday that bad weather had prevented him from getting through. Because it was essential that they be in on discussions about the situation, Mr. Troutman told them to expect the Pacer the next morning (Saturday). Charlie was glad he was not totally unfamiliar with landing and takeoff procedures at the Baliem. His recent trip accompanying Al in the Sealand now took on added significance, and seemed providential.

Both Charlie and Dave were exhausted when they showed up at home for supper about 7:00. Friday had been a long day. Yet there was a kind of restlessness—a feeling of being at loose ends, of wanting to do something when there was nothing anyone could do—until morning. We were preparing for bed when a caller arrived to brief Charlie on the search thus far. Showing obvious concern, he pointed out on a map the areas the Catalina had already covered in its afternoon search. This was most helpful.

Alarms were set for 4am Saturday morning. Because it took time to tow the plane to the lake and transfer the plane from the trailer into the water, the two pilots didn't get airborne until close to 6am. They searched carefully along the route used to get to the Baliem, but saw nothing of the Sealand. Dick Lenehan, the Sealand's mechanic, met them as they landed on the river. Dick had flown in with Al the day before the plane disappeared, to take a little break for a couple days.

Discussions focused first on how to meet the needs for continuing service. All recognized the much smaller capacity of the Pacer when compared with that of the Sealand. Just what were the priorities? How could MAF best meet them? Answers were not immediately clear, although all agreed that the Baliem station must somehow stay open and continue to be supplied. It was decided that Dick should return to Sentani—his help in searching on the way back to Sentani would be especially valuable since he had flown with Al many times and knew the route. However, because the Pacer could take only one passenger out at a time, Dave stayed behind and spent the night in the Baliem. Charlie planned to return for him the next day.

Along the way to Sentani, Dick and Charlie searched in and out of valleys, but saw no trace. The Catalina meanwhile searched along the Edinburgh River. Another float plane, a Beaver operated by KLM, joined the search late that day. At the end of the day the pilots of the various search planes (Pacer, Beaver and Catalina) met together to coordinate plans for the next day's more thorough search.

Charlie was up again at 4:30am on Sunday and managed a 6am takeoff, with the help of Bill Widbin. Myron Bromley, a C&MA missionary who had been waiting in Sentani to be taken into the Baliem, helped search along the way. Sadly, even with three planes searching all day, no trace was found of the Sealand. Hope for Al's survival was dwindling. Yet, where was he?

The search remained a top priority as concern for Al's safety—and survival—increased. I couldn't help thinking this was a most awkward time for the Mellis' expected baby to be due. I also realized that babies many times arrive during crisis situations. Privately, Charlie and I had prayed about this, asking the Lord to time our baby's arrival at a "least inconvenient" time—whenever that was. But all of us were praying for Al, for his wife Mary, and for those involved in the search.

The intense concentration and strenuous flying produced considerable emotional drain. The pilots' fatigue was building. Reluctantly, after four straight days of searching (Saturday through Tuesday), Charlie and Dave felt compelled to rest for a day, despite the fact that each passing day meant finding Al alive was less likely.

This decision was made late Tuesday afternoon, and the Lord timed the birth of our fourth son Gilbert early on Wednesday morning—that "rest" day! So Charlie was able to be present during his birth, and could rest for the remainder of that day before resuming the search with Dave on Thursday morning.

That was the day rumors began to circulate that the Catalina's participation in the search was to be cancelled. Charlie hoped that wasn't true, even though the designated area had been thoroughly searched. It was disappointing to think of losing their help, but the search should go on. Charlie decided to ask Vic to come across in the Wewak Pacer and bring Bob Hutchins to help. There was one ridge they had not been able to check because it rose too high, beyond the float plane's capability. This would be only a short flight, but the presence of the Pacer on wheels would also enable them to catch up on "wheel-work" that had accumulated. It would also allow the plane on floats to focus specifically on meeting the needs at the two water landing sites: Baliem and Archbold. Moreover, with all four pilots on hand (Charlie, Vic, Dave and Bob), they together could plan a strategy for meeting the needs in DNG in the light of the Sealand's loss. All four realized that MAF would, temporarily at least, need to assume responsibility for C&MA's needs by incorporating them into MAF's services.

As Charlie pondered the situation in the western half of the island (DNG), he realized C&MA's Wissel Lakes area could no doubt be served once again (as they had been before the Sealand's arrival) by the KLM Catalinas—at least for a while. It was the Baliem that needed MAF's attention. Charlie's discussions with C&MA's field leadership led to an idea for an interim plan: MAF would care for the flight needs for the next few months while the mission developed its replacement plan. At the same time, everyone recognized that the little Pacer on floats—even with regularly scheduled help from the Wewak Pacer—would be woefully inadequate for the task. Charlie wrote,

> Everyone is holding his breath hoping that the government won't order C&MA out of the Baliem because of the lack of a supply line, and [lack of] evacuation possibilities. The gang in there is pushing ahead on a small airstrip from which we could probably evacuate three at once—if we could use wheels.

As Charlie thought in terms of possible governmental limitations, his mind drifted to other related matters: the need for airstrips (for wheel landings) would become urgent. Weather factors encountered and increased service responsibilities would necessitate a review of equipment choices. What should be MAF's strategy? Charlie put some of his thoughts on paper as he wrote to our families at home:

> After completing most of our search on Monday, May 2nd (weather is really only good until about 10 or 10:30am when the clouds keep us from seeing any-

thing much of the ridges), we landed at the Baliem again and spent several hours there. Myron Bromley stayed with the plane while Jerry Rose took Dave and me down to their camp in the outboard. From there we walked about 25 minutes to the proposed airstrip site. Dave had already seen it, so I double-checked it and we figured it was usable. They've got a lot of stones to move, but no big trees. It will be a lot of work, but a lot of missionary strips have been worse. Jerry thinks they can finish it in two months. He figures they can get about 30 local people per day to work on it ....

After returning from the walk, we had lunch there and then left about 1:45pm. It was a beautiful day, and we still did a bit of searching on the way home. I am impressed with the fact that all the talk about "impossible" weather conditions and other barriers surrounding the forbidding Shangri-La are a lot of fairy tales. The gaps are lower than the ones into the Wahgi Valley [in Papua] that we use regularly and the weather is no worse. (It's not too often that we can get out of the Wahgi after 2pm.) I'm sure that with the proper procedures—and that's the whole secret of safe missionary aviation—the Baliem is no more formidable than any other inland valley. The only problem is the lack of alternatives between here and there. That's why I love those floats—there are lots of water alternatives.

My first takeoff from the Baliem River was pretty rough. The next two have been better. I now have no trouble getting on the step. But hauling it off the water is still a problem, due to the built-in downwind. This plane is definitely marginal for this work. But since most of our loads will be inbound only, we'll be OK until something else is sent out. And once we get the airstrip, all outbound loads will be on wheels.

Vic and Bob arrived on Friday, May 6th (1955). After Bob made a wheels trip to Sengge in the Wewak Pacer, Vic and Dave flew it to Manokwari to finish the drops at Testega for TEAM that had been abandoned 10 days earlier. Bob stayed behind in Sentani to fly with Charlie, since both of them were checked out on floats.

The fellows continued to search, even though the government's participation had ended. Then, very unexpectedly, someone in town reported he heard—even saw—a plane return from the direction of the Baliem that fateful day the Sealand was missing. This raised a new question: could it possibly have disappeared in the Hollandia area, practically under our noses?

Hopes revived, and attention was diverted from further inland searching while the fellows checked out the reported sighting. The more they learned, the more they wondered if the plane had possibly gone down in Lake Sentani. All agreed that the weather that day had been very bad. And everything about the report sounded logical and even appeared quite reliable. Although they weren't entirely convinced, they felt they had to pursue any such possibility. Because the reported details fit together so well, the fellows even reconstructed a scenario of what could have happened. It had to be checked out.

They first conducted a search locally by air, and noticed oil spots in the water. These they initially discounted. And yet, should they, when so many variables were involved: fatigue, equipment problems, misjudgment of distances, etc. But it was the location of the oil spots, the placement of the trees along the shore, the angle of turn (causing a wing to catch in the water)–all seemed to fit together to lend plausibility to the report.

The fellows decided to enlist the help of the DCA officials who asked for Navy divers and grappling equipment. Eight dives were made, but nothing was found. Clearly the government responded in every way possible with full cooperation of time, money and effort. We in the mission family were most grateful. But the mystery remained unsolved. What had happened to Al Lewis and the Sealand?

Finally, on June 2nd (1955), more than a month after the Sealand disappeared, Charlie had time for a letter home. He wrote,

> The big news–almost a week old now–is that we found the Sealand. It wasn't in the lake after all. Apparently, from what Dick says now, they [had] approached from the direction of the lake earlier in the week–and apparently the witnesses just have their dates mixed. Anyway, an operator from Lae that flew his Anson over here on a charter flight, was then chartered by C&MA to fly in [Mr. Troutman, Dick Lenehan and Charlie all went] and look over the higher parts of the ridge that we couldn't reach with our plane on floats. (On wheels we could top everything, but we weren't crazy about offering to do it when we were so relatively sure he was in the lake.)
>
> We headed for the gap, about 13,000 feet, and then started East. We hadn't gone but four or five miles when we spotted it below us–something over 10,000 ft. We had been right by that spot twice on our earlier searches–once above 10,000 ft. But the wreckage lay in such a position that you can't see it unless you're well above it. On our third pass over the wreckage, we positively identified it as the Sealand (at first we thought it might have been an old army wreck). Al obviously hit straight in with no chance of survival.

It was good to find the plane and to know Al had not suffered. At the same time we all mourned the loss of our friend and missionary colleague. The month with all its unknowns and uncertainties had been difficult for everyone, but it must have been especially hard for Al's wife Mary. C&MA conducted a memorial service for Al in Sentani on June 6th, and field leaders of various missions (including Charlie) took part. Joining the mission family at the service were a number of government officials and townspeople, including the acting Governor (the Minister of Inland Affairs) and his wife. (The Governor was out of the country.)

Later on, arrangements were made to get to the site to bring the body out. At that time, those making the trip would determine the worth of salvaging any of the scattered cargo.

The search was over, but in the aftermath of the accident Charlie and Dave found themselves busier than ever. Additional flights would be required to meet needs beyond those originally planned. Not surprisingly, the building of airstrips for wheel landings took on a new urgency.

29
A Task Accomplished

Almost immediately after the Sealand was reported missing, Charlie realized he needed to ask that our concession with the government be amended—it would now need to cover service into the Baliem Valley. Unofficially, MAF's flights into the Baliem, beginning with the emergency trip for consultation, continued and soon became routine. Charlie flew there usually two (sometimes three) times a week; and Dave, now checked out on floats, made trips to Archbold Lake on alternate days.

Then, one week, this schedule was interrupted by a government request for an emergency flight to Sengge where, according to some well-confirmed rumors, the hill people in that area were massing to attack the government's patrol post at nearby Waris. The government officials, eager to reinforce their garrison at Waris, asked MAF to help with an airlift of extra police. Accommodating the government's request meant changing from floats to wheels, but it was an opportunity to show MAF's willingness to cooperate with the government. Evidently the arrival of the extra police either inhibited or squelched the anticipated uprising, for there was no further news about the matter.

Once the plane was back on floats, we heard an epidemic had broken out at that same location (Waris), and we were asked to deliver a package of medicine. This presented no problem. It wasn't much out of the way—only 35 minutes from Sentani—and could be delivered by "drop" on the way home from the Baliem.

In addition to flying regularly, Charlie kept up a barrage of correspondence with L.A. At this point it was particularly important to keep the office abreast of the current situation in DNG in connection with ongoing discussions with C&MA relative to their Sealand replacement plans. Charlie knew the L.A. office expected to be approached about a possible joint operation. In fact, that inquiry surfaced when a couple of the C&MA leaders flew to California to confer with Grady Parrott, MAF's president. Subsequently, on June 2nd, we in Sentani received a wire informing us that C&MA had placed an order for a Cessna 180, a plane similar to the planes used in the Madang program, although with a larger engine. It was the type of plane MAF originally recommended for their Sentani-based program, prior to their decision to move ahead with the purchase of the Sealand. Although we knew no details of the new arrangements, we realized they could be the beginnings of answers to earnest prayers—not only of recent prayers, but probably prayers extending over several years! We learned later that MAF had agreed to assume responsibility for supplying the pilots for the joint venture.

By the end of May (1955), Charlie realized that a number of loose ends were coming together, including the granting of our long-awaited concession. In a letter written June 2nd, Charlie indicated he had not yet seen the English translation, but understood it to be "quite favorable." And in reference to Dave's taking over the program, he added,

> There just isn't too much left for us [personally] to do, except to check Dave out on the Baliem [River] and make a trip to the Wissel Lakes. We've been fondly hoping we might [finish our assignment and] get away from here on June 30, but that is just a bit doubtful....We still have stopovers to make in the Territory [Papua] and in Melbourne, so it will take us two weeks to reach Los Angeles once we leave here.

> We found we have sunk a lot of roots in three years, even in our nomadic situation. So while it is exciting to think of going home, it also leaves us a bit breathless. But the Lord has provided a bunch of wonderful replacements and we're eager to see them carry on. Dave may be a bit short-handed here, but there are several possibilities of getting help for him; we are quite sure we can work that out in the next three weeks.

Dave's Baliem checkouts were completed within the next few days. On one of those flights Charlie suggested they try taking off upriver. They tried several takeoffs and were delighted. Both agreed that upriver takeoffs worked much better than takeoffs downstream. Charlie commented,

> The wind seems to affect us much more than the current, so it's better to go upriver and upwind than downriver with a downwind. On the last takeoff we had 220 lbs. aboard—30 lbs. more than the heaviest load we took off [with] during the search; and we had much better clearance. Of course, the flatter prop we're using now helps some. But we're glad to know that we can take out any one of the fellows safely if any of them should get sick. I now feel that I have pretty well completed the checks I wanted to make about takeoff possibilities.

> And just in time. Because right after that trip, the river dropped a couple more feet—to a point where several sand bars are now showing. I went in alone again

on Friday, and got a chance to study the situation....As far as we can tell, we probably won't have any trouble even at lowest water—the way we're taking off now [that is, upriver].... We don't think we'll have any trouble with sand bars or too-shallow water. Our biggest worry now is submerged snags. But of course the fellows will check the channel each time the river drops another foot to be sure it is free of such. Last year they just forgot about the river after it dropped below a certain level because the Sealand couldn't use it. But we draw a lot less water. Friday it was three to four feet below the Sealand's minimum landing level. And I think we'll be able to use it even a bit below that.

With our family's time in New Guinea drawing to a close, the fellows set aside a day to drive into Hollandia. Charlie wanted to introduce Dave to some of the officials he hadn't yet met. And there was one more trip to Manokwari with Dave on Charlie's agenda. He wanted to try a different route this time. He had in mind, following the bend of the coast west and south of Geelvink Bay to take a look at a place called Nabire whose location at the southernmost point of the Bay seemed ideal as an eventual sub-base. That was the place Charlie had tried to reach by launch the previous September. Going to Manokwari by way of Nabire was a bit like going around an elbow to reach a thumb, but Charlie thought it was important for Dave to look at the site with him. As it turned out, they were glad they took that route. Nabire actually did become an important MAF sub-base—within the next year.

In Manokwari, Dave flew all the trips into Anggi Gigi alone, and these trips concluded his checkout in the Bird's Head. Back in Sentani, Charlie watched Dave settle very capably into the routine of the Baliem and Archbold trips. It was clear Charlie had complete confidence in Dave's ability to handle the DNG program. He had only one remaining concern: what if Dave got sick? Knowing that it was imperative that MAF maintain continuous uninterrupted service, Charlie decided to check Vic out on floats the next time he flew over from Wewak. This was a precautionary measure since the one-plane situation in DNG was especially critical. At least in Papua there were two Lutheran Cessnas and the Wewak Pacer to fall back on in a crisis.

When all the checkouts were completed, Charlie turned his attention to arranging our departure schedule from New Guinea. His target date was June 30, 1955. In setting that date, he was allowing time for a final flight with Vic to attend a conference in Papua—at Tari. Their week together would also give opportunity to discuss some personnel matters that would provide closure as he left the island.

As usual, his planning was designed to make the most of the time that remained. But, to fit this in, he would have to leave Sentani a week ahead of the rest of our family. And because he planned to meet our Qantas flight in Madang rather than return to Sentani, it meant that finalizing everything for our family's departure from DNG would be left to me. I must admit that I was not overjoyed by this prospect. At the time, all I could think of was that he was really "dumping a load" on me. I thought about the routine demands of meals, laundry, etc. for the four boys and myself (including our six-week-old baby). And I thought about the responsibility involved in deciding what to pack and what to leave as we brought to an end our time in New Guinea. It seemed I was being handed a monumental task to take care of alone! Feeling overwhelmed, I'm sure my attitude was less than positive. In fact, it was easy for me to see this as one more instance of insensitivity on Charlie's part, and to blame him for his misplaced priorities. Yet, from Charlie's perspective, there was no alternative—if we were to keep our end-of-June departure date. There was no question but that he genuinely believed this trip was important to finishing up our task well. And he did remind me that Janet (Steiger) would no doubt do what she could to give me a hand, though I was not altogether convinced because I knew she had her hands full too. I wanted to "understand," particularly because I didn't want to thwart the Lord's leading, but I still found it hard to accept. While I am not proud of my attitude in this situation—my impatience, even self-pity, must have been very apparent—I continued to struggle for a good many more years with what I considered was a lack of balance between family and work priorities.

Nonetheless, Charlie left as he planned. It was obvious he was pleased with the outcome of the conference, for he wrote:

> Actually we had no known reason for accepting the invitation to Tari for last weekend. It might be called a hunch, but both Vic and I felt it was the Lord's leading. We suspected the Lord's reason had something to do with the long-talked-about [southwestern] Papua program, but we had no plan in mind. A complete survey was out of the question. But in a most unexpected way, things "broke" for that Papua program. We got a trip to what will probably be our base. Now I've seen it and can visualize the things Vic writes about as he develops this program. And I can make the initial contacts in Port Moresby as we pass through. It has—without any exaggeration—worked out perfectly....

As happy as we were to be on our way home, both Charlie and I experienced mixed emotions about leaving New Guinea. On the one hand we were grateful to be concluding our assignment with so much accomplished. But, we were leaving behind colleagues and friends we'd miss, particularly because of the many experiences we had shared together. All that remained before leaving this part of the world was a final opportunity for Charlie to confer with the AMAF Council in Melbourne.

One of Charlie's greatest desires throughout our three years in New Guinea was to see AMAF reestablished on a solid footing. He wanted to see them participate as full partners in mission aviation. He often blamed himself for the intermittent communication breakdowns, but he was also impatient with the AMAFers on occasion as well. Although we didn't understand a whole lot about cross-cultural differences at that time, or how best to build bridges cross-culturally, we were aware that "Yanks" all too often tended to exhibit know-it-all attitudes. I have even wondered whether Americans sub-consciously put forth greater effort in trying to avoid that image when work-ing with people whose language is totally different (for example, when deal-ing with Pidgin-speaking people, or Dutch New Guinea government officials). I know Charlie wished he had been able to relate as comfortably with the AMAF office and home Council as he had with Vic. Admittedly he found it hard to communicate easily with the men in Melbourne. As I suggested above, this difficulty may have had more cultural overtones than we realized at the time. We may have assumed that our common language predisposed us to look at things and interpret things in the same ways. But that isn't necessarily true—as we were to learn some years later. However, in 1955, the extent of Charlie's inner anxiety about this last face-to-face encounter with the men in Melbourne became apparent when he referred to the meeting as "the Granddaddy stomach-jumper of them all." In a final letter from New Guinea to our parents, he shared his feeling by writing,

I still have no assurance that the outcome will be happy, but I do have a growing peace about the session—perhaps less fear … about what is required [of me]. After three years of determined sugar coating, it's not easy to go back to the forthright approach which came more naturally in my twenties.…

We're sure praying earnestly. Despite all [the] recent encouragements, I'm fear-ful of the outcome. Hope it's not weak faith. But the Lord's will be done—even if it doesn't fulfill our dreams. At least we've tried to move with complete unselfishness, and I'm sure the Lord wanted us to make that effort first.

Once the Melbourne meeting was over, Charlie was able to say,

> The meeting in Melbourne went well. It left something yet to be desired, but Rome wasn't built in a day.... They're now more realistic about some weaknesses ... and have taken a long step toward correction. [From my point of view] their attitude toward Vic could stand improvement, but at least it's coming. And, meanwhile, Vic is big enough to "grow on it.".... But I'm glad it's over.... It seems mighty strange to move away from our last three years' work. Guess we'll get used to it. Meanwhile, we're already becoming aware of the fact that not all the tensions are on this side of the Pacific. The only redeeming factor is that hopefully we've learned better how to live with them, and how to exercise some patience.

Arriving back in L.A. we found ourselves caught up almost immediately in the whirl of activities at MAF's headquarters. Charlie picked up his duties as Secretary-Treasurer of the organization, and our New Guinea experience receded a bit from our minds, although in many ways it had marked us for life. We didn't know it then, but less than 2 years later we would be given another, though shorter, cross-cultural assignment.

30
Another Assignment

Arriving back in L.A. we found ourselves having to house-hunt and get acquainted with a new community, since MAF's headquarters had meanwhile relocated to Fullerton—which lies to the south, although still within the greater L.A. metropolitan area. Property adjacent to Fullerton's airport was purchased and permission given for direct access to the runway.

Scarcely six months after we returned from New Guinea, in January of 1956, the world was rocked by news of the deaths of 5 missionaries in Ecuador at the hands of the savage "Auca" Indians, now know as the Waodani.[1] Nate Saint and his wife Marj, along with the four other missionary couples, suddenly were the focus of intense interest worldwide. Nate had been the pilot of the MAF plane used to make contact with the tribe. Not surprisingly, MAF leaders were suddenly besieged by reporters seeking information. Grady, as President of MAF, left immediately for Ecuador to represent MAF and care for organizational affairs there; Charlie and Jim Truxton (the other two principal officers of MAF) handled details at headquarters; and Hobey and Olivia Lowrance and their family prepared to take over Nate's flying responsibilities, at least temporarily. Almost instantaneously, MAF, a previously little-known organization, had been thrust into the world's spotlight. As Christians around the world processed and pondered the loss, MAF began to receive inquiries from Christian pilots who wanted to "take Nate's place."

About the same time, mission agencies in Africa began to approach MAF for help with their transportation needs. Up until this point, MAF-US had not given much thought to work in Africa; Sudan Interior Mission had a plane in Nigeria, and BMAF (British MAF) was working in East Africa. BMAF's resources, however, were fully engaged in East Africa at that time, particularly

---

[1] For more detailed accounts, see *Jungle Pilot* by Russell T. Hitt, and *Through Gates of Splendor* by Elisabeth Elliot. In 2006, in commemoration of the 50th anniversary, other resources became available: *Beyond the Gates of Splendor*, (DVD), *End of the Spear*, a major motion picture (which tells the story from the perspective of the Waodani [Aucas]), and *End of the Spear*, a book by Steve Saint, son of martyred pilot Nate Saint.

in the Sudan; it could very well take some years yet before they could consider expanding into West Africa.

In 1956, BMAF made a decision to replace its Sudan plane, a Rapide, with a Cessna 180. Two MAF-US pilots (Ernie Krenzin, together with his family, and Betty Greene) were already flying in the Sudan—on loan to BMAF. After considerable discussion of how best to assess the need for MAF-US to enter the West Africa scene, a decision was made to ship BMAF's new Cessna to Lagos, Nigeria, for assembly. BMAF's leader, Stuart King, also their chief engineer, would fly over from the Sudan to supervise the assembly. It was further decided that Charlie could be spared from the US office for up to a year. If he were to meet Stuart in Lagos, it would not only give him opportunity to assess needs for service in that area but the two men would be able to conduct additional surveys together across central Africa as they flew the plane back to BMAF's base in Malakal, southern Sudan.

Plans for a year-long commitment called for Charlie to spend a few months in the Sudan, a few months back in New Guinea, and additional time for meeting with mission leaders in Indonesia (Jakarta) before returning to the Philippines to complete the investigation that he began before we left New Guinea a couple years earlier. Since he was reluctant to be away from the family for a year, and since our children were all under 12 (which considerably reduced air fares), it was decided we would go as a family. This time I would home school 3 boys.

Late April of 1957, Charlie and I, with our four boys (ages 11, 9, 5, and under 2) flew first to New York where Charlie met with mission leaders. I vividly recall waiting in the N.Y. terminal to board our flight to London. Charlie was in a phone booth making one last phone call to L.A.—which seemed to go on and on. I suddenly panicked when our name was shouted out over the loud speaker for final boarding. In desperation I signaled Charlie—and we each grabbed our parcels and ran! We were out of breath, but we made it.

During our few days in London Charlie conferred with BMAF leaders there, including Steve Stephens who was in charge of the London office. Our flight to BMAF's base in Malakal had several segments; there were stops in Paris, Rome, and Benghazi in North Africa before arriving for an overnight at a mission home in Khartoum. The next morning we flew on south to Malakal, near the confluence of the two rivers which form the White Nile.

BMAF's families lived in three adjacent houses in Malakal; the airport was a distance away. Stuart and Phyllis King (BMAF) and their family occupied one of the houses; the Krenzin family, on loan from MAF-US, lived in the second house; and the third was the home of Gordon and Jean Marshall and their family. Since they were on furlough, their furnished home was available for our family to use. Betty Greene, also on loan from MAF-US, lived with a mission family in town.

Charlie spent the first few days after our arrival conferring with Stuart, and then flew alone to Lagos, Nigeria, where Stuart would soon join him to supervise the assembly of BMAF's new Cessna. The boys and I remained in Malakal while Charlie and Stuart conducted joint surveys on their return flight to Malakal.

Our 4 boys and I soon settled into a routine in Malakal that included home-schooling (7th grade, 5th grade, 1st grade, and "interruptions," otherwise known as "mischief" from our 2-year-old). I was especially grateful for the young man who was to help us. He was one of God's gifts—rather quiet but very conscientious. I learned he had previously worked for another mission family, so was at least somewhat acquainted with European customs and food—and he spoke some English! He did our laundry and much of the cooking. (He even knew how to make delicious cinnamon rolls!) During our time in Malakal, he even showed us how to make peanut butter. The boys and I discovered we needed to shell a "heap of peanuts" to make a tiny amount of peanut butter! We also learned to watch out for scorpions and snakes. Instead of windows, the house had screens all around to allow for circulation of air. These were normally propped up like awnings. However, when it rained, we needed to go outside and lower all the screens to keep the rain out of the house—which was a bit tricky when trying to do it at night by flashlight.

Meanwhile, in French West Africa, Charlie met with a number of field leaders to assess transportation needs of the US missions located there. As planned, he and Stuart met in Lagos. Once the Cessna was assembled and test flown, the two of them began flying east, gathering information and conducting surveys across central Africa en route back to Malakal. Charlie wrote a number of detailed letters along the way (from Bamako, Niamey, Dakar, Cameroon, Libenge, Leopoldville, and Tshikapa). Portions of his summary report from Malakal include:

Malakal, Aug. 24, 1957 – to Jim/Grady: Re: Completion of African Survey

… The fact that our time [in Africa] has not been divided just as we planned it is not, of course, a criteria for determining whether we've finished the Lord's plan.

...It seems pretty obvious that [Kenya] should follow hard on the heels of Ethiopia—and still within the BMAF sphere.

By the same token, the Lord caused us to spend the most time in survey where we expected to spend the least—FWA [French West Africa]. And there we found the most genuine need. The Cameroon need is considerably less, and the CIM field much less yet. See the picture: We've found the logical expansion fields of BMAF on this [East Africa] side ... and we've found the neediest field for our attention farthest west, so there's no conflict of interest. From these vantage points, we'll begin a pincher movement toward each other with our chains describing a southerly arc in each case. Oddly enough, this is exactly what Stuart and I talked about as an ideal when we were discussing a map of Africa soon after I first arrived....

Charlie's letters to Grady and Jim in the home office (during the survey trip across Africa) were not, however, confined solely to matters in Africa. They indicated he was actively engaged in thinking about New Guinea operations as well. He shared thoughts about Highland basing, aircraft replacement, and personnel problems (particularly the choice of who best to fill in for Dave Steiger during his furlough). His correspondence with L.A. also dealt with setting goals for the TNG program [the eastern half of NG], particularly those that related to Lutmis (Lutheran Mission) operations. Beyond these concerns related to Africa and New Guinea, the ongoing correspondence between Charlie, Grady, and Jim indicated discussions about personnel for Ecuador. (Hobey Lowrance had been filling in temporarily after Nate Saint was killed, but now was needed elsewhere.) Through it all came a growing recognition of the wisdom of placing an experienced man on each of MAF's bases in Latin and South America—even though that would inevitably necessitate moving some pilots around. (One may wonder if this was the origin of the well-known acronym for MAF: "Move Again Friend.")

Once the Africa portion of our trip was completed, our family flew on to New Guinea (via Addis Ababa, Aden, Bombay, Calcutta, Bangkok, Manila, and Biak). Charlie expected our stay in New Guinea to last a few months, since he wanted to be thoroughly updated and familiarized with the current situation and also allow adequate time to confer with AMAFers, particularly Vic Ambrose.

That Charlie's mind was still on matters in Ecuador when we arrived in Sentani [DNG] is clear from what he wrote to Jim (Grady must have been out of the office). Convinced of the importance of certain principles, he wrote:

CJM to Jim T, from Sentani [DNG]: Nov. 11, 1957,

1. We must guard against being idealistic—of placing the standard too high. The more I get around in mission circles (and we've really been around this last six months!!), the more I'm impressed with the way the Lord does His work through men who are in jobs a notch or two over their heads. Without engaging in any false modesty, but in some realism, isn't it true of all of us whom the Lord has chosen to lead MAF? Furthermore, Scripture seems to indicate that it is designedly that way— [in other words] unless we're thrown on the Lord because of being in over our heads, we're certain to go off without His leading on many important matters....

2. We must guard against looking for a "pattern." We're not necessarily looking for a man to fill Nate's shoes. MAF is built around the "team" idea anyway. But to use a team effectively, we're going to have to make at least some changes, no doubt.... Two principles are involved: First, from the leadership standpoint, real leadership diffuses responsibility (not mere jobs) as much as possible. Retention and concentration of responsibility is a weakness in leadership and definitely limits growth potential. Second, from the personnel standpoint, we can't get the most out of our personnel (the amount the Lord can bring out in them—usually well beyond their normal, human potential) unless we give them a real opportunity to "make a contribution." ...

3. I don't see how we can justify "wasting" Hobey in Ecuador much longer. No, I'm not going back on my first paragraph and down-grading Ecuador. Nor am I saying we made a mistake to date. But Hobey's "contribution" is in Fullerton. He's wading in water only to his chest and possibly because we're afraid to throw someone in over his head where he'd have to swim, like all the rest of us.

Other letters written to the home office during our time in New Guinea included the need for clarifying arrangements with C&MA (in DNG) after being asked to take over the aviation work following Al Lewis' death and the loss of the Sealand. Other correspondence dealt with topics which are indicative of the increasing complexity of service, such as: personnel and scheduling; aircraft choices, including the matter of floats; ownership and use of the Sentani hangar; the need for a business manager to handle purchasing, accounting, and distribution of goods for all the missions served there; inventory requirements; the need for vehicles; discussion covering charges for service, and the like.

It was obvious from his correspondence with the office that Charlie was "thinking details" in his great concern for MAF's future throughout that entire area. MAF's responsibilities were expanding at an amazing pace—particularly with the new need now surfacing of overseeing business matters for the various missions served in Dutch New Guinea. But there was also the matter of how to unify the TNG program in the eastern portion of the island. Charlie was beginning to believe this overall development could require the presence of an administrative officer of MAF–at least for a while. As it turned out, Grady and Maurine Parrott did go to Dutch New Guinea for a year–not only to oversee new developments but to assure uninterrupted service during the Steiger family's furlough.

After our few months in DNG, we boarded a Dutch freighter bound for Singapore. It made a number of scheduled stops at Biak, Manokwari, Serui, and ports surrounding the north coast of Borneo. At Labuan, an island off the west coast of Borneo, the boys and I left the ship and were flown by a Borneo Evangelical Mission (BEM) plane to its base in Lawas (Sarawak). We were to wait there while Charlie continued on by ship to Singapore. From there he flew to Jakarta to investigate potential needs for MAF's service in other parts of Indonesia. During our stay in Lawas, our two older boys stayed with one aviation family (the Parsons) on one side of the airstrip, and our two younger boys and I occupied the guest room in the home of the other pilot's family (Bruce and Ruth Morton). I had not looked forward to "imposing" on these families, but God gave us good rapport, and a warm friendship developed. Following his time in Jakarta, Charlie joined us in Lawas. Bruce briefed him about BEM's aviation setup there and even took him along on a few flights. He wrote to L.A. to report on this visit and his disappointment in Jakarta:

> As you know, my trip into Indonesia was an apparent failure [he hadn't been able to get to the locations as planned, or even make productive contacts]. However, after my visit to Lawas, I think [I am] beginning to see how the Lord's hand was in this (as we know, of course, that it was). We went to Lawas just to visit the work there. Bruce had indicated he wanted to discuss aircraft types. But as it turned out, we discussed (under the leading of the Spirit, I feel sure) quite a wide range of subjects.... Let me say that we had a grand time of fellowship in the Lord. We had a liberty in discussing [a number of] matters candidly, [more so than on] any similar occasion I can recall.

From Lawas, we flew to the Philippines. Charlie expected to spend about a month there to follow up his previous visit two years earlier (during our time in DNG). At that time, he had concluded that it wasn't yet time to press ahead with plans for a program there. This time, as he conferred with mission leaders in the Philippines, he could report on renewed contacts, provide additional information, and touch on a variety of other subjects. The subject of one letter revealed a concern for a better approach to MAF's basic orientation of new personnel.

Manila, Feb. 19, 1958

... I remember how in the early days we just plain hangar-flew with our candidates. In the course of the give-and-take we got the ideas across.... Another good technique is to discuss, without drawing conclusions at the time, but make notes. Then in just a few well-spaced sessions, sum up some of the things you've particularly noted that they might need to think about in terms of MAF policy.... But it takes repetition and definiteness....

There's no doubt that this year's trip—which has shown me M.A. [mission aviation] up-to-date in *scope*, as the previous 3 years showed me in *depth*—is a perfect prelude. My thought of a S.A. [South American] jaunt was in terms of completing this. But that's by no means essential.... Your emphasis on orientation materials rather than on the manual as such also appeals to me. The latter should probably be an outgrowth of the former; and the former are more desperately needed....

When I went through the obstacle course with Grady before leaving, and as I study over the present flight orientation outline, I'm impressed with the fact that a disproportionate amount of time is spent on procedures-for-a-pinch, and not enough on *normal* procedures. Worse yet, I'm afraid these aren't carefully enough *distinguished*. Both Hobey and Grady say that they emphasize over and over again, "This isn't how we do it all the time—this is what you do when necessary." ... One solution, I feel, is to break the orientation course clearly and firmly into two sections, and not start the unusuals until the normals are firmly implanted. Then perhaps there should be a further period of reviewing the normals. Another solution, I feel, is to make "margins" a concept on a par with our emphasis on "pressure." Jim, I'm afraid this has been the biggest weakness in our program. We've tended to get carried away with our own publicity—delighting in the tight strips instead of determining to find a way to improve them....

At which point he referred to a statement made in one of MAF's promotional films that had troubled him. One of the pilots was quoted as saying, "You've got to be right—every time." In his letter, Charlie added, "That's OK for publicity— if we didn't make the mistake of thinking it's true."

Other letters from Manila during our month there revealed thoughts on a wide range of subjects: personnel suggestions for New Guinea and the Philippines; his meetings in Singapore with C&MA leaders from the States relative to their program in New Guinea; vehicles for Hollandia (financing, insurance, rental arrangements, and thoughts about who should be in charge of ownership papers). Anticipating his return to Fullerton, he wrote Grady and

Jim to plead that time be set aside during the first couple days after his return to debrief as an executive committee.

In a letter to Vic in early March (1958), written to share our travel dates for returning to L.A., he also verbalized his hope that a decision would be forthcoming for Grady to take over in DNG during Dave Steiger's furlough. He thought it would have an added advantage—that of enabling Grady to "finish orientation that had been incomplete earlier due to pressures to get personnel on the field; to work on further arrangements with Lutmis; and to help decide further personnel movements and assignments" for both portions of New Guinea (TNG and DNG), and also for the Philippines.

Other letters went to Betty Greene in the Sudan (Mar. 10, 1958) commenting on the situation in Malakal, and to Steve Stephens in the BMAF London office, to tell him about our Borneo visit, sharing especially about contacts with individuals Steve would know.

It is no doubt clear, from the above glimpse of his prolific correspondence during our year of travel, that Charlie was very much a part of wide-ranging discussions and decision-making processes as MAF grew and expanded. Except for very occasional cables and wires, written correspondence was the sole means of communication. No wonder MAF's leaders (Grady, Jim, Charlie, and Betty) began to give consideration to positioning one of them *on site* for a period of time as new areas were entered and being developed.

It was the middle of March, 1958, when our family returned to the States. Once again, Charlie settled back into his role of Secretary-Treasurer at the headquarters office in Fullerton, California. He remained in that office until 1967. In a planned transition to younger leadership for the organization, he assumed the title of Executive Vice President between 1967 and 1970, and then President in 1970. Although this latter office was intended to last 3-5 years, he chose to step aside completely in 1973, at the end of three years.

* * * * * * * * * *

As I have implied throughout, Charlie was "more than a pilot." To illustrate his administrative role in MAF, and to give an idea of who he was as a person, his gifts and how he used them in leadership, I am devoting the next several chapters to some of his writing—in his own words.

In my final chapter I will share personal reflections from a wife's perspective. But first, a glimpse of Charlie, as MAF leader and administrator.

31
"Approve the Things that are Excellent"

Like many other of the new "faith-missions" that came into being following World War II, MAF was a member mission of the Interdenominational Foreign Missions Association. In 1956, Charlie, then Secretary-Treasurer of MAF, was invited to present a paper at IFMA's annual meeting in 1956 at Haverford, Pennsylvania, on November 1. This paper is reproduced in full because it represents Charlie's ability to reflect on and communicate in a formal paper something of the significance of mission aviation to the post WWII missionary movement, particularly in the areas of technical professionalism and inter-agency cooperation.

COOPERATION BETWEEN MISSIONS, AND BETWEEN MISSIONS AND SERVICE AGENCIES
By Charles J. Mellis Jr.

Missionary aviation, as a significant movement, is now ten years old (though the pioneer efforts date back another eight years to the pre-war period). Where has ten years of growth taken this young servant?

Like any new field, missionary aviation went through a sifting period in its earliest years. Some had a tendency to look on this challenging tool as a cure-all; to over-sell it. They tended to minimize the problems, the limitations, the hazards, and the need for realistic standards—even to look on it as an automobile with wings.

The results were tragic. At least 45 missionaries and their children have lost their lives in missionary aviation activities since World War II. An analysis of these fatalities gives a significant picture.

Thirty-six fatalities occurred in transport-type planes between the homeland and the mission field. This type of operation had already been considered questionable by a majority of mission societies and missionary aviation leaders before the fatalities occurred. It has now been wisely abandoned in favor of available public facilities.

Of the remaining nine fatalities, seven occurred in four light planes piloted by missionaries who had relatively low technical experience when they began field operations. The lack of adequate training and solid experience was probably a major factor in each of these cases. (Operational experience without adequate training and supervision can develop and accentuate poor techniques.)

The other two were experienced pilot-specialists. Though the exact causes of these accidents cannot be determined with certainty, there is considerable evidence that weather-flying and fatigue were the most significant factors.

This unfortunate record graphically illustrates what are probably the three most important factors in the utilization of this modern, potent missionary tool: 1) selective usage, 2) adequate qualifications, and 3) sound operational principles. Let's discuss the degree of growth in each of these areas.

1) Selective usage. Probably the greatest gains have been made in this area. Largely through your encouragement as mission leaders, few air services are now being organized until adequate surveys have been made. The purpose of these surveys has been to give an intelligent basis for selective usage. The goal is qualitative rather than quantitative growth. The result is better stewardship and improved safety.

In discussing selective usage, special mention should be made of the relationship of missionary aviation to indigenous objectives. We know this is a matter of utmost importance to all of you. We want you to know that we who are specially engaged in aviation service functions share your burden for these objectives; and we agree that this alone will and should dictate against air-aid in some areas.

2) There have also been definite gains in the matter of qualifications. The record has forced prospective missionary pilots to recognize the need for somewhat higher standards. But the normal human tendency to take short-cuts is still with us. We of the Missionary Aviation Fellowship believe that the answer to this problem lies largely with you mission leaders. We will be glad to help you determine what the standards should be. But then only you can make them stick.

Standards have been established in two mission fields to date. In one of these, they have been watered down to meet the status quo. In the second case, the standards are adequate; but since they were adopted, there have been a number of exceptions. While these cases have not involved members of this Association, it is well to note and guard against this trend. Often the urgent need to get a man to the field to fill a gap is the reason for short-circuiting the standards.

This suggests a particular word about the use of specialists in this field. We of MAF are grateful for several leaders of this Association who advised us in our formative years to emphasize this type of development. The Lord has certainly put His seal on this. Consequently, we have encouraged this as the major method of missionary aviation development. We particularly stressed it in the early years of hasty ventures. Since then, we have not discouraged exceptional cases, providing adequate standards are adhered to. However, we've noted that "exceptions" are on the increase again. There's a reason for this. Aeronautical facilities are improving in many places. But we still feel it wise to comment on the inherent difficulties of maintaining adequate standards on a non-specialized basis—even if original qualifications are rigidly enforced by mission leaders. The divided responsibilities create frustration, and too often result in neglect—either of the airplane or the mission work. In this connection we might quote a standard aviation training poster: "Flying is not inherently dangerous; but like the sea, it is terribly unforgiving of any incompetence or neglect." And in the last analysis, mission field situations which combine: 1) adequate facilities for safe operation by non-professional pilots, and b) a continuing, proven need for missionary aviation, are still the exception rather than the rule.

3) The growth and standardization of operational principles has been a problem—at least outside the confines of individual organizations. Personalities and personal opinions—not to mention pride—have been greater factors here than in the establishing of qualifications. This is probably inevitable in individuals, and seems to constitute one of the main human reasons for the comparatively better record of the larger group operations (SIM, JAARS, MAF, etc.). "In the multitude of counselors there is safety" (Proverbs 11:14).

It should be noted that essential "operational principles" go beyond such technical considerations as: alternates, procedures, margins, limitations, devices, etc. It also includes such things as economic factors. Inadequate fiscal policies can create unfortunate pressures on the pilot which result in corner-cutting. This has actually been a significant factor in at least one fatal accident.

So it is evident that the ten-year development of this specialized activity has pointed more and more in the direction of inter-mission cooperation. For safety, economic, and other reasons, this tool lends itself particularly to cooperative and service agency development.

And such cooperative development is particularly feasible in this field. Several years ago, the leader of a group that tends to keep to itself on the field expressed this fact. He suggested that here was the best area to aim for wider inter-mission cooperation—in transportation and other service functions, rather than in education, literature and other areas where doctrinal emphases are involved.

This has not only happened, but it has begotten further cooperative results. In one field, tensions were forming between two societies over a comity question at the same time a cooperative air service was being formed. During the course of the committee meetings called to plan the air service, the groundwork was also laid—privately—for the resolving of the comity question. In another field, an actual inter-mission fellowship has grown out of the cooperative air service.

After our five colleagues gave their lives for the Lord in Ecuador last January, the Ecuadorian missionaries of a denominational group that belongs to the National Council contributed an article to their church paper on the incident. The burden of the article was: Inter-church councils talk ecumenicity—here it is practiced. They pointed to the two mission groups involved in the expedition, the service agency, the reporting and aid of Radio Station HCJB (plus their hospital which serves all the jungle missions), and the functioning, purposeful Inter-Mission Fellowship of Ecuador.

We have felt humbly grateful when the Lord allows us to be in the midst of these cooperative movements among missions. However, we do feel it is important that service agencies refrain from seeking this function. Our proper sphere is cooperation between our agencies and the missions we are called to serve. In seeking to achieve this, we of MAF have tried to lay special emphasis in our candidate program on what we call the "servant concept." We stress that our calling is not only to be faithful servants of Christ, but also servants of the missionaries.

Even with the best orientation, missionary servants will sometimes fail to measure up to this ideal—and possibly more often in the eyes of the missionaries being served. This is especially true in fields like aviation where safety is such an important consideration. The hard considerations of safety may sometimes have to take precedence over desired service—and the pilot's desire to serve. And frequently the safety considerations are hard to explain without sounding like so many "excuses." Pilots can even appear to be "babying" themselves, whereas actually our men are under orders to control their flying hours.

There's an axiom in aviation that is particularly applicable to pioneer missionary flying: "Fatigue can be as toxic as alcohol."

It is for such reasons as these that the missionary airman is in a better position to maintain safety standards when directly responsible to a specialized agency. We've been interested to see how mission leaders have appreciated this factor. In one case, MAF arranged to begin a program for a mission. But when we had trained their men, they asked that we take these men under our wing as associates and continue to carry full responsibility for the operation. Their reason was principally the additional safety factor inherent in the independent service agency approach.

At the same time, this places a responsibility on the service agency to see that its members render effective—as well as safe—service. Probably the first step in achieving this is recognition—recognition by the service agency that its members are only human, and that in their field assignments they have less personal supervision than the missionaries they serve. We feel this suggests that service agencies need to be very highly selective in appointing personnel, with at least as much emphasis on spiritual qualification as on technical ability. Then, as we've already mentioned, orientation is of extreme importance, more so in some ways, than for missionaries who will be under closer personal supervision.

A further important ingredient, we feel, is a closer liaison between missions and the service agencies. The latter should welcome—yes, encourage, observations, questions, suggestions, and even criticism from the missions they serve. Probably this is normally best handled between the homeland leaders to avoid embarrassments and personality factors. But we'd encourage that problems be brought out as early as possible before they develop to more sizable proportions. In our own experience, the relative freedom from difficulties in the service agency-mission relationship has been most gratifying.

This close liaison can also be helpful in the matter of planning. I'm not thinking now of expansion plans; here the need for liaison is obvious. We're thinking of the day-to-day and month-to-month operations. It's more a matter of getting the most out of the service function. Normally the service function is, and should be, planned around the existing needs of the mission work. However, the mission work can sometimes benefit more by certain adjustments to the new dimensions provided by such service. In fact, sometimes, with a little imagination, a project considered impossible may become feasible. Or a whole new approach or method may become possible.

I'm sure that we're all equally thrilled with the fact that Bible-believing Christians have led the way in utilizing tools like radio, recordings, and aviation in mission work. I'm sure we also rejoice in the opportunities afforded to work closer together through these and other media such as literature. In the years ahead, other tools will probably be developed, and new service agencies proposed. I'm sure we shall all welcome—with open minds and hearts—these new possibilities, while at the same time carefully studying the proposals objectively in the spirit of Philippians 1:9, 10, "… in knowledge and all discernment; so that you may approve the things that are excellent."

32

The First Oil Change after "Hanging a New Engine"

Charlie took over the Presidency of MAF on April 1, 1970. A few months later, at the Corporation meeting, he took time to describe some of the significant changes that had been taking place in MAF, recognizing the initial discomfort of absorbing a third year in a row of change.

MISSIONARY AVIATION FELLOWSHIP
(President's) Annual Report
September 25, 1970

Thus far, the year 1970 has been a year of expansion, a year of consolidation (including some subtraction), and, for the third year in a row, a year of substantial organizational change ... with the last six months involving an absorbing of that change.

In Rhodesia, a former sub-base became a full-time program under Dave and Janet Steiger, ministering to a developing area among a transplanted people. Don and Phyllis Beiter have arrived in Afghanistan as a tentative step toward establishing air service for the Medical Assistance Program. Full establishment of this service is still dependent upon the supply of funds needed for the aircraft and other program establishment costs. Funds have been provided, and an aircraft recently purchased, for the eagerly-anticipated and challenging program that Jack and Jeannette Walker will be establishing in northwest Colombia soon after the turn of the year.

In Indonesia we received permission to expand into East Kalimantan ... also, sub-based services, extended to Timor and surrounding islands by our West Irian personnel, have opened up some exciting possibilities for next year. It's anticipated that our Australian MAF colleagues will play a substantial role in these developments.

Surveys in Haiti and Nicaragua have not yet received full Board analysis and decision, but do represent interesting challenges. We've also had an invitation to enter West Brazil, deep in the heart of Amazonia …, a situation that for many of us will bring to mind Mexico, Peru, Ecuador, Dutch New Guinea and/or other parts of Brazil during those periods we nostalgically, and perhaps some unrealistically, refer to as "the good ol' days."

Again, our staff has grown numerically (8 couples and 3 single men). As we know from experience, this adding to our fellowship brings qualitative growth as well.

The growth of our aircraft fleet has been less dramatic. Only two new units have been added, but there has been upgrading of our fleets in Congo, Honduras, and Brazil. This lesser activity in fleet development was inevitable for two reasons. The previous year we had above-normal replacements due to the series of accidents. But there is also the consideration, due to the "changing scene," in which we live and work, to extend the life of our aircraft somewhat … you'll see this reflected in the area reports, and we'll be discussing it later in this meeting. This in turn could perhaps be listed as one factor in speaking of this as a year of "consolidation."

Consolidation of our services in the northern part of South America has brought a decision to phase out our work in Guyana, due to improved government and commercial air service, and marked reduction of foreign mission staff for a variety of reasons, including an altered political outlook. At the same time, just across the border in Roraima Territory, Brazil, our work is thriving to the point where we will be placing a second couple there early in the new year. We face the problem of low usage in northeast Brazil, the Philippines, and Rhodesia (northern base). These will have to be carefully studied during the coming year, particularly in relation to our overall operational losses. Meanwhile, we have locations temporarily inoperative, or operated on a part-time basis.

"Consolidation" is also upon us in regard to personnel requirements. The immediate need here involves headquarters staffing, which reached a peak this past summer. Part, but not all, of this is due to transitional factors. For in our headquarters operation we have been absorbing additional changes beyond the overall structural change (financial revision, revised orientation approach, etc.). We have already begun a phased reduction of the headquarters staff. By next summer (as compared with this last summer's peak) we will have a net reduction of at least seven regular staff members and four to five employees. Our expenses from undesignated income—always the critical part of our revenue—will be reduced to approximately $4,500 per month (total savings will be somewhat higher than that).

The question of whether most of the functions of the headquarters Technical Department could be better carried out (quite apart from financial considerations) through a commercial entity is still being carefully studied. If such a move should be made, another four to five headquarters staff members would be removed from the MAF "payroll" along with one to two employees. This would result in a further reduction of expense against undesignated income of $3,000 per month.

Now let me hasten to add that all of the above-listed anticipated staff reductions will be by normal attrition—none by requested separation. Some will be by overseas appointment or re-appointment. Dave Ellichman and Carl Schoonover will return to the business world from which they came to assist us in our transition. Ted Lepper and Jean Firth have been called to full-time preaching ministries. Let me further add that the above figures are net figures. There will probably be a few additions along with the changes.

In speaking of staff consolidation, I've put the headquarters picture first because it is already underway. But total staff consolidation seems to be pretty much "upon us" also. Here I'm not speaking of attrition, but of a leveling off. I've recently re-read the "performance and trends" report that Research prepared for management last year. This indicated a fairly straight line growth to 1972, a lesser growth to 1975, and a leveling-off-come-reduction from '75 to '80. (This report spoke only to activities in which we are presently engaged.) These trends appear to be quite parallel in terms of operations, aircraft, and personnel. Another year's experience seemingly confirms the validity of these trends for planning purposes—in terms of operations and aircraft. However, there's some evidence that we will "top out" earlier on personnel—at least as far as North Americans are concerned. 1975 may arrive two or three years early! International candidates are one significant factor here.

As indicated at the outset, we have passed through a third continuous year of significant change. I am certain that every one of us has found this cumulative experience traumatic—though the form of the trauma may have varied widely. Since April 1, I've tried to give priority attention to *absorbing* the last structural change.

Thus far I can only measure progress in terms of the management team itself. Here I feel we are absorbing this change fairly well. I'm looking forward to hearing reflections from you on this subject during the coming week. I won't be surprised if you feel we've not yet emerged from the transition. In some cases—some that most affect you—I've consciously by-passed "instant results" for what I felt promised longer range benefit.

Within this new team, we're learning more about "individual responsibility and control." Committee meetings have been reduced to a minimum. Selective consultations have preserved the advantages with much less time consumption. But actual management decisions are largely being made by the responsible individual … and, for the most part, comfortably. Of course, there have been exceptions!

It's my earnest hope—and working goal—that in the months immediately ahead, all of you will feel, in a renewed and vital sense, comfortable in *your* responsibilities.… and in your relationship to the new administration. It takes a little time for a new pair of shoes to be as comfortable as the pair it replaced. This is normal expectancy.

Let me change the figure … to one suggested by Bob Johanson before he returned to Indonesia: "When I hang a new engine, I'm never quite sure I trust it as much as the old one. I've got my ear in it every flight … a little skeptically. That's the way it is up until the first oil change and I get a look at that screen."

Perhaps this week of fellowship and discussion together will, to some degree, serve as such an oil change.

CHARLIE MELLIS

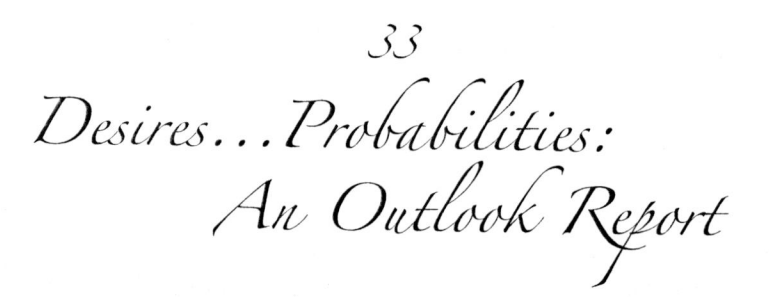

33
Desires...Probabilities: An Outlook Report

This presentation was made during the early months of Charlie's tenure as MAF's President. In it he expressed a few of his "dreams" for the organization along with some hoped-for goals, and a challenge to deal responsibly with inevitable "changes."

MISSIONARY AVIATION FELLOWSHIP
AN OUTLOOK REPORT
at the meeting of the Corporation
September 28, 1970

Outlook, yes. For "the 1970's," no. I'm not prepared to speculate ahead a whole decade. But I do feel some responsibility to go on record as to some of the things I foresee for MAF in the next *few* years.

And, I'd like to divide this outlook into two segments; first, what I'd *like* to see happen; second, what I feel probably *will* happen. In the latter case, I trust I'm not just interested in playing prophet, hoping for the ego boost of possibly being right ... no; I hope, rather, that somehow it will help us to be *prepared*.

My first wish for MAF, and each of us as its people, is that we shall know a new sense of <u>commitment</u> ... and that this will be a purified, single-minded commitment to our living Lord ... and to Him alone.

It's my observation that within our evangelical churches and missions, this sense of commitment has suffered some in recent years. And not at the hands of "worldly" distractions alone. Rather, too often, the good—even the very good—has been the enemy of the best. With high motivation, we become committed to good spiritual causes: to a worthwhile program, to an important task, to a people, to a geographical area or place, to an organization, or, more all-inclusively, to "a calling."

Such commitments can hardly be faulted—except on one ground. They are all subject to revision by the Sovereign Lord of the harvest. Unless we are crystal clear on our *primary* commitment, we may never recognize a change of orders when it hits our "in" basket.

My second yearning is to see us experience a new depth of faith ... in our personal lives, and also in our united task.

Here again, I feel the churches and missions from which most of us have drawn our nurture, have experienced some slippage. In this case, it's a little harder to analyze. But I'd like to propose a possibility. In rejecting the greedy materialism that surrounds us, have we perchance approached an equating of faith and finances? That's the title of an MAF brochure ... and guess who proposed it? Guilty!

I would even be so bold as to suggest that an emphasis on faith-in-regard-to-finances (particularly within the faith missionary movement) may well have inadvertently *contributed* to a lesser exercise of faith in some far more important areas. Could it be that the ever-subtle devil has taken this originally-fine motivation and used it to distract and divert us? Each must examine this question for himself, of course. But as a matter of personal testimony, I've learned more about real faith-life in the past year than in any previous two. Home staff has been on "salary" (though hardly a princely sum!) for a year. The timing correlation may be purely coincidental.

During recent months, I've had to ask myself in full honesty whether the quality of my faith went beyond present—and future—financial security to include such things as: the lifestyles of my adult children ... enough confidence in the Lord to progressively release my other children from excessive sheltering ... the Lord's choice and timing for a second career (when I think I see what I most want right now) and, most of all, the confidence that the Holy Spirit of God can—*and will*—develop and demonstrate the Christian graces to an equal or superior degree in my physical and spiritual descendants, despite any limitations seemingly imposed by their culture or sub-culture.

My third wish for myself and for you-all, is somewhat linked to the last. To borrow Lincoln's words in another context, I'm asking the Lord to give us a new birth of freedom. Most particularly, a freedom from fear, that only a *broad* faith can breed. Freedom from fear of "they" ... of the untried ... of the unpopular cause, and of mistakes ... even apparent failure.

At IFMA last week, Walter Frank, one of the new officers, led the prayer sessions. At one, he suggested that we center our prayers around the thought, "Lord, loose us, and let us go!" I immediately thought of the Lord's own words: "If the *Son* shall make you free, you shall be free *indeed*." The italics, of course, are mine. But it seems to me that the final word in that inspired, authoritative declaration *genuinely* "looses us" ... far beyond anything the liberal academician can know in his unending quest for *academic* freedom. So let's breathe the free air of this God-ordained freedom, which He graciously gives us as His willing bond-slaves!

My fourth and fifth desires parallel those in Paul's prayer (Philippians 1:9-11) that we prayed together earlier.

Paul prayed that we'd know a *growing* love. I believe this has been—and is today—a substantial reality in MAF, despite divergent outlooks on individual questions. Let's continue to pray that it will always be so. And let's remind ourselves of what an aid *growing* love is to some of the other matters we've been speaking of. That total *love* of God that includes heart, soul and mind will keep the primacy of our *commitment* straight ... it will produce a truly broad-based *faith* life ... and, as John reminds us in his first letter (4:18), "Perfect love casts out *fear*." This, in turn, contributes further to our *freedom* in Christ.

Then, finally, Paul asks that this growing love will be characterized by some realistic qualities, resulting in some guided-but-responsible decision-making. In English, at least, the words are descriptive and pungent: knowledge ... discernment ... approve ... excellent.

To me, this says that a growing love must produce more than warm and friendly feelings (though it must, of course, produce these *too*). It must seek to understand (discern) what God is doing in His world today. It must make conscious choices that are not only good, but best (excellent). More often than not, such choices have a substantial price tag. The tariff is usually more personal than economic.

This is a good point [at which] to turn to the probabilities for the years ahead. I don't want to go dramatic on you and try to play Winnie Churchill with his promise of "blood, sweat, and tears." But frankly, I don't see any feather beds down track either! I *do* see some things that are not inclined to produce ecstasy in *any* of us.

Let me bluntly hit the bugaboo first: change. I know the word rankles—partly because we've overused it. (If it's any comfort to you, it "gets to" me at times also—even though I've played the role of advocate and initiator.)

Perhaps we can handle this problem better (in a change-oriented, sometimes change-crazy age) if we face the fact that there are two major aspects of largely-unwelcome change. If we fail to separate them in our minds, change can overwhelm us. If we carefully sort them, we've at least got a shot at dealing with this constructively.

First, there's the change we <u>can't control</u>. It happens apart from us—maybe in Washington, maybe in Moscow, maybe in a government office in Kinshasa. If it's a bad change, we can regret it. But it's beyond our power to undo it ... beyond our control. Does that mean it's beyond our *responsibility?* Very often not. If the change affects us (and these are really the only ones we're discussing) we must *respond* to that change. This produces tension, frustration, even resentment. And that resentment often ends up directed against "change" itself.

Do we need to respond? Why not just ignore it? But even that is a response. It might possibly be an adequate response. Or it may be the very worst. In any case, it is impossible to avoid *some* response. The question is: *How* should a mature, growing Christian respond? God's Word through Paul says, "Knowledge ... discernment ... approve ... excellent" (and, of course, disapprove the wrong). It would seem that we are responsible to respond—as much as possible—by conscious decision rather than by default.

But then there are the things we see that we think <u>need to be</u> changed. "Elective maintenance," if you please! How elective? We put it back through the sieve: "Knowledge ... discernment ... approve ... excellent." The Lord's voice is clear—we can't just cop out. But there's one more sieve here (as with our elective aircraft maintenance): timing. Fit it in without upsetting the flight schedule. At the same time, not every elective job has the same amount of slippage before becoming critical.

Let me share with you a promise—and a prayer. As God gives wisdom, I will do my best to space our necessary elective changes so they don't fall right on top of the can't-wait responses to non-elective change. We'll also try to prioritize the elective items and effect them *before* they become critical, can't-wait items (when it's so much harder to make the *best* decision).

My prayer? It's a paraphrase of the daily morning prayer used by A.A. (which, of course, is equally good for us more sober types!):

Lord, give me today ...

the grace and understanding to respond usefully and
helpfully to change that I cannot control ...

the courage to voluntarily initiate (or resist) change
where it clearly falls to my responsibility ...

and the wisdom to discern the difference ...
lest I allow this age of rapid change to become a blur,
regard change as an enemy, and be tempted to retreat from reality.

In the days ahead, I also foresee that MAF will have to be even more <u>mobile</u>. Changed assignments may be for very different reasons than in the past. Yet, despite the obvious difficulties of changing cultures, language, etc., I foresee that fewer of us are going to experience the "settled" life. That's hardly a welcome prospect!

If this projection proves correct, it will certainly further test our commitment. But we must also meet such challenges with realism—particularly in regard to family life. One result may very well be less long-term tenure (there are, of course, other reasons for this also). And because of this, I see it as deeply important that the "failure" stigma of shorter missionary careers be minimized by adequate sharing of biblical truth. Salary and retirement structures must also respond to these probabilities.

MAF has always played a servant role. I know some of you feel we down-graded that with the publication of our statement of Character and Policy. I urge you to read it again—particularly after we share with you (within the next few weeks) an article by Dit Fenton of Latin American Mission. I foresee for us a much <u>more difficult servant role</u> in the years ahead. Some of our Congo people will tell you that "the years ahead" have already arrived! We have much need for not only further knowledge and discernment—but abundant grace! We Americans have been richly endowed by God for our missionary task in many particulars. We also have some substantial (and not always readily recognized) liabilities!

We will of necessity become <u>reproducers</u> in many places. Daws Trotman [founder of Navigators] used to have a very interesting statement for those he led to the Lord. It went something like this: "Study the Word! But study is no substitute for activity. And activity is no substitute for production. But never forget, even production is no substitute for reproduction!" As MAFers, we're basically activists and producers. Let's do look ahead.

This doesn't by any means *cover* this subject. That would take a small book. If I've left out a subject of particular interest to you, please ask about it. Maybe others have the same question. Feel free to ask even personal questions, such as "where do you stand on ... ?" Either now, or later. My principal objective here is full and open communication. Then, despite some of the gloomy attempted realism of part of this report, we can work confidently together in the years ahead, looking to our Sovereign Lord for new victories.

34
Communication Challenges in the Early 1970s

Samples of Staff Memos

Charlie used frequent memos to communicate with the Staff. The first one below shows Charlie's desire to find the right balance of sufficient and effective internal communication in a growing world-wide organization. But it also shows something of his own *detailed* style of trying to *cover all the bases* on a subject—in this case the *felt need* content, the frequency, and the cross-directional flow of information. Note in each memo, the invitation to MAF staff to dialogue with him and with each other about issues presented in his memos.

March 12, 1971
To: MAF Staff
From: Charlie Mellis
Re: Staff Communications

We want to make some changes here. We trust they'll all be good changes from *your* viewpoint.

As you know we're purposefully moving not only toward a "de-centralized" concept of managing and operating ... but also toward an increased "individual responsibility and control." We're not *talking* as much about these concepts lately, but we're trying to plan so that we find them "happening." What we do about communications can have a big effect on this. That's the goal of these particular changes.

On the one hand, "Communicate more" can mean just deluging you with mimeograph. Here we have to face some facts: *some* information is important for everybody, even apart from felt need; a lot of it is selective based on felt need; some people want more information than others do; different bits of information have different relative importance to different people. We could go on and list other similar "presuppositions."

198

We're going to attempt to solve these problems by a little better "break-down" of different kinds of information. And we're going to add some new items. Here's how the breakdown will look.

1) news as such—personal and operational
2) information to note
3) information to save
4) interaction

"News" is pretty self-explanatory. You might say this is a continuation of the narrative D-2 with the informational items taken out. Incidentally, we've talked about possibly having someone design a special heading and new name for this staff letter. (Anybody want to submit an "entry"?) What? And bury our beloved "D-2"? How tradition-busting can you get?! OK, so if you are sentimentally attached to dee-too, say so. That's the kind of thing we want to know.

The "information" of categories 2 and 3 will go *beyond* that which is removed from the old D-2 format. We expect to convey through this a lot more "management" information. Let me give you just a brief history here.

When we were smaller, and basically headquarters-managed, management information got shared regularly through group meetings. A year ago, as we moved toward our new format, we found a gap in our knowledge of what was going on in other departments. To correct this, we established a weekly management memo. This has bridged a gap.

However, we now feel the need for sharing much of this information on a wider basis. As indicated above, not all of it is important to everybody. But sometimes it's pretty hard to be selective and be sure that everybody who needs the information is covered. Hence we plan to put more management information out to the whole staff. Where discretion is called for in handling this information, we know you'll treat it that way.

The two-category information sheets will be easily distinguishable: the ones to save will be punched on the left side for a three-ring binder. This will identify them and possibly facilitate your filing. *How* you file them is up to you. Just so you *do* file them. These "save" items will *also* have a page number in the upper right hand corner, progressive through each year: 17-1, 17-2, etc. We will communicate from the *assumption* that these pages (and only these) are kept handily filed by each family.

On the "news" communications and the "information-to-note" communications, we will continue to use some numbering system for those of you who <u>choose</u> to save these also for reference. But this is not required.

You'll find the first information sheets in the new format in the next second-class air mail. As you'll see, we are going all out to make it easy to read and refer to, using adequate white space even though it will take more sheets to do it this way. We feel this is important.

Now, introducing a new "rag": interaction ... feedback ... crossfeed. (Again, maybe you'd like to suggest a name for it.) The idea is to break out of the one-way nature of our group communications. We share our ideas with you. Now you share *yours* with all of us. Letters to the editor? Yes, that's OK—answer, comment on, disagree with our sharings. But also initiate fresh ideas of your own for discussion.

Any limits? Let's try it with only one qualification. We're interested in *your* thoughts. (Brief quotations are fine as a part of this.) We won't even put a word limit down—let's see how it goes.

Editing? Not unless you *ask* for it. Then only to condense or help get your point across; no "censorship."

How often? Every other second-class air mail. Or every one if we have the contributions!

So let's chat, huh?

> In Him,
> s/Charlie

* * * * * * * * * *

The next two memos reflect Charlie's attempt to lead the organization in asking good questions—and listening biblically to possible answers—in the aftermath of two fatal accidents in 1971.

Mar. 25, 1971
To: MAF Staff
From: Charlie Mellis
Subject: "What is the Lord trying to tell us?" [re: accidents]

There was the question <u>again</u>: "What is the Lord trying to tell us?"

It was barely 30 minutes since I'd heard of Hatch's Homegoing. But the same question has been asked any number of times since Don Roberson was called Home 3½ years ago—and particularly since the series of accidents 2 years ago.

I'd like to record here some of the thoughts I've personally heard expressed during this period ... by various members of our fellowship ... and then perhaps add a few thoughts of my own.

Is it testing ... to test our dedication? Are we really willing to put our lives where our mouths are?

Is it instructional? Were we subconsciously drifting–despite all we said–to a place where we really felt a fatal accident wouldn't ever happen? Could this have induced a creeping decrease in vigilance? Did we need to be faced with stark reality to check a subtle drift?

Are we really as professional as we think we are? Are we living off our image?

Is it pride? With our words we insisted our long no-fatality record was of the Lord. But the true thoughts of our hearts often deceive us. They don't deceive the Lord.

Is it chastening ... to wake us up regarding some place or places where we're missing God's way for us? Particularly, are we running ahead of Him ... or in the wrong direction?

Pris (Voth) Larsen asks an opposite kind of question in a recent letter: "Do you think MAF is doing such a job for Christ that Satan is trying to hinder?"

Someone else carried this thought a step further: could these incidents actually be evidence that we're on the verge of more effective service in the days ahead? Are we perhaps getting <u>too</u> close to real, current effectiveness for the devil's comfort? (I think it was C. S. Lewis who suggested that our tempter may be less interested in getting us to do "bad" things ... than in keeping us doing "good" things that are losing their meaning or effectiveness.)

Historically, we have some points of identification with that particular thought. We learned a lot of "lessons" through the Waco repair in 1946-47. But think of our feelings: one month flying; 12 months repair. Even 25 years later it's hard to ignore the element of satanic attack on an emerging, since-proven-effective tool–at a point when we were potentially vulnerable. Yet <u>God</u> meant the attack for our good. We grew on it.

More dramatically, there was January, 1956–the first of 3 times now that death has come to MAF in pairs. At that time we were beginning to "break out" in progressive expansion. Our service was apparently effective.

The scene I remember occurred just 10 days after Nate Saint fell to Auca spears–our very first experience of this kind. Grady Parrott was with Marj in Ecuador. Two weary guys–Jim Truxton and myself–were still at the office late in the evening trying to collect our thoughts for the next day's priorities. We couldn't yet see what an impact would result from all those hours spent with the press and others. My own feelings were mostly grief and weariness.

The phone rang. It was Dan Derr calling from Mexico. Vi had just been called Home following the birth of Marilyn. As Jim hung up, I remember laying my head on the desk and crying aloud: Lord, if the devil thinks this will stop us, he's got another think coming ... he'll have to try something else ... by Your grace, we're not backing down. There was little doubt of spiritual attack.

But is it necessarily the Devil either? Does it have to be any of this? Could it be testing of a wholly different kind? Could it be a testing of our ultimate view of God? How do we view God's sovereign love? And do we have a truly Christian view of death? Does God want to enlarge our view of Himself... and His ultimate purposes?

Here it's natural to remember Job. Interestingly, the Sunday before Hatch left us, Claire and I completed an 8-week Bible study course, centered mostly in Job. There's probably a view of Job for every 3 readers ... maybe for every one! But in this very helpful study, several things came through in a fresh and forceful way to me (which I'm only sharing ... not "selling").

1) God was not playing a mere game of chess with Satan ... or with Job. He had purpose—regardless of whether or not His purpose is seen to be disclosed to Job and the reader.

2) Job's 3 "friends" were dead wrong in their insistence that Job was suffering because he had sinned.

3) Their error seems to stem from placing more confidence in their cherished convictions (even their convictions about God) than in God Himself. Even Job had this problem—trusting his doctrine more than God.

4) Jehovah hardly touches on the questions raised or the convictions discussed. He basically just presents Himself!

As Pastor John Tebay pointed out at Hatch's funeral, Satan no doubt thought he won at Calvary. (Also at Stephen's stoning.)

So did a couple of the Lord's disciples en route to Emmaus: "But we were hoping he was the one who was to come...." All the evidence—natural, logical, even Scriptural (as they currently understood it)—said this wasn't the way after all. But Jesus gave them new insights from the same Scriptures—concerning Himself. Is God perhaps giving us a fresh vision—and commission—as He did to Isaiah in the year of King Uzziah's death? "I saw THE LORD high and lifted up ... then I said, 'Here am I! Send me.'"

What do you think?

* * * * * * * * * *

A few months later, on Aug. 13, 1971, Charlie followed up on this previous memo with another one, a portion of which dealt with concerns related to a second fatal accident. A copy of the accident report was enclosed with the memo. I have purposely left the pilot unidentified.

To MAF Staff
From: CJM

… I wish we could just leave it there. But we can't.…

[We are reminded in the report that] we can't know what actually happened during the last few minutes of that flight. But we do know what happened the previous few days. [The pilot] had begun to show some resistance to reason-able instrument rules. He had been cautioned by his checkout pilot who, of course, shared [this information, following the accident]. Quite independent-ly, he had been gently cautioned by a buddy. [He had been] counseled firmly on the subject, 41 hours later the accident occurred. We learned from a passenger that on the intervening day, he had broken the rules.

Let me anticipate two logical questions. First, were checkout procedures adequate [for the pilot in this case]? I don't want to anticipate a technical report, but Hobey is *pleased* with present [program] procedures—which were followed. (As you know, Hobey has strong feelings on this subject.) Should [the pilot] have been grounded rather than just counseled? After reading the very thorough accident report, my conclusion is "no." It will be a sad day if we come to the point of having to take mechanical disciplinary measures for first offenses.

Believe me, gang, it hasn't been easy to write the above about a well-liked brother. It was tempting to just file that report. But I couldn't do that. *We need* the reminder of *our* humanity. We are neither supermen nor super saints. At the same time we *all* are targets of Satan's devices.

There is one reminder that we probably especially need. We live in the midst of a crisis of authority. This didn't *start* at Berkeley in 1964—but the curve has certainly steepened since then. If we feel this is just a problem of the "hippies" … or "the world" … we're of course kidding ourselves. These crises of history inevitably spill over into the Church—into *good churches*.…

On the authority question, we evangelicals already had a running start with which to catch the world. For one thing, we can spiritualize our independent spirit via the Reformation emphasis on the individual priesthood of all believ-ers. Then, too, separations (of both churches and mission agencies) brought on by doctrinal defections in the major denominations, have tended to give an "independency" to our movement. This isn't all bad, of course. And for that reason the temptation to follow our current cultural problems regarding authority can be very *subtle*. And subtlety, we know, is one of Satan's chief characteristics. Let's be on guard.

When we think of authority, we think of laws or rules. I'd like to add a word about the latter. Rules cannot guarantee safety. That requires attitude—including attitude toward rules. Personally, I believe that even technological rules, like flying regulations, are subject to what Jesus Christ said about rules: the letter kills; the spirit gives life.

Yes, I well know that people tend to use that statement to cop out on rules. They use it to *water down* the letter. But look at it again in context. Jesus meant it to *increase* responsibility. The Pharisees were copping out on *mere* letter-keeping. Sadly [this pilot] failed even that test. But our responsibility goes well *beyond* that.

If this experience serves to bring into clearer focus the balance between our horizontal responsibilities (subject to one another as unto Christ) and our vertical relationship (individually responsible to maintain the spirit that gives life), it may not be in vain. Let me assure you that I'm speaking to myself also. For the applications of this in the midst of our present culture, go far beyond flight rules. I'm sure you agree.

s/Charlie

* * * * * * * * * *

Early in 1972, the Board initiated an evaluation of the then-current management. Questionnaires returned from MAF overseas staff were collated and shared with the Board and the management team. Charlie wanted to share the results with MAF staff; the Board wasn't sure this was wise. This prompted another memo to the MAF staff about principles of leadership accountability.

March 30, 1972
CJM to MAF staff
Re: Response to Board-initiated evaluation of current management

Several months ago, Chuck sent you (overseas families) a Board-instituted questionnaire, asking your help in the Board's evaluation of management. The results were shared with the Board and the management team as planned. All involved were very grateful for your help in this.

In filling out the questionnaire, some of you expressed interest in seeing a summary of the results. I felt this would be a good idea. But as I took it to the Executive Committee (representing the Board), I found that the non-management members had some questions as to whether this was necessary—or wise. Let me hurriedly assure you that this had nothing to do with any desire to be "secretive." There was full recognition of the need for "openness" in many more areas of our lives than we normally practice. But at the same time, there was a feeling that we should wrestle with the Scriptural principles involved in the selection and evaluation of Christian leaders.

Identifying and confirming those whom God has equipped and selected is a complex matter at best. As one of our Board members said, the Bible is not a handbook on leadership—but on serving. This is brought out so clearly in the first two verses of 1 Corinthians 4: "This is how one should regard us, as servants of Christ and stewards of the mysteries of God. Moreover it is required of stewards that they be found trustworthy."

But then in verse 3, Paul—very conscious of his ordination to Christian leadership—says that it is a "small thing" that he should be judged by them. That's pretty authoritarian to 20th Century American ears! At the same time, it is quite clear that Paul did *not* consider their opinions inconsequential. If he did, he could hardly have written his second letter to this same church—or his letter to the Christians at Galatia. Since all of this was written under inspiration of the Spirit of God, we cannot pass it off as mere human "defensiveness."

It would seem that there are some things which we have to hold in "tension" here: God's ordination, confirmation of fellow Christian leaders (elders), and sensitivity to the whole Body of Christ—particularly those directly involved in one's ministry. As indicated, we are given no "formula" for balancing out these tensions; there is no "simple" answer.

As I said at the outset, my first reaction was very favorable toward sharing the results of this evaluation with you. And I'm happy that this was the decision of the Executive Committee. You'll find it enclosed.

At the same time, I praise God that He has given us a Board which takes so seriously its God-given responsibility for overall leadership, including its key role in the certification of staff leadership. In this task, the Board obviously considers your viewpoint important—as *one* of its inputs. Having considered *all* of its inputs, the Board must then be led by the Spirit of God as it meets together to seek that leading. Then as it appoints leaders—it appoints them to *lead* ... according to their gifts and temperaments. At times this may even require shielding them from the necessity of popularity, or the potential tyranny of polls.

I'm sure you'll understand that the Board is concerned here about a principle. Since the question was raised at this time, it was felt that it would be a good time to discuss these principles—apart from any specific personality or situation. (They didn't yet know of my plans for July, '73.) There was also the feeling that we should, in recognition of these principles, point out that future evaluations may or may not be shared (just as other inputs to the Board may or may not be shared) as the Lord might lead. The criterion should be: what is necessary and wise—what is the best expression of Christian love—to benefit the whole Body of Christ?

If you have questions about any of this, please do write.

In Him,

s/ Charlie

Charlie

[A P.S. referred to an attached summary of the evaluation of management appropriate to the place served—whether on the field or at headquarters—which is not included here.]

* * * * * * * * * *

On August 25, 1971, Charlie's memo revealed his doctor's recent diagnosis that probably signaled the "beginning of the end" of his life's ministry. At the time he was not overly concerned, but it is interesting to note that his earthly ministry ended just over 10 years later, when the Lord called him Home (in December of 1981). A couple excerpts from this staff memo reveal Charlie's attempt to be transparent about his own health, while recognizing that others were facing similar struggles.

August 25, 1971
To: MAF Staff
From: Charlie Mellis

Dear Gang,

I saw a cartoon in a Christian magazine several years ago. A teacher was enrolling a boy of 10 or 12 in an MK school. He was saying, "Let's see; I had malaria, amoebic dysentery, hepatitis ... you know, the usual childhood diseases."

Perhaps I was feeling left out—or lacking in status. I had picked up malaria in Mexico way back in 1947 ... and had it again in New Guinea in 1953. But that's not where it's at today. Malaria is out. Hepatitis is in.

So a couple of weeks ago I got a call from the doctor. I'd just had my annual physical and he had the lab reports. How did I feel? Fine. A little tired still from the trip [7 weeks in Africa] and the meetings; but otherwise, fine. Well, it seems that two different blood tests both showed a typical pattern of hepatitis. A repeat test was still "elevated" though slightly better. The test could possibly be affected by the anti-malarial I took on the trip, or it could reflect a very low-grade actual infection. Until the re-tests come down I'm supposed to be on a reduced schedule.

So I've been staying home half-days (even sleeping in some days), catching up on reading and correspondence that accumulated for 12 weeks. Man, if you have to get sick, this is definitely the way to go! Seriously, I'm very grateful for the lightness of the infection (if any), and mindful that a lot of you have had some tough bouts with this recently. We're praying! …

35

Organizational Growth

Charlie's second opportunity to present an annual report to the Corporation occurred in 1971. Although he dealt primarily with organizational growth in terms of personnel and finances, he expressed appreciation for the resources, both human and material, that God provided. He was especially desirous of laying a biblical foundation for relationships with constituency that would enable adequate support. To this end, he prepared an outline for a joint Bible study, hoping for valuable input from, and a consensus among, the career staff—in seeking to be faithful to God's Word together.

MISSIONARY AVIATION FELLOWSHIP
President's Annual Report to the Corporation
July 23, 1971

Since our last Annual Meeting, two anticipated new services in Afghanistan and Columbia have become operational. Other new services are planned, as brought out in the area reports. Two services—Sao Luiz, Brazil and Mindanao, Philippines—have been suspended; Mindanao may be re-activated later.

Our staff has grown by 9 couples, a single man, and one bride! Welcome, all! Three families are now serving the Lord elsewhere, as anticipated at our last meeting.

Not anticipated was the Homegoing of four of our staff colleagues. . . . I almost hesitate to include this with this statistical portion of my report. For we haven't lost just so many shoulders on a collective wheel; we've lost friends, brothers, individuals with distinctive gifts who have made distinctive contributions. We will be reflecting on their personal contributions to us a little later in this meeting.

Personally, the loss of our brethren has served to further heighten my awareness of, and appreciation for, each of you as individuals. I want to be more aware of (and more expressive concerning) your accomplishments and your felt needs. This is what made my Africa visit [earlier in 1971] such a memorable experience—getting reacquainted with each of our families, and entering into both the challenges and problems they face individually. I feel that some of our people there will face tough and complex situations for the next several years.

It's going to require stamina and patience. My hat's off to them. More importantly, I know better how to pray for them now.

But the Africa trip was a learning experience, in addition to the sharing. It was personally interesting to re-visit places I'd been to 14 years ago ... some of them 34 years ago! Beyond that, it was instructive to observe mission/church relationships and third-world nations at closer range.

In the realm of finance, we have approached the problem of the income/expense gap in the Operating Fund from two directions. Most of our cost-cutting efforts were aimed at streamlining the headquarters staff. As you know from previous communications, this effort was more successful than predicted at our last meeting. However, this has not closed our gap. The cost-cutting program is not yet complete, but further anticipated savings represent only a small percentage of total budget. Any additional cost-cutting would involve salary reductions at a time when the opposite is needed.

Increasing our income—the other side of the coin—is a major subject for prayerful consideration at this meeting. As reported, the creative efforts of Information Services have been used of God to increase undesignated giving encouragingly. But again, this rate of increase has not closed the gap, nor is it apt to apart from a sizable informational effort that would itself be costly, and probably out of character for MAF.

It is my personal conviction that the remaining gap must be closed by the further development of income; that the quality of this development is more important than the speed; and that the primary areas of development should be two:

1. Further development of personalized support, based on the proposal we'll be discussing at this meeting. As you know, I'm proposing that overseas staff (while abroad and while on furlough) be responsible for adequate constituency *relationships*; but that Information Services carry primary responsibility for adequate *support*. The latter can begin to happen when a decision is reached on the proposal.

2. Supplementary income. Even though I have *personal* assurances of God's guidance in this matter, it would be inappropriate for me to make a proposal to the Board unless there is some reasonable consensus concerning the biblical principles. If the Lord brings us to that point through this meeting (and follow-up correspondence), I will be giving a major portion of my time the next two months to proposals for our October Board meeting.

I see these two approaches as inter-related. I also foresee that they will take *time*–particularly in the light of (a) present economic conditions, and (b) the fact that development of supplementary income *must* be subservient to the accomplishment of our primary service goals. (To me, *one* indication of God's guidance lies in the fact that some of our goals seem quite compatible with such a step.) My proposals to the Board will include time projections and recommendations regarding interim resources.

I'm sure you realize that these proposals for closing the income/expense gap over a period of time are made in full confidence that our God can short-circuit these plans with direct, special provision at any time. It depends only on His *choice*. As indicated, I have felt led to make these proposals–in terms of the faith-with-its-boots-on that I find in the teaching of James ... [and in] the example and teaching of Paul.

Let's return briefly to our human "resources" ... you–and me. As you know, I am deeply concerned that our people have the same options as other late-twentieth-century Christians have in exercising their stewardship ... the option of *voluntary* contribution, of developing and using their varied gifts, of raising and training their children, of length of service. All these are at least implied in our goals, and some are explicit in current proposals. As the Lord leads, I expect to translate the rest into specific proposals in the coming year.

Finally, I would like to acknowledge especially fine contributions by several of our people this past year. Wes Eisemann did outstanding "double duty" in the midst of difficult times. The opportunity this gave for overall management coordination and language study opportunity for the Parsons is greatly appreciated. Bob Gordon achieved an amazing record at School of World Missions; and it was more than fine marks–his papers were geared to contribute to the mission movement.[1] Even as I write this, I'm aware that others certainly have also achieved in special ways that are less visible to me.

May the Lord help us all to achieve His purposes for us and in us during the coming year ... with joy!

Charlie Mellis

* * * * * * * * *

---

[1] One such paper written by Bob Gordon that Charlie found "intriguing and probing" was entitled, "Anybody Know What to Do with a Pilot?"

July 14, 1971
To: MAF Staff
Re: Bible Study at Annual Meeting

As indicated on the tentative agenda, two subjects are related to the proposed Bible studies. But let's list the actual subjects for study this way:

1. Principles involved in the <u>relationship</u> between the church(es)–sending or receiving, as applicable–and the individual messengers.

2. Principles involved in the <u>support</u> (physical, financial) of the messengers.

I hope you'll have a chance to study the following passages (and any other references you find that I didn't) before Monday, July 26. It's not really as much reading as it looks like. Remember, this is to be a study together.

Needless to say, the bulk of our study sources will involve Acts and the Epistles, after the Church was born. But we have some background material on item 2 as follows:

Sending out the 12:	Matt 9:35-10:15 (and to end of chapter)
	Mark 6:7-13
	Luke 9:1-6
Follow-up:	Luke 22:35-38
Sending out the 70:	Luke 10:1-12; 17-20

For further background, consider that the original messengers (the apostles...

1. Were called solely by Jesus Christ before a Church existed.
2. Were commissioned (sent) directly by Christ (Matt 28:18-20);
   Mk 16:15; Lk 24: 46-48; Jn 20:21; Acts 1:8
3. Were told to wait for what proved to be the birth of the Church
   (Lk 24:49; Acts 1:4-8)–though final commissioning
   was still by the Holy Spirit rather than the Church.
4. Chose a 12th (Acts 1:15-26).

Original financial basis of the new community (no aspect of sent-witnesses yet apparent),

> Acts 2:44-46
>   4:32-37 & following in chapter 5 (Voluntary, not required–see 5:4)
>   6:1ff (trouble in the distribution)

A sent teacher-messenger ... Acts 11:21-26
Financial sharing, non-local ... Acts 11:27-30

Church commissioning sent ones/receiving their reports.

    Acts 12:25-13:4
            14:21-23; 26-28
            15:3, 4, 12, 30-33

Support through hospitality and work.

    Acts 16:15
            18:3, 11, 18, 24-26

Effect of the Gospel on a city's economy, and the messenger's conduct there.

    Acts 19, especially vv. 23ff
    Acts 20:17-38

Relationships with various churches

    Acts 21:3-6; 7-14; 17-26

Miscellaneous references to Paul's financial status

    Acts 24:26
            28:14-16, 30, 31

Now let me just list, without introduction of system, passages I found in the Epistles that may have some bearing on our subjects. Key passages are marked (*).

Romans	12:1-13; 13:6-8; 15:24-31; 16:1,2
I Corinthians	3:5-9; *9:3 to the end; 16:1-19
II Corinthians	1:8a, 11-16; 6:3; *chapters 8 & 9; 10:15, 16; 11:7ff
Galatians	6:6-10
Philippians	1:3-8; 2:19-30; 4:10-20
I Thessalonians	2:9, 10
II Thessalonians	3:6-13
I Timothy	… Several refs to financial qualifications in chaps. 3, 4, & 5 … particularly 5:17-22
II Timothy	2:1-7
Philemon	4-21

* * * * * * * * * *

36
New Management Strategy

The following report reflects overall satisfaction with the newly inaugurated decentralization of management. But Charlie also mentions wide-ranging concerns in other areas, most notably an observed improvement in organizational unity.

MISSION AVIATION FELLOWSHIP
President's "Position Report"
to the Board of Directors
October 4, 1971

I'd like to share first what to me have been the most significant—and encouraging—internal results of the past six months since we last met as a full Board in April.

1) Our decentralized approach to management is now fully operative. Roy Parsons has completed his language study and is resident at Kinshasa. My visit to Africa assured me that this will meet a felt need for all concerned. Hank Worthington recently took up residence in San Jose, Costa Rica. Hobey Lowrance is now fully established within the Asian area, and the "readings" from there by mail indicate a high degree of satisfaction.

2) Our second major target in our new management concept—individual responsibility and control—has also taken a large step forward. This is not only true in the areas but also in the headquarters unit. My physical absence from Fullerton for a seven-week period played an important role in this. We are currently taking further steps to augment this.

3) The discovery and correction of earlier deficiencies in our purchasing and shipping department has been a crucial development. Overseas staff confidence had fallen to a low ebb with a tendency to blame this on the "new regime." Rebuilding of confidence must be by demonstration over a period, so it is not yet an accomplished fact—but there is encouragement.

4) The further revision of our candidate and furloughee programs, which will now take place only once per year during the summer months, brings opportunity for development of all our personnel efforts. Simultaneously, the experiment in inter-agency orientation that we had the most significant part in planning has generated considerable interest within IFMA-EFMA circles[1]— even though the breadth of involvement in this first program was limited by late finalization and announcement.

5) My trip to Africa was a very rewarding experience. It's been 12 years since I've been abroad; 14 years since I was in Africa. It was an appreciated learning experience. But the most significant part of the trip was the opportunity to spend two or three days with each of our families. There had been a considerable degree of "un-ease" among our African staff. I feel this has been significantly reduced. Some of this had already begun before my trip. Let me cite one highlight. One of our men had been very openly critical of the changes within MAF—not only to others but also by letter direct to headquarters. Shortly after I arrived at his base, he indicated that he owed me and others at headquarters some real apologies, and then added, "I just want you to know, Charlie, that I'm back on the team!" Everything he did and said during the remainder of the visit proved that he meant it.

6) The spirit of the Annual Meeting in late July gave further evidence of substantial uniting behind MAF's new configuration.

Let me add at this point that I see this "substantial uniting" as 1) a near elimination of the negative (resistance to changes), 2) a very substantial acceptance of the new condition. This I see as a good but essential neutral factor. I do not believe that we have yet achieved (though I see encouraging progress) a positive posture among a substantial majority—a posture we must achieve if MAF is to even retain the relevancy it has enjoyed during its first quarter century. Like other Spirit-led movements, ours was built on vision. Today we have a great deal of dedication to tasks—tasks with which we are comfortable. We have yet to see a majority of our people accept the discomfort of God's cutting edge where vision is again perceivable.

---

[1]IFMA and EFMA originally designated the Interdenominational Foreign Missions Association & the Evangelical Foreign Missions Association respectively, but, as with many organizations in recent years, these names have undergone revision.

My greatest disappointment in my own performance centers in the financial area. I have not been able to give this the attention I wanted to. Jim Lomheim has faced a succession of frustrations too numerous to mention here. In spite of this he has made real progress in identifying the problem areas. Some progress has also been made toward solutions. For both Jim and myself the next five months will be crucial. Barring circumstances completely unforeseen, we will at last be able to turn from fighting brush fires and give some real attention to building the fire breaks. We are both keeping our schedules clear for this.

As you'll see by the final audited financial statement (promised in time for our meeting), we've taken a considerable step toward a consolidated statement; we should complete this process within this fiscal year. Meanwhile, Jim is providing an internal statement with notes.

You'll find several proposals enclosed, with the principal one being the one I promised centering around financial development. Both Jim and I will have additional data available at the meeting. However, we have fallen short of our target of having scheduled, dollarized projections toward a balanced budget. It is realistic to complete this by March and present it with the new budget.

Charles Mellis, President

37
Crafting a Policy Statement

When a policy statement was considered necessary to clarify the organization's position on a current issue of concern, it was developed through an in-depth study of Scripture by a Board appointed ad hoc committee. Charlie's memo to the staff and the policy statement that was crafted are presented below.

December 30, 1971
To: MAF Staff
From: Charlie Mellis

Dear Gang,

Some time ago the Board recognized that a study should be made of what is generally referred to as Neo-Pentecostalism with a view toward a new definition of our relationship to people of pentecostal persuasion. Grady [as Board Chairman] appointed an ad hoc committee for this purpose: John Tebay (chairman), Art Glasser, and myself. This committee has now completed its work and the Executive Committee, acting for the Board, has issued the enclosed statement. This statement will be reviewed by the full Board at its next meeting, March 17-18. Any comments that you would like to share will be very welcome.

As you'll see, we've confined our statement essentially to speaking in tongues since it is this one of the charismatic gifts that has most frequently created a tension in relationships between Christian brethren. As you will note, we recognize that any of us can be the cause of this tension—no matter what our view or experience is. May God guide us all as we consider these matters prayerfully before Him....

MISSIONARY AVIATION FELLOWSHIP
Policy Statement on Tongues

As members of the MAF Board of Directors we desire to be sensitive and responsive to the insights and experiences which fellow Christians are having in all parts of the world in our day. Many are speaking of a new freedom and power in Christ. Who knows but that the Holy Spirit is preparing the Church for the spiritual renewal which she desperately needs. We should be open to the possibility of this renewal coming in surprising ways and through unexpected channels. "No eye has seen, nor ear heard, nor the heart of man conceived, what God has prepared for those who love Him" (1 Cor. 2:9).

Quite candidly, we fear that at times we have limited the work of the Holy Spirit in our thinking and practice. And we are conscious that in addressing ourselves to the question of tongues, we are dealing with only one small segment of a vast body of truth that has enormous potential for us all. We plead therefore, for a prayerful mutuality of respect and affection. In confronting this subject we all must display an openness toward those whose spiritual experiences differ from our own. Even though spiritual gifts may be abused, this does not mean that they should be prohibited. Those who speak with tongues have valid contributions to make to the spiritual vitality and unity of MAF. Our task is to be open to the new lessons the Spirit of God may be teaching us through each other.

We have but one caution to raise. Whereas our sole appeal is to Scripture, we would suggest that to ascertain the will of God for MAF we must give primary attention to its didactic rather than historic parts. "What is described in Scripture as having happened to others is not necessarily intended for us, whereas what is promised to us we are to appropriate, and what is commanded us we are to obey" (John R. W. Stott).

Therefore, we invite your attention to the following propositions:

1. Scripture teaches that the manifestation of the Holy Spirit through all of the gifts is for the purpose of bringing unity and edification to the whole body of Christ (1 Cor. 12:12-26; 14:1-5, 12-19).

2. Scripture teaches the essentiality of diverse gifts to allow for a full expression and manifestation of the Holy Spirit through the Body of Christ (1 Cor. 12).

3. Scripture teaches that not all speak in tongues, just as not all participate in any other gift (1 Cor. 12:28-30).

4. Scripture teaches that speaking in tongues is good, but prophesying is better, and love for God and men is best of all. From the silence of the gospels and of the great majority of the epistles on the subject of the gift of speaking in tongues it appears that it occupied a subordinate place in the life of Christians in the apostolic age (1 Cor. 12:31; 14:1-5, 18-19).

5. Scripture teaches that we should not forbid speaking in tongues (1 Cor. 14:5, 39).

Conclusion:

We therefore conclude on the basis of Scripture that the practice of speaking in tongues should be neither despised nor forbidden; on the other hand, it should not be emphasized nor made normative for the Christian experience.

Therefore:

1. Since our written doctrinal statement does not discriminate against Pentecostal or Neo-Pentecostal views, membership is not limited on this basis.

2. However, in view of the broadly cooperative nature of our fellowship and service, we encourage those who believe that speaking in tongues is a *normative* Christian experience to seek service through some other agency.

3. It is our responsibility to resist that which brings division to the Church whether that be through excessive promotion or rigid rejection of speaking in tongues.

4. We do not exclude from service or cooperation those of Pentecostal or Neo-Pentecostal persuasion or experience.

* * * * * * * * * *

"We believe the Scripture teaching to be that the gift of tongues is one of the gifts of the Spirit, and that it may be present in the normal Christian assembly as a sovereign bestowal of the Holy Spirit upon such as he wills. We do not believe that there is any Scriptural evidence for the teaching that speaking in tongues is the sign of having been filled with the Spirit, nor do we believe that it is the plan of God that all Christians should possess the gift of tongues. This gift is one of many gifts and is given to some for the benefit of all. The attitude toward the gift of tongues held by pastor and people should be 'Seek not, forbid not'"–A.B. Simpson, as quoted in the *Alliance Witness*, May 1, 1963, p. 19.

12/23/71

38
The Transition Period Comes to an End

This memo to the staff was intended to share the Board's actions relative to the anticipated end of Charlie's three-year transitional term as MAF's President, in 1973.

March 23, 1972
To: MAF Staff
From: Charlie Mellis

Dear Gang:

The MAF Board meeting last weekend was a great experience. All 15 members were present, and I heard several comments during coffee breaks about how the Lord has given us such a well "balanced" Board.

We also had a well "balanced" meeting. There are times when we've felt a bit frustrated with so much of our time spent on financial matters—even though this, too, is very important. This time we had a real good balance between discussing our ministry *per se*, on the one hand … and the financial means of making it possible, on the other. This was greatly facilitated by our earlier decision to spread this meeting over two days: from 2:00pm Friday to 3:00pm Saturday. This greatly relieved the time squeeze, and we plan to repeat it in the future.

As you know, our Board meeting was preceded by almost three weeks of joint management planning with all three of the Area Vice-Presidents here. This also proved very effective and will no doubt be repeated. This was helpful not only for our annual planning and budgeting … but also in overall management coordination. Some of the proposals that came before the Board were a result of this planning session.

When we planned our management revision in late '69, it was communicated (at the annual meeting and elsewhere) that I'd accept the Presidency for a transitional period of three years. Subsequently, I've been encouraged by members of the Board, colleagues in management, and others of you to think in terms of a longer period. This has been flattering and appreciated. Also appreciated was a positive response on the Board-initiated evaluation questionnaire (we'll be sharing a summary of that with you shortly). For a time I felt that I could enjoy extending my term to a five-year period if this was desired. But during the past six months the Lord has progressively, and very strongly, confirmed to me that His original guidance was valid and still stands. Consequently, I asked the Board to plan toward relieving me by mid-summer of 1973. In order to have a specific target, I suggested July 31st. I'm sharing this now for one purpose: so that we can all pray together that the Lord will guide us concerning future leadership. I share this with the confidence that our discussions will be motivated toward a finding of God's will for MAF tomorrow … and free of the type of campaigning that our news media are so full of in this leap year.

As indicated above, the Lord's guidance to me in this matter has been very clear. It is made up of many components too complex to put on paper. Some of the reasons are personal. None of them involve unhappiness with MAF. Basically, it's a matter of recognizing that I have made my contribution … and that my particular gifts can now be more validly exercised elsewhere. Just a *part* of my decision is a recognition that I have not been able to perform as well in my present position as I did when I was "No. 2." Consequently, I've asked the Board to give me some help for my remaining months in office.

Acceding to my specific request, the Board has appointed Bob Lehnhart Director of Operations. This is a temporary position which will probably continue only through my remaining time in office. It does *not* imply that Bob is being "groomed" to take over. (He is, of course, one of several possible candidates.) I trust you will all accept this at face value. I have asked for his help because I need it and he "fits" the job. His task will involve coordination of the management team. He will take over my *management* (as contrasted with *leadership*) responsibilities. He will continue his responsibility as Director of Planning and will also do whatever is possible in the realm of New Developments (we're limited here at present for financial and other reasons). Chuck [Bennett] will also be taking some of my responsibilities in the area of internal communications.

This letter has been centered on certain aspects of what has *happened* here the last few weeks. We wanted to share that. But we were also deeply conscious that we had good meetings because you-all were praying with us and for us …

even as we were remembering you and your activities. Praise the Lord for this privilege to share together in His work....

> ... and in His love,
> s/Charlie

* * * * * * * * * *

A few months later, in Charlie's final annual report as President, he communicates his realization that MAF as an organization has reached adulthood—and suggests what that may mean for MAF in terms of responsibilities to the larger mission community.

MISSIONARY AVIATION FELLOWSHIP
President's Annual Report
July 24, 1972

Allow me to omit any statistical summary. The past year's record lies in other areas. Yet we're thankful for new friends and helpers. And not unmindful that some who shared our task faithfully for many years are no longer directly serving in this way.

We should note, with special gratitude to God, that in the 12 months since we last met, our accident record has been the lowest of any year since 1961. God has worked *through* the conscientious dedication of each one of you to give us this further improved record. Undoubtedly our new safety program has played a part also.

At the same time, we have again witnessed the clear prerogative of our loving God to make His sovereign choices ... particularly in two widely-separated events: the miraculous survival of Dave Olson and his passenger from an act-of-God-induced crash ... and the Homegoing of little Grace Karetji, along with the apparent speedy recovery of her mother, Netty. For me personally, this year has brought further and fresh insights toward a Christian view of death ... as an integral part of life.

Financially, we've closed a fiscal year with the largest deficit in our history. The fact that this outsize figure is accentuated by two unusual items scarcely makes it more palatable. Rather, our encouragement comes through the present year's budget. By God's grace, working through the efforts of many, we expect to finish *this* year with a *balanced* Statement of Operations. Via Bob Lehnhart's persistent efforts we are *now* experiencing the huge savings of a self-insured workmen's compensation program. Other cost-reducing programs, though less dramatic, have continued through this year.

Increased income has been another item of praise. I've been reviewing my report of last year, and am humbled to find that my rating as a "prophet" is hardly 40%. The Lord did work through our discussions and decision regarding salary/support—and a heartening response by our constituency—to substantially increase our income. On the other hand, this was *not* the year for increases in the "supplemental income" we discussed at some length last year; the trend, in fact, was the other way. But then I was delighted to be wrong in my somewhat pessimistic view as to how the national economy would affect our general giving.

The remainder of income improvement in our present budget is resulting from efforts not yet planned a year ago. Norm Olson and his crew have done a fine job here—and have not allowed our goals or our character to take second place to income development *per se*. Other programs will become more visible in the months ahead.

Our recent trip through Asia was an experience Claire and I will long remember. The memory of *places* visited is dim compared with the consciousness of 24 wonderful families—and a much-loved son[1]—who shared their lives with us for a few days, some in the midst of over-crowded schedules. It's been hard to come back to a desk!

As you know, God has been working tremendously throughout Indonesia. Yet I come away with a feeling that even greater things are on the horizon there. Our visit to Kabul, Afghanistan, also gave us a strong sense of God at work. Even in our Laos and Palawan programs, where there have been multiple problems and discouragements, we saw signs of stirrings in diverse areas.

Perhaps this is symptomatic of what's ahead for MAF. Hand-size clouds are forming on the horizon. Will we recognize them? It's my impression that relatively few large movements of God's Spirit come in easily-recognizable, expected form—like today's movement on the Canadian prairie. You Narnia fans will recognize this as the outlook of lay theologian C. S. Lewis as represented in his Aslan. But during the next two days, we'll look at this subject directly from the Scriptures (which Lewis merely expounded in unique ways).

---

[1]Charlie and Claire's son Jim was at that time serving in Sentani, (New Guinea) for a 2½ year period as MAF's bookkeeper.

Probably this is one of my two greatest concerns (neither of them related to our Asia trip) for MAF in the years ahead: our sensitivity ... even our willingness ... to perceive God's hand, not only in that part of history that preceded us, but in that part of history for which we have direct responsibility. I'd recommend a study of Isaiah 43:18 & 19 in every version you have access to.

My other concern is related to this. It involves our continuing (though considerably lessened) reluctance to take our responsibility—commensurate with our attained experience and maturity—as *participants* in the discovery of God's will for His Body today. Historically this is understandable. In our mid-years, we inadvertently shifted the direction of our strong sense of servanthood from God Himself to a group of people. This, too, was understandable; we were then adolescent. In trying to correct this in recent years, we in leadership made some poor word choices (like "co-leaders")—which clouded rather than clarified. This is past history.

My concern today is this: do we recognize that MAF *has* reached adulthood? And that adults must accept adult responsibilities? A close friend of MAF wrote of our new posture, "It seems like the case of a truck driver who suddenly takes over the presidency of the firm." I found the extremity of this analogy a help in clarifying the issue. Isn't it rather, "Over a period of 27 years, the truck driver gradually rose through the ranks and became a contributing member of management"?

In the business world we laud that. Why are *we* so reluctant to take our place of responsibility at the conference table? We have insights of *breadth* (we work face-to-face with more groups than any other agency within missions) which add a needed dimension to the *depth* insights of the groups we serve. Let's look at this, too, in the light of Scripture this week. Properly understanding our adult role will, I'm convinced, take nothing away from our responsibility for full technical competence.

I'm looking forward to these three days together—and to the year ahead. Not just because it's my last ... but because it's another year to serve our wonderful Lord in fellowship together. Let's make the most of it ... with joy!

Charlie Mellis

39

Reflections of an Observer

by Charles Mellis

This may have been presented as a "paper." It was not dated, but would have been written between 1978 and 1980. It is included since it provides a glimpse into Charlie's thinking and strategizing about missions following his departure from MAF in 1973.

In 27 years of mission administration, I barely touched the world of Islam. This is partly because the nature of Mission Aviation Fellowship's task caused us to focus on the jungle. But it is also due to my preoccupation, for at least 20 years, with *do*-ing. It has only been a little more than a decade since I became a conscious observer, and eventually a reflector. For less than a decade my observations and reflections have included Islam. My mounting interest has been based on 4 factors: intuition, information, interest among youth, and the study of mission strategy.

What can one say about INTUITION? It's a term we so often use when we are unable or unwilling to cite reason. Yet we all recognize its validity, particularly in the role of leadership. Intuition is most thoroughly validated by eventual results. But in the interim it may also be corroborated by the independent intuitions of others who have a track record of "good intuitions" (keenness, sensitivity, etc.). As a highly-interested "outside" observer, my sense of expectancy for the Spirit's working in Islam derives, in part, from an observed significant consensus of such expectancy among Christian leaders.

I sensed this in some of your papers as I edited them for *Missiology* two years ago. But, of course, I found more than intuition there. I found also solid INFORMATION, some of which was new.... I had also begun to view very differently the mid-1960s movement in Indonesia—[recognizing that] a movement of substantial proportions has taken place. God has done a new thing.

But perhaps my most surprising discovery came from my new relationship to mission-interested Christian students when I was asked to head up the Summer

Institute of International Studies [from 1974-1977].[1] Within this circle, and among other Christian young people, I am constantly finding significant INTEREST in relating to the Muslim world.... I have not been able to trace it to one or even just a few sources (though I do not claim to have done significant research here). It *seems* that the Spirit is giving this interest to a great many young people.

There are questions to be answered here that are beyond my purpose. For example, why aren't these people applying somewhere? ... Do we need that many westerners, particularly Americans, surging into Muslim lands? ... My purpose here is only to note the apparent widespread INTEREST as a sign of the Spirit's activity.

So we come to my fourth basis for mounting interest in the current Christian encounter with Islam: the study of STRATEGY. Like anyone else who has studied at the School of World Mission in Pasadena, I've become excited about the potential of some of the tools that are now in our hands: missionary anthropology, cross-cultural communication skills, church research studies, etc. Not that I am a 100% convert. But then, who is? There is no "pure" consensus of a "Church Growth viewpoint" even among the professors. And that is only to say that they are human beings! But in my own case, my areas of reservation stem primarily from my suspicions about the American business community. I do not eschew entirely insights from the latter that may be applied to our task; but I proceed here with a great deal of caution. For in the American church we seldom stop to reflect on how the so-called free enterprise system has invaded and pervaded our overall world view....

Nevertheless, I am still enthusiastic about the potential. The identification of the *principles* of the *theory of mission* that we usually call the Church Growth School give me a base from which to grow and think. My favorite expositor of these principles is Dr. Alan Tippett, now retired in his native Australia. I have been particularly helped by the emphasis he gives to the "fullness of time" principle, also referred to as "evangelistic opportunity"—the principle that not all peoples are ready (not all harvests are ripe) at the same time. This throws the emphasis less on our planning or strategizing than on our *discovering* the present strategy of the Holy Spirit.

---

[1]The Summer Institute for International Studies later became known as the Institute for International Studies at William Carey International University, Pasadena, California. The New Perspectives courses, developed from these initial offerings, are currently offered at various locations nationally through the U.S. Center for World Mission (Pasadena).

My studies have also punctured my neat little organizational mind (focused on "decently and in order") with the recognition that C.S. Lewis was right: Aslan is *not* a tame lion! I stand in awe of what, from my finite viewpoint, I call the risks of the Spirit. For example, what the Spirit is doing in the African independency movement, partly at least, to correct the "orderly" we made there. One need not draw any final conclusion about the T'ai P'ing movement in China to recognize that we made unfortunate, history-changing moves based more on cultural viewpoints than on any openness to the freedom of the Spirit in working through "fallen" men. In this same vein, I was tremendously challenged by John Wilder's article in the April, 1977, *Missiology*. Are we ready to be "left out" of the Spirit's movement in Islam? Is our study of strategy primarily to *recognize* a movement which most of the church would probably reject? Is it to prepare us to be the friendly bridges John [Wilder] speaks of—no matter what risk we face from a non-comprehending Church?

These, then, are the strategic questions that challenge me most. For all our learning by intensively reflecting on the mission of the people of God to date, we may find ourselves only prepared to recognize—and accept—the surprises of the Spirit.

Finally, I want to pose [and leave with you] a *question* of strategy. As some of you know, my background in the structural aspect of missions (even though I now view this very differently than I used to) has led me on to think of effective mission structures for the future. I've written on this subject, particularly emphasizing the "committed communities"/orders/brotherhoods that we see recurring throughout history.[2] This interest, in turn, brought me into relationship with Chaeok Chun.... I was particularly fascinated by one paper [she] wrote ... in which she compared the primary Korean view of the Church (the family model) with the Muslim frame of reference [in which she] speculated that the brotherhood model might be a better cultural fit. I would love to hear a group like this interact on that thesis. Does this suggest patterns for the Muslim converts that have not yet been incorporated into existing church structures?

---

[2]See *Committed Communities: Fresh Streams for World Missions*, by Charles J. Mellis. Pasadena: William Carey Library (1983), originally written as a thesis for his M.A. degree in Missiology at Fuller Seminary's School of Intercultural Studies (formerly the School of World Mission) and first published in 1976.

40

More than a Pilot—
A Wife Reflects

Our New Guinea experience in the 1950s opened our eyes to far more than we anticipated (at 30 years of age); it gave us a shove that moved us beyond the confines of our own culture and value system. And it convinced us that further stretching lay ahead. Then in the 60s, we read an article written by the chancellor of U.C.L.A. about what he called paradigm shifts that shifts through the years brought significant changes to Western-European society. He noted that in the 17th century, beginning about the time of Descartes, intellectual pursuits of thinking and reasoning were highly regarded, to the extent that a person's sense of being was described in terms of, "I think, therefore I am." With the arrival of the industrial revolution, a noteworthy societal shift occurred. A person's sense of being now was expressed in terms of activity—in doing, and producing ("I do, therefore I am"). This emphasis lasted well into the mid-1960s when it too was replaced. Young people in particular were discovering the importance of feelings and relationships, and began seeking ways to "find themselves"—often through drugs and communal lifestyles. This new reality—"I feel, therefore I am"—was another paradigm shift that was to have a global impact.

Charlie and I belonged to the generation of *do-ers*, as did our parents. Charlie's father was an entrepreneur builder whose top priority was his business, although he also had a deep interest in Christian missions and missionaries. Charlie was work-oriented too, as well as a *do-er* by temperament. I discovered he had been influenced by the modernist/fundamentalist controversy of the 20s. Possibly as a result he was ready to take a firm stand for what he believed—any compromise of his Christian faith would be unthinkable! This had further application in his finding it hard to let go of a decision he believed in when there was a difference of opinion.

* * * * * * * * *

Many will recognize that few in our generation found it easy—or comfortable—to reveal themselves or share very deeply; it was far too risky. The tendency to internalize feelings and frustrations was widespread. This reluctance to share pervaded our society up until the mid-60s when changes began to appear through growing interest in small group sharing and in building relationships. As more information became available about the effects of stress and tension on health, I began to connect some dots, wondering if the many pressures Charlie experienced (both internally and externally induced) together with residual damage from tropical health problems (e.g., malaria and dysentery) may have contributed to his early death at age 60.

※ ※ ※ ※ ※ ※ ※ ※ ※ ※

At Charlie's memorial service, in December of 1981, one of his MAF colleagues on the "management team" suggested two traits that had characterized Charlie's life. One was: "He always gave himself 100%; whatever he believed, he believed passionately." I agree. For, in addition to an underlying commitment to the Lord, Charlie's life exhibited an extraordinary love for MAF—he poured himself into the organization. Firmly convinced of MAF's purpose, goals, and reputation, he often accepted an assignment of implementing a difficult decision for the good of the organization. This I found hard to accept when I saw it becoming a pattern. However, if I dared question him about why he seemed to "always be the one"—he'd remind me that if a tough decision had to be carried out, someone had to do it. Then he'd reassure me by saying that the Lord understood his reluctance, and that he wasn't trying to win a popularity contest. He was more concerned about Whom he wanted to please.

Holding firm convictions (such as determining to please the Lord) may be strengths; but they don't always translate into appropriate actions. For example, Charlie's colleagues respected and valued his analytical ability and his desire to achieve goals. He was aware of that and found it both gratifying and satisfying. However, strong convictions that make letting go of a position or accepting a compromise more difficult, may possibly contribute to perceptions of intimidation, aloofness, or unapproachability.

I'd like to include here a personal letter that seems to provide clues about how he viewed himself. It was written on February 23, 1956 after he returned to L.A. from a visit with his father, then seriously ill with cancer in St. Louis:

Dad, I appreciate your sharing your thoughts with us about how to handle your affairs when the Lord calls you Home. It's good to have these things in mind whether it is two months or two years. And by the same token, it's a time when I (living away from St. Louis) am thinking in terms of wanting to express to you how much I appreciate all you've been and done through the years. Of course, I expect to see you again next month, but even then it won't be too easy to say it face to face, 'cause I'm a 'chip' after all.

But Dad, I do want you to know that there's an awful lot to appreciate: your provision, care, guidance. But even beyond that, I appreciate the heritage I've received from you: missionary interest, drive, sense of economy, and overall conservatism, to mention only a few. They've marked my life and laid out my ministry, for which I'm most grateful.

But beyond all of that, I appreciate your love, Dad. We're really going to miss you when the Lord does call, even though we know your glory will be way past that of this life's.

Meanwhile, if my letters and conversation seem to indicate 'business as usual,' I'm quite sure you'll be pleased and not think that I'm unaware of your discomfort and lack of health. I'm quite sure, because I'm after all your junior edition.

More than a few MAFers were recipients of his personal concern. He may have had a "business as usual" demeanor, but if a matter gained his attention, he was capable of spending a lot of time and energy—plus considerable time in prayer—to find solutions, give counsel, or arrange for help of some kind.

I've implied his extraordinary ability to concentrate deeply; he could be physically present, but totally oblivious to what was going on around him. A family incident will illustrate his proclivity to intense preoccupation. We were eating dinner together as a family in Sentani one evening when our young (3-year-old) Gordon decided to tell his dad something about his day. "Dad," he began … and then realized Charlie wasn't listening (no doubt trying to solve an organizational problem!). Gordon tried again … "Father…" Still no response. But he didn't give up; he was obviously intent on sharing. When he began again, it was with slightly elevated volume: "Charlie …" Then he stopped—still hoping for eye contact. It was no use; Charlie's intense concentration continued to block everything else out. Finally, in thorough exasperation, Gordon blurted out, "C-J!"

That worked! Charlie abruptly turned his attention to his little son who apparently wanted desperately to share something with him. The rest of us couldn't help laughing at that point, but it did remind Charlie that he was important to his family and needed to be available to us—especially at dinner time.

* * * * * * * * * *

Charlie's role as head of our family was never disputed, although we both knew that greater responsibility fell to me whenever he was away. I found (as have other MAF wives) that it's not easy to move in and out of the authority role as one's husband comes and goes. Sometimes this shifting back and forth is disruptive, particularly if a father returns to an unknown situation. In which case, the mother should follow it through. But a father can find it equally diffi-cult to handle a situation when he has not had his hand on the pulse of the fam-ily for a time. In our case, I tried hard to fill in gaps for Charlie. But it meant a lot to me that he wanted to be involved and brought up to date. It takes work, doesn't it, to be partners in building strong family relationships.

* * * * * * * * * *

It saddens me to recall that I allowed some resentment to build over the years over one particular issue. I knew Charlie was determined to "put the Lord first" in everything, and had no quarrel with that. My discontent lay in the fact that, in practice, "the work" seemed to have greater priority for him than our family—that was what ranked. I was so convinced that God also cared about families that I resented it whenever I felt the family got left out or shortchanged by "the work." Realistically, I knew that many in Christian ministry gave far less time to their families than Charlie did. But I was sure there had to be a better solution—perhaps a better balance than we were finding—out there some-where. Good intentions can get sidetracked so easily, particularly if personal desires—or egos—get in the way. In hindsight though, I realize each of us viewed "balance" a little differently.

Over a period of years, Charlie and I both made a number of adjustments. I seized opportunities to encourage his greater involvement with the children, and he began to schedule time for special occasions. It was gratifying to know that, by the time he died, he had been able to build close and strong adult/adult relationships with our two older sons. His relationship with our younger two sons and our daughter (born after our New Guinea assignment), while not yet at this level, must have had a worthwhile impact. I hope he is somehow aware that all of our children have chosen to be Christ-followers and involve themselves in Christian ministry of one form or another. Interestingly, it was the children who suggested the verse for his grave marker, and all of us agreed it should read: "His goal … to please the Lord. 2 Cor. 5:9."

The second trait mentioned at Charlie's memorial service was his openness to change. Although I'm not entirely sure how to account for it, I think I can identify a few contributing factors. In the first place, our whole society was undergoing change in the 1960s (the Free Speech Movements on college campuses, the peace and anti-Vietnam demonstrations, and the appearance of the counterculture and "flower children"). We were more concerned at the time about how these would affect our children than we were about their effect on us. A seemingly trivial incident, however, apparently startled Charlie into some introspective thinking. He shared a conversation he had with son John (attending Wheaton College). John, then an emerging adult, had risked challenging Charlie's use of the word "obviously" by carefully explaining that what seemed obvious to Charlie at that moment wasn't really that obvious to him. Though taken aback at the time, Charlie had listened, and pondered....

I also recall our first small group experience. Although initially apprehensive, we learned to share and soon began to appreciate relationships that were deeper (less superficial) and mutually supportive. We saw the value of affirmation and caring, particularly among believers—members of the Body of Christ. And we came to understand more fully that God wants His children to use the gifts He gives them.

In 1971, I discovered I was in for a major surprise when Charlie returned from a seven-week trip to Africa. He asked me to sit down—and then told me he had done a lot of thinking while he was away. He said he wasn't happy about having "taken me for granted" for so many years, and told me he intended to make some changes. "Sure," I thought.... But he made a start by affirming me more, in front of the children as well as when we were alone. He began to encourage me to use my gifts. (However, the idea of gifts was so new to me that I hadn't begun to identify any yet.) Nevertheless, I was deeply touched, to be "appreciated"—and to realize he did value my insights and contribution to the family (and to MAF). He seemed to enjoy our conversations and companionship more. He was now more tolerant of my "poor" logic (which I had perceived as a put down!) after we learned through reading and small group interaction that there was more than one valid logic system. This insight—that different ways of thinking and doing things may be just as acceptable as our own—not only increased our understanding and appreciation of each other, but encouraged greater acceptance of our children, friends, and even strangers.

Two books Charlie read during this time of social upheaval (in the early 60s) undoubtedly affected his openness to change. One was *Self-Renewal,* and the other, *Excellence: Can We be Equal and Excellent Too?* Both were written by John Gardner, then US Secretary of Health, Education, and Welfare. In reading, Charlie's mind was always busy making applications. He now began to wonder: If God cared more about people than He did about tasks (even well-executed tasks), might He also be more concerned about whether a task was really the *right* task? In trying to apply this concept to MAF, he rephrased the question this way: Are MAF's operations helping to build the Church or are there instances where MAF's activity is somehow hindering the growth of the Church (or even of a local church)? Put another way: Was MAF as an organization possibly placing too great an emphasis on "doing the job right" rather than making sure it was "doing the right job" in the first place? He decided it would certainly be worth examining!

※ ※ ※ ※ ※ ※ ※ ※ ※ ※

Occasionally I've wondered if the idea of turning the organization over to emerging leaders of the "next generation" derived perhaps in part from the new emphasis on using one's gifts that gained momentum from the relational movement. Regardless of how it happened, Charlie encouraged a five-year plan designed to transfer leadership from the hands of MAF's original leaders (Grady, Jim, Betty, and Charlie) to a very capable younger management team. In 1967, as the plan began to unfold, Charlie became Executive Vice-President. Then, in 1970, Grady accepted the newly created position of Board Chairman; Jim assumed other duties within the organization; and Charlie became President, expecting to leave that office after five years. It was during his second year as President (1971), that long-time colleague and friend, E. W. Hatcher was killed in a plane accident while flying with a candidate. Charlie, as MAF's president, accompanied by Hobey Lowrance, shared the news with Penny ("Hatch's" wife). As he entered into the grief and subsequent struggles of the Hatcher family in his capacity as president, Charlie realized God intended this very difficult time to be another stretching experience.

Charlie believed he should leave MAF completely at the end of the five-year transition period, rather than take another assignment within MAF. He was convinced that it would give his Board-appointed successor greater freedom to lead if the former occupant of the office was not looking over his shoulder.

This view was not without merit of course; but in hindsight, it may have been too drastic a step for us. We realized only after the fact that by intentionally cutting ourselves off from what had been our "family"—and our "life" for 27 years—we had actually cast ourselves adrift from a vital support network. It was hard to realize we suddenly didn't really "belong" anymore.

※ ※ ※ ※ ※ ※ ※ ※ ※ ※ ※

During those final years in MAF and in the years to follow, Charlie began to enjoy reflecting on missions, on mission theology, and on ideas for alternative structures in missions that might have greater appeal for young people. He was intrigued by the community aspect of the counter-culture movement of the 60s and early 70s. Could any strengths of these communities be incorporated into Christian missions? He decided to explore that idea in the context of a master's degree program at the School of World Mission, a part of Fuller Seminary in Pasadena. Through his studies, and through a close association with his friend and mentor, Dr. Arthur Glasser, he gained a fresh and deeper appreciation of the Church, and was increasingly motivated to want to enlarge Christ's Kingdom. And his concept of "mission" was colored by his newly acquired view of the importance of the Church of Jesus Christ. His master's thesis was later published as a book: *Committed Communities: Fresh Streams for World Mission.*[1]

Charlie's desire to see an expansion of the Church now dominated his thinking. He wanted to see young people adequately equipped for missionary service. When asked by Dr. Ralph Winter to direct a summer program, he did so for five years (1974-1978). "The Summer Institute of International Studies" was designed to provide pertinent information (and offer college credit) to college students considering a missions ministry.[2] Faculty was recruited from among experienced mission leaders and credentialed professors throughout the States.

Then, in 1978, Charlie was invited to become the Director of Missionary Internship[3] then located in a suburb of Detroit. Through a continually developing

---

[1]Pasadena, CA: William Carey Library, 1976.

[2]Graduate students as well as undergraduates could earn academic credit for courses covering subjects such as: The Biblical Basis of Missions, Cross-cultural Communication, Mission History, and Demographics of the World's Religions. These early "Summer Institute" courses were later expanded and developed into the "New Perspectives" program now offered through William Carey University.

[3]MI subsequently moved to Colorado Springs and was renamed Missionary Training International.

curriculum, MI still offers cross-cultural insights, including coping skills and language acquisition techniques, for accepted candidates of mission agencies and church boards—to enable greater confidence and ease the transition to life and work in different cultural settings.

In recalling our rather brief time at MI (1978 through 1980), I believe God brought together another set of threads for Charlie which fit this task: his interest in the Church of Jesus Christ, his interest in young people finding their way into missions, his own mission experience, and his gift of administration. Characteristically, when Charlie believed his contribution at MI had been made, he encouraged the transition of Missionary Internship into the hands of a younger leader: Dr. John F. (Jack) Robinson.

* * * * * * * * * *

When we returned to California at the end of 1980, we did not know that Charlie's earthly life would come to an end just one year later. We both worked on editorial projects, and Charlie served as west coast representative for MI. He also read and pondered the idea of servant-leadership, hoping to develop a leadership style that would reflect a greater sensitivity to people. We knew his condition was "uninsurable," but remained confident that the Lord was our "rock," and that He was accompanying us through this dark valley. We prayed for his recovery—that he would be healed. But we also prayed for wisdom to "cope." Occasionally I wondered about my future if I was to be left alone, aware that I had no formal résumé of work experience to be employable, for Charlie and I had always loved being involved together. I also recall Charlie's response to the question (a couple weeks before his death) about his greatest fear at the moment: he didn't want to leave me (and our daughter) alone.

During those final months, I read and practically devoured the little book *Not My Will,* by Andrew Murray, which I'm sure God used to prepare me to accept His plan, whatever that might mean. As a result, I could tell Charlie, as he lay in a coma in the hospital, that if the Lord was calling him home, he should not try to hang on for me—that I was confident the Lord would take care of me and provide all I would need. I didn't expect a response, of course, but he did react, appearing startled and abruptly opening his eyes for only a moment. A few minutes later he breathed his last, and I had become a widow. My next challenge—and an ongoing one: how to "live out" what I said I believed.

Charlie wrote out a prayer in 1969, just before he assumed his duties as president of MAF, that he shared only with the Lord. I came across it while sorting through files for this book. I found a memo attached to it noting that he had shared it with colleagues on MAF's management team, at the end of his three-year tenure as president (in 1973). As I read it, I was struck with his honesty before the Lord. I'm sure those words accurately represent his ongoing concern for MAF; they express his earnest and genuine intent to intercede for those who were to follow. Each time I read it, I am freshly aware of my great respect for Charlie and of the depth of the love we shared. How can I adequately express my gratitude to God for a wonderful husband, for our precious children and grandchildren, and for the gift of 37 years in meaningful ministry together?

Here follows Charlie's prayer:

> Loving, merciful Father
> I come to You today as a leader in transition.
> I thank You for
> The privilege of evidently significant service
> By Your mercy, substantial success
> Some apparent, some less so.
>
> Help me to rest this with You—and only You
> And to rest in Your smile of acceptance.
>
> I also thank You—and You know that, for me,
> this is a lot harder—for
> The sting and disappointment of failure
> The hurt of faithful correction by colleagues
> Their patience in other instances—Yours in all
> The shame of less obvious failures known
> only to family—some, only to You.
>
> Help me to rest these, too, with You alone
> To be secure in Your forgiveness ... and purpose
> And so to accept the judgments of history—
> right or wrong—without defensiveness.
> Surely other errors *will* come to light.
>
>   ✻   ✻   ✻
>
> O Father, I thank You for my/our successors
> Gifted ... dedicated ... sensitive ... aware
> Human ... fallible
> Growing, learning, able to change.

Help me to "allow"—and *defend*—their right
  To be themselves
    To their own leadership styles
      To err—their own errors.

In counseling, may I
  "Hear" the matter as *they*—see—and feel it
    Identify it with *relevant* experience—
      and spare them the rest!
    And be primarily a catalyst for
      decision-making.

✻   ✻   ✻

O Lord, give them a "double portion" of real success.
  I believe their achievements will outstrip ours
    (But help me not to "expect" too much of them).
  Give me the grace to truly rejoice in this
    And not for hope of reflected credit,
      Or their credit,
        But for Your glory!

SIGNIFICANT DATES IN THE LIFE OF CHARLIE MELLIS

1921	Born September 25 in St. Louis, Missouri, to Charles J. Mellis, Sr., and M. Selina Mellis.
1937	As a teenager, spent 9 months traveling with his father–visiting mission stations and missionaries in Africa supported by their church in St. Louis.
1938	Met Claire N. Schoolland at Christian camp in Estes Park, Colorado.
1941	Gained private pilot license on May 2.
1941	Entered Wheaton College where he joined FMF (Foreign Missions Fellowship).
1942	Enlisted in US Army Air Corps; Received wings, and was commissioned 2nd Lieutenant, January 1944.
1944	Saw active duty in England as B-17 co-pilot; flew 32 missions over Germany (May-October); awarded DFC.
1944	Became Instrument Flight Instructor, Bryan AFB, Texas. Engaged to Claire Schoolland in November of 1944.
1945	Married June 9, 1945 in Boulder, Colorado; Learned of CAMF (Christian Airmen's Missionary Fellowship); Released from military service mid-September.

✳✳✳✳✳✳✳✳✳✳

1945-46	Volunteered, as Mid-West representative for CAMF in Chicago area. [First son, John, born March 15, 1946.]
1946	Moved family in mid-May to Los Angeles, California, where Charlie became Treasurer of CAMF. (CAMF's name was changed to MAF in 1947.)
1948-67	Served as MAF Secretary-Treasurer. [Second son, Jim, born April 1, 1948; third son, Gordon, born March 13, 1952.]
1952-55	Family moved to New Guinea to launch a series of new MAF programs there; [Fourth son, Gilbert, born in Dutch New Guinea, May 4, 1955.]
1956	Invited to present paper to interdenominational mission leaders on the subject of cooperation between mission organizations. (See Chapter 31.)
1957-58	Made surveys and contacts, accompanied by the family, in Africa, Pacific, and Asia. [Only daughter, Esther, born March 2, 1963.]
1967-70	Served as Executive Vice-President of MAF.
1970-73	Served as MAF's third President during planned transition to next generation leadership. (Succeeded J. Grady Parrott and preceded Charles Bennett.)

✳✳✳✳✳✳✳✳✳✳

1973-75	Enrolled in masters degree program at Fuller Theological Seminary's School of World Mission in Pasadena, California.
1973-74	Served as Director of UPCMS (United Presbyterian Center for Mission Studies).
1974-77	Served as Director of SIIS (Summer Institute of International Studies).
1974-78	Served as Assistant Editor of *Missiology* Journal. (Arthur F. Glasser, Editor.)
1975	Awarded Master of Arts Degree in Missiology from Fuller Seminary's School of World Mission (which has since become the School of Intercultural Studies).
1976	Thesis published as *Committed Communities: Fresh Streams for World Missions*, published by William Carey Library.
1978-80	Served as Director of Missionary Internship, Farmington, Michigan.
1980	Resigned from MI and relocated with Claire and Esther to Fullerton, California.
1981	Attended dedication of new MAF headquarters in Redlands, California, in mid-October. (This was his last public appearance.)
1981	Entered the Lord's presence on December 22, 1981.

FOR MORE INFORMATION

Contact Author:
Claire Mellis
Email: morethanapilot@gmail.com

Contact MAF:
P.O. Box 47
Nampa, ID 83653
(208)468-0800
(800)FLYSMAF
Email: MAF-US@maf.org
Website: www.maf.org

Contact Publisher:
R.C. Law & Company, Inc.
4861 Chino Avenue
Chino, CA 91710
Phone: 800-777-5292
Website: www.rclawco.com/pilot